P9-CDV-278

ESSAYS IN
LEGAL PHILOSOPHY

K
235
.S86
1976

ESSAYS IN
LEGAL PHILOSOPHY

Selected and edited by

ROBERT S. SUMMERS

Professor of Law,
University of Oregon School of Law

Tennessee Tech. Library
Cookeville, Tenn.

UNIVERSITY OF CALIFORNIA PRESS
BERKELEY AND LOS ANGELES

WITHDRAWN

University of California Press
Berkeley and Los Angeles, California

© in this collection
BASIL BLACKWELL, OXFORD, 1968

California Library Reprint Series Edition, 1976
ISBN: 0-520-03213-6
Library of Congress Catalog Card Number: 68-31075

Printed in the United States of America

Printed in the United States of America

Contents

vi   *Contents*

Editor's Preface

The editor wants, first of all, to thank the authors and publishers who granted necessary permissions. He wishes also to record his gratitude to the authors for advice and encouragement in putting this volume together, though he, of course, assumes full responsibility for error or misjudgment in its preparation. In particular, the views expressed in the introduction are his, and it is not to be inferred that any contributor agrees with them in all respects.

What criteria were used to select the essays? One of the important functions of a collection in this Age of Collections is to make otherwise inaccessible materials readily available to students for teaching purposes, it being generally better that they study original work in this form rather than at second-hand through 'summaries' authored by text writers surveying the field. Accordingly a chief criterion was that the essays should be suitable for assignment and discussion in seminars and courses in law schools and in philosophy and social science departments. Another criterion was that the essays should contribute to the over-all plan of presenting a representative cross-section of the work now being done in this field. Thus, an effort was made, in Part One on conceptual studies, to present work on a variety of *concepts* reflecting use of varied *approaches*, and in Part Two on rational justification, to present studies dealing with a variety of types of *institutions* and *practices*: community establishment of processes for resolving disputes, legislative use of criminal law to enforce morality as such, judicial resolution of constitutional questions, administrative and judicial efforts to comply with legislative mandates, and citizen refusals to obey particular laws; also, fundamentally different types of *justificatory appeals* are explicitly made in these studies, e.g., to the 'nature of things', to forms of utilitarianism, to 'principle', to legislative intent, to logic, to justice.

It was also a part of the plan of this book to present essays both by lawyers interested in philosophy and by philosophers interested in law. Finally, the selections were made with an eye to stimulating further interest and work in this field. For this reason, an essay was not excluded merely because polemical in tone. But it must be recorded, with regret, that many fine essays did have to be omitted, even ones that other editors would certainly have included.

A word on footnotes and bibliography. Because of the purpose of this volume, many more footnotes appear in it than is usual in such collections. However true it may be that some *professionals* are better off if they work something up from scratch without first 'reading up the literature', students in law schools and philosophy and social science departments are not yet professionals. Among other things, the abundance of footnotes in most of the essays will give further leads which many students can pursue with profit. Also to this end, bibliographical notes appear at the back of this book.

Finally, the editor wishes to thank the University of Oregon Office of Scholarly and Scientific Research for support, and Miss Kristen Nelson for efficient assistance in preparing the manuscript.

Note on Abbreviations

The abbreviated forms of titles of journals are self-explanatory, e.g. HARV. L. REV. for HARVARD LAW REVIEW; L. Q. REV. for LAW QUARTERLY REVIEW, etc. Other abbreviations used are as follows:

App. Cas.	– Appeal Cases	Q.B.	– Queen's Bench
Ch.	– Chancery	T.L.R.	– Times Law Reports
Eng. Rep.	– English Reports	W.L.R.	– Weekly Law Reports
H.L.	– House of Lords	Wms. Saund.	– Saunders'
K.B.	– King's Bench		Reports annotated by
P.C.	– Privy Council		Williams

Legal Philosophy Today—
An Introduction

ROBERT S. SUMMERS

What is law? What is justice? What are good kinds of reasons for official actions? For purposes of punishment, what conduct is intentional? Such questions of legal philosophy have occupied social theorists from Plato's time to the present day. As an academic discipline, legal philosophy now flourishes in America and in Britain as never before. Its practitioners are found in faculties of law, philosophy, and the social sciences. Some are concerned principally with law, or philosophy, or political science *as such*, and contribute only occasionally to the literature of legal philosophy. Others devote a large part of their time to the subject. Both types have made a variety of significant contributions.

Output of published work in legal philosophy in the past ten years has, compared with that of immediately preceding decades, been immense. A great deal of it has appeared in specialist journals, but there have been important books as well, including Hart, *The Concept of Law*, Fuller, *The Morality of Law*, and Lucas, *The Principles of Politics*. Also, the 'Nomos' volumes of the American Society of Political and Legal Philosophy have appeared annually for several years, each devoted to a single topic or theme such as responsibility, equality, rational decision.

It would be wrong to say that all this work is of precisely the same *genre*. This introduction deals only with the kind of legal philosophy represented in the essays collected here.

SCOPE AND METHOD

To take up scope first: The essays in this volume consist of conceptual studies and exercises in what will be called 'rational justification'. Analysis of existing concepts is one kind of conceptual

I

study; conceptual revision another.[1] The first deals with the conceptual *status quo* only, while the second goes beyond it. In both, the relevant subject matter consists of concepts of and about law. These may be concepts entertained by laymen (see Kenny's essay here), or by lawyers and judges (see MacCallum's essay), or by legal philosophers. Consider the following illustrative listing:
(1) Concepts used in formulating theories of law, e.g., sources of law, rules, adjudication, minimum efficacy, sanctions.
(2) Concepts used in characterizing theories of law, e.g., imperative, positivist.
(3) Concepts used in criticism of law and its administration, e.g., justice, equality, freedom, morality, natural law, 'the rule of law'.
(4) Concepts central to the administration of law, e.g., legislative intent, *ratio decidendi*, *stare decisis*, discretion, justification.
(5) Concepts of general significance which are more or less creatures of law, e.g., ownership, corporation.
(6) Concepts widely used in formulations of substantive laws, e.g., intention, causation, possession.
(7) Concepts used to demarcate basic legal relations, e.g., right–duty, power–liability.
(8) Concepts used in classifying laws, e.g., criminal, civil, substantive, procedural, public, private.

So much for the general subject matter of conceptual studies. What kinds of intellectual *activities* come into play in 'analyzing' aspects of the conceptual *status quo*? Like most cover words, 'analyzing' suggests more unity than actually exists. 'Analyzing' is not a single activity but a family of related activities. As the essays in the first half of this book clearly demonstrate, analyzing not only includes breaking concepts down into constituents (when possible), but also distinguishing and differentiating related concepts, correlating or tracing connections between concepts, identifying conceptual unities, classifying concepts from various points of view, charting their implications and 'logical bearings', and more. All of these activities (or fruits thereof) are illustrated in this book.

Because of surface similarities, conceptual analysis is sometimes confused with legal interpretation. For lawyers, it is important to point out several differences. When a thinker engages in conceptual analysis he is simply not doing the kind of work that the lawyer does when he interprets a statute or some other authoritative text.

[1] It is not suggested that there are no other types of conceptual study.

First, the sources of their problems are very different. The lawyer's interpretational problem arises because, for example, there is in-consistent usage of the same word in the text, syntactical ambiguity, or evidence of a difference between what the authority intended and the usual meanings of the words used. The conceptual analyst's problem does not arise in this manner. Instead, it may arise be-cause he is genuinely puzzled or confused about what is involved in the general content of some concept or about how it contrasts with and relates to other concepts. Alternatively, his problem may arise not because he is antecedently puzzled or in a fog, but rather because he simply wants to articulate a clear analysis of something he has set out to investigate.[1] Second, the lawyer can almost always frame his issue in terms of a choice between two alternative interpretations each of which he readily grasps and fully understands. This cannot be true of the legal philosopher whose problem arises because of antecedent confusion or puzzlement. Moreover, his analysis—his 'solution', if it can be called that—can hardly be described in terms of a choice between alternatives. The complexity of the activities involved in analysis defies such simplicity of description. Third, the lawyer will use techniques in his 'analysis' that are hardly appropriate for the legal philosopher. Thus, interpreting a statute, the lawyer can be expected to invoke canons of statutory construction, canons obviously foreign to con-ceptual analysis. Also, the lawyer might involve himself in the old methodological dispute between purposive and literal interpreta-tion.[2] But the conceptual analyst could not even be a party to this dispute if he is analyzing the conceptual *status quo*, or, indeed, even if he is recommending the adoption of a better conceptual frame-work for representing reality. In both cases, he is plainly not trying to determine what a specific person on a particular occasion meant or should be taken to have meant by a specific use of a term. Furthermore, the lawyer, in interpreting a statute, may quite rightly marshal and rely on relevant arguments of public policy. But it would be inappropriate, indeed, for a legal philosopher to try to establish a *conceptual* connection between, say, the concept of law and the concept of general rules, by invoking considerations of 'public policy'. Similarly, it would be queer, indeed, for him to differentiate the concepts of purposive and reckless behavior

---

[1] See generally, WARNOCK, ENGLISH PHILOSOPHY SINCE 1900 147–57 (1958).
[2] See generally, *Heydon's Case*, 3 Coke 7a, 76 Eng. Rep. 637 (EX. 1584).

'as a matter of public policy'. It is proper that within *the substantive law's* own conceptual scheme, connections and distinctions be influenced by specific policies and purposes of duly constituted authorities. But it does not follow, in fact it is surely false, that all connections and distinctions within any conceptual scheme are exclusively creatures of specific human policies or purposes of the moment. Whether or not there is a conceptual connection between the concept of law and the concept of general rules, and whether or not the general concepts of purposive behavior and reckless behavior can be differentiated, are *not*, as such, questions arising within the conceptual scheme of the substantive law. Moreover, while over the long run such connections and distinctions are influenced by general human purposes, they have a reality of their own[1] which is not governed by short-run, transitory, practical policies or purposes of the moment. Of course, whether or not these connections and distinctions are to be recognized and embodied in the substantive law, and thus made subject to such policies and purposes, is an entirely different question, and itself one of policy.

Conceptual revision is the second main type of conceptual study.[2] Sometimes the scholar will go beyond the conceptual *status quo* and try to devise ways of *more faithfully* conceptualizing legal phenomena in which he is interested.[3] The necessity for this work can stem from at least two sources. First, our existing state of understanding—our existing conceptual framework may not have got things right initially. Second, things change, and our understanding—our conceptualization—sometimes lags behind, thus becoming outmoded.

Some things none of us yet understands satisfactorily. It is not that we have been *misinformed* about them, but that we have from the beginning *misconceived* them in some way. When so, a conceptual schema more faithful to the facts is needed. While providing it will involve going beyond the conceptual *status quo*, it will

---

[1] For useful discussion, see CRAWSHAY-WILLIAMS, METHODS AND CRITERIA OF REASONING 103–27 (1957).

[2] Conceptual revision as here conceived differs from (a) the reconstructions of philosophers via formal logic, see Strawson, *Construction and Analysis* in THE REVOLUTION IN PHILOSOPHY 97–110 (Ryle intro. 1957) and (b) the wholesale efforts of metaphysicians to 'redraw the whole map of thought on a new plan', see THE NATURE OF METAPHYSICS 21 (Pears ed. 1957).

[3] cf. Nowell-Smith, *Philosophical Theories* 48 PROCEEDINGS OF THE ARISTO-TELIAN SOCIETY 165 (1948).

not necessarily involve introducing wholly new concepts or even devising new terminologies in which to express concepts. Sometimes a new word or phrase will be invented, or an old word or phrase put to a new use.

Understandably, legal philosophers frequently present improvements upon our ways of faithfully representing legal phenomena in the form of criticisms of each other's views. For example, in the first essay here, Professor Dworkin shows in detail how a conceptual schema of law which leaves principles and policies out of account and focuses exclusively on rules must inevitably distort law in modern societies. Yet *many* legal philosophers (and lawyers and judges) have, it seems from the very beginning, thought of law as consisting of a *body of rules*.[1]

Conceptual lag, as well as the failure to get things right in the beginning, can also give rise to the necessity for revising conceptual schemes.[2] To illustrate: One of the central problems of jurisprudence is the problem of explicating the nature of law itself. Law—the phenomenon of law—unlike elephants or triangles, is a mode of social organization and therefore is itself subject to some change, even fundamental change over long periods. Because of this, our understanding of law, our conceptions of it, may ultimately require revision. Hence, in criticizing a theory such as John Austin's that law consists of sovereign commands, there are two possible dimensions of criticism. It is not merely that Austin might have gotten it wrong in the first place back in 1828. It is also possible that some features of his theory might need to be revised specifically to account for basic developments since that date.[3] For example, any general account of the nature of law in modern industrial societies must make a place for the pervasive impact of new administrative institutions with their varied structures and paraphernalia of orders, rulings, and regulations.

Rational justification, the other main type of intellectual endeavor undertaken in contemporary legal philosophy, is exemplified in essays in the second half of the present collection. Consider the following questions: What, if any, is the rational justification—

---

[1] John Austin, the 19th century British jurist, is an influential example. See AUSTIN, THE PROVINCE OF JURISPRUDENCE DETERMINED (Library of Ideas ed. 1954).

[2] See generally, Corbett, *Innovation and Philosophy* 68 MIND 289 (1959).

[3] See generally, Hexner, *The Timeless Concept of Law* 52 J. POLITICS 48, 62–63 (1943).

the 'case'—for civil disobedience?[1] What, if any, is the rational justification—the 'case'—for the social practice of punishment?[2] What, if any, is the rational justification—the 'case'—for *stare decisis*?[3] Questions of this nature call for one to marshal and articulate general justifying arguments, rather than to analyze the conceptual *status quo* or construct new conceptual schemes with their accompanying terminologies. Of course, *argument* figures in conceptual studies, too, but in rational justification it is deployed distinctively to build up cases *for* or *against* general social institutions, practices, choices. Despite this and other differences, conceptual studies and rational justification can be closely related in particular cases. For example, while the essay by Professor Mac-Callum on 'legislative intent' appears in the second half of this book because concepts of legislative intent figure prominently in *justifications* of statutory interpretations, the essay itself is largely conceptual analysis.[4]

We may differentiate rational justification from the familiar day to day justifying done by the so called 'man of action'. First, the philosopher works on a general type of question, e.g. what, if any, is the rational justification—the 'case'—for civil disobedience? The man of action, however, addresses himself to a more immediate and specific form of this general question, e.g., is it justified to disobey the local ordinance against mixing races in public hotels? Second, the man of action, in the nature of things, takes a stand on the merits of his specific question, whereas the philosopher need not take a stand at all. His job is completed when he has formulated and marshalled the relevant arguments. While this task necessarily requires that he evaluate the *rational* plausibility of possible arguments, it does not *call* on him to take a stand on the ultimate question or to grind an axe of any kind.

Rational justification is now a major concern of legal philosophers.[5] This is a recent development and a welcome one, for the

---

[1] See, e.g., the last essay in this volume, and CAMPBELL, OBLIGATION AND OBEDIENCE TO LAW (1965).

[2] See, e.g., Hart, *Prolegomenon to the Principles of Punishment*, in PHILOSOPHY, POLITICS, AND SOCIETY, 2nd series 158 (Laslett and Runciman eds. 1962).

[3] See, e.g., WASSERSTROM, THE JUDICIAL DECISION: TOWARD A GENERAL THEORY OF LEGAL JUSTIFICATION Ch. 4 (1961).

[4] Similarly, some of the essays in the first half of this volume involve rational justification.

[5] In particular, see, in addition to the essays here, NOMOS—RATIONAL DECISION (Friedrich ed. 1964) and LAW AND PHILOSOPHY, Part III (Hook ed. 1964).

ideological sources of irrationalism have been numerous of late: the logical positivist dogma that *rational* justification is not even *possible*; the familiar doctrine of ethical relativism; misplaced libertarianism: 'A man is *free* to adopt any position'; pseudo-Freudianism: 'We don't know what our *real* reasons are, so they can't be very important'; misplaced egalitarianism: 'One man's view is *equal* to that of any other'; deterministic 'futilitarianism': 'We *can't help* choosing as we do, so rationality can have no role; deductivism: 'No argument is valid unless *deductively* conclusive'. Legal philosophers seldom undertake to refute any of these views as such, but much of their work today stands in opposition.

Turning away from the types of intellectual endeavor within legal philosophy as represented in the essays here, what of methodology? It cannot be said that the thinkers involved share some basic technique or formula. But their activities, especially their conceptual studies, do reflect recent methodological advances in general philosophy, advances which are best described in terms of deeper insight into the basic nature of conceptual inquiries, and a keener awareness of certain 'sources of error' in conducting them. These sources of error are familiar to professional philosophers, but perhaps for other readers several of them can be profitably explained: (1) the urge to convert conceptual questions into straightforward questions of fact, (2) the urge to 'grind axes', (3) the influence of misleading models, (4) the reductionist impulse, (5) essentialism, and (6) misuse of definition *per genus et differentiam*. It is not claimed that no other influences are at work in the examples that will be used to illustrate the foregoing. Nor, of course, is it claimed that the errors involved are errors *because* of the influence of the sources of error identified. Whether an example illustrates an error obviously depends on the merits. For present purposes, however, it is not necessary to argue merits; error is therefore assumed in each example, and the focus is on its source.[1]

The urge to convert conceptual questions into straightforward questions of fact

There are differences between conceptual questions and straightforward questions of empirical fact. It may be true that, despite the

---

[1] The term 'error' is not ideal, here, but there is no other equally concise term of reference. The discussion of sources of error which follows is based largely on Summers, *The New Analytical Jurists* 41 N.Y.U.L. REV. 861, 877–87 (1966).

long history of philosophy, these differences have never been satisfactorily drawn. But it is clear that they exist. For example, we must first decide what constitutes intentional behavior, before, say, setting out empirically to find particular instances of it. For reasons we shall not try to explore, many earlier thinkers tended to succumb to the urge to convert conceptual questions into straightforward questions of empirical fact. To cite an important example, John Austin and some of his followers were led to say that having an obligation consists merely of being threatened by a sanction if one does not act or forbear as indicated.[1] This is a faulty analysis, for one may quite rightly say a person has an obligation even if there is no possibility that a sanction will be imposed for noncompliance. What probably accounts for this analysis is the urge to translate the conceptual question, 'What constitutes having an obligation?' into the straightforward empirical or sociological question, 'What is likely to happen if citizens do not act or forbear as indicated?' Unlike the former question, this is plainly a *straightforward* empirical question calling for sociological research into human behavior. Once such research (or, more often, speculation) shows that, as a matter of cold, hard, empirical fact, sanctions normally follow noncompliance, then it is but a short step to the tempting but faulty analysis that 'having an obligation' consists merely of being threatened by a sanction and that, therefore, it is not possible to have an obligation if no sanction for noncompliance is likely.

A recent example superbly illustrates the widespread tendency to convert conceptual questions into straightforward empirical ones. It arises in one of the celebrated exchanges between Professor Lon L. Fuller and Professor H. L. A. Hart. Hart wrote:

If social control . . . [through legal rules] is to function, the rules must satisfy certain conditions: they must be intelligible and within the capacity of most to obey, and in general they must not be retrospective, though exceptionally they may be. . . . Plainly these features of control by rule are closely related to the requirements of justice which lawyers term principles of legality. Indeed one critic of positivism has seen in these aspects of control by rules, something amounting to a necessary connexion between law and morality, and suggested that they may be called "the inner morality of law." Again, if this is what the necessary connexion of law and morality means, we may accept it. It is unfortunately compatible with very great iniquity.[2]

---

[1] For a faithful statement and incisive criticism of this view, see HART, THE CONCEPT OF LAW 79–88 (1961).   [2] op. cit. p. 202.

Interpreting this passage, Professor Fuller concludes that: 'Certainly one could not wish for a more explicit denial of any possible interaction between the internal and external moralities of law than that contained in the last sentence.'[1] This, however, is a false interpretation. Hart is not saying, as Fuller takes him to be saying, that law and morality do not, in fact, affect each other. He is only saying that they do not *necessarily* affect each other and that good law in the sense of intelligible, prospective law, is *logically* 'compatible with very great iniquity'. Yet Fuller wants to convert Hart's proposition into a straightforward empirical proposition of fact.

The urge to grind an axe

Conceptual questions are also sometimes, consciously or unconsciously, converted into questions of value. Earlier legal philosophers have, from time to time, smuggled their own value preferences into what they seem to want to present as conceptual analysis. While purporting to analyze concepts, they have really been evaluating and recommending. Examples of this abound; one of the most spectacular appears in the work of Thomas Hobbes. Hobbes published his *Leviathan* in 1651, a period of great civil strife and turmoil. In this book, Hobbes' value preference for order emerges with luminous clarity, yet he pretends to be analyzing the concept of law within the framework of his day.[2] Thus, Hobbes wrongly contended that it would be *conceptually* illegitimate to speak of a right to revolt.[3] While we may sympathize with Hobbes' desire for order in a time of great civil disorder, his is not really an analysis; rather, it is an indirect way of endorsing values. There is nothing *conceptually* illegitimate in the notion that citizens living under law have a right to revolt. This notion does not have the same kind of sound as 'round–square' has.

Of course, the urge to grind an axe is not necessarily inconsistent with conceptual analysis. Indeed, it may provide the motivation for careful and, on its merits, wholly defensible analysis. But it may also distort an analysis, particularly if the axe at hand is one the analyst holds dear.

The influence of misleading or irrelevant models

The influence of irrelevant or misleading models has been a fertile

---

[1] FULLER, THE MORALITY OF LAW 154 (1964).
[2] See HOBBES, LEVIATHAN 172 (Oakeshott ed. 1946). [3] op. cit. pp. 113–15.

B

source of error in legal philosophy. Thus, the model of scientific knowledge embodied in general laws has sometimes led jurists to seek more unity and universality than exists in the nature of the case. Austin, for example, was led to think that there *must* be certain principles of positive law common to all developed systems.[1] Mathematical models have played their part. Indeed, Kocourek lamented that jurisprudence had not sufficiently imitated mathematics and formal logic.[2] Because of this, he was sometimes led to insist on what *he* conceived to be 'logic' at the expense of conceptual felicity. For example, he wrote as late as 1937 that the 'proposition, that "sovereign power is incapable of legal limitation", while often denied, is an inescapable proposition of logical truth.'[3] Similarly, Bentham thought that the activity of rational justification was essentially a process of calculation. We are to *add up* the pleasures and pains involved, *count* the number of persons affected, *multiply* this number by the relevant pleasures and pains, and act accordingly.[4] 'The law giver . . . [and] the geometrician . . . are both solving problems by sober calculation', according to Bentham.[5] At the other extreme, some jurists have been influenced by the so-called 'Boo–Hurrah' model of 'justification', according to which *rational* justification is simply not possible.[6]

The influence of the criminal-law model has been pervasive. Among other things, it has led some thinkers to neglect the vital role in a legal system of rules that, unlike the rules of the criminal law, confer powers rather than impose duties.[7]

The foregoing are only illustrative of how models—conceptualizations—have led earlier thinkers astray.

The reductionist impulse

Reductionism is not all bad. For example, generalization or systematization may be in order, and for purposes such as these it may be necessary to throw *different* things into the *same* category—

[1] See AUSTIN, THE PROVINCE OF JURISPRUDENCE DETERMINED (Library of Ideas ed. 1954).
[2] Kocourek, *The Century of Analytic Jurisprudence Since John Austin*, in 2 LAW, A CENTURY OF PROGRESS : 1835–1935, pp. 195, 210, 221 (1937).
[3] op. cit. p. 200.
[4] BENTHAM, AN INTRODUCTION TO THE PRINCIPLES OF MORALS AND LEGISLATION 30–31 (Hafner Library ed. 1948).
[5] BENTHAM, WORKS 19 (Bowring ed. 1859).
[6] See, e.g., KELSEN, GENERAL THEORY OF LAW AND STATE xvi (Wedberg transl. 1945).   [7] See HART, THE CONCEPT OF LAW 27–41 (1961).

to 'reduce' one thing to another thing.[1] But for other purposes, distinctions may be more important than similarities. Succumbing to the reductionist impulse, the analyst may obscure important differences, and even ignore some things altogether. Thus, reductionism can be a vice. As such, it plagued the efforts of earlier legal philosophers such as Austin who sought, for example, to reduce all types of directives having authoritative force in a system of law to 'commands'.[2] This obscured the very great differences between such things as orders, rules, rulings, principles, and regulations. He also sought to reduce the various factors that account for compliance with a system of law to 'habits'.[3] This obscured the differences between, and indeed ignored altogether, such differing factors as the desire for order, the inclination simply to do as others do, the wish to be respected, and so forth. Austin sought to reduce the diverse things citizens do with legal rules to that of 'obeying' them,[4] whereas what is done with rules includes many other activities as well.

Essentialism

For some thinkers, to analyze a concept was to search for an ideal form—an essence. They assumed that all of the diverse things to which any general term is applied *must* have some defining property or properties in common.[5] While it may be true that essences can be found for some concepts, it does not follow that an essence can be found for every concept.

Austin seems to have been a searcher for essences where none could be found.[6] Consider, for example, his analysis of the concept of law. In Austin's day, many diverse societies existed to which this word was applied. Austin undertook to determine properties these societies had in common by virtue of which they were said to have law.[7] He concluded that it was not possible to

---

[1] See *Symposium—Reducibility* ARISTOTELIAN SOCIETY SUPPLEMENTAL VOL. XXVI 87–138 (1952).

[2] AUSTIN, THE PROVINCE OF JURISPRUDENCE DETERMINED 10–33 (Library of Ideas ed. 1954).

[3] op. cit. pp. 191–361.   [4] ibid.

[5] See, e.g., PLATO, MENO, in 1 DIALOGUES OF PLATO 852–3 (Jowett transl. 1937).

[6] See generally, Morris, *Verbal Disputes and the Legal Philosophy of John Austin* 7 U.C.L.A. L. REV. 27, 36 (1960), and Chloros, *Some Aspects of the Social and Ethical Element in Analytical Jurisprudence* 67 JURIDICAL REV. 79 (1955).

[7] AUSTIN, THE PROVINCE OF JURISPRUDENCE DETERMINED 367–8 (Library of Ideas ed. 1954).

conceive of a system of law without the following properties as 'constituent parts': duty, right, liberty, injury, punishment, sovereignty, and independent political existence.[1] This was Austin's 'essence' of law. He was apparently led to search for such an essence because he assumed that the propriety of using the same term for diverse phenomena must inevitably turn on the presence of some property or properties *common to all the things* to which the term is applied. But with many terms of interest a search for an essence is likely to prove fruitless. This is certainly true of 'law' itself. Of course, the various societies to which the term 'law' is applied cannot lack all or even very many of the pro-perties normally present in legal systems and still be legal systems. Yet even at this date no one has established that there is some de-fining property or properties which all things properly called legal systems have in common and which must therefore be present for the term to be correctly applied. Austin seems to have stressed the property of 'unlimited sovereignty' more than any other, but even this is not present in many legal systems.

The influential Ludwig Wittgenstein, in one of his attacks on essentialism,[2] offered 'family resemblances' as an alternative type of unifying factor. While there are still other types,[3] Witt-genstein's has been more widely discussed in philosophical litera-ture than any other and is therefore singled out:

Consider for example the proceedings that we call "games". I mean board-games, card-games, ball-games, Olympic games, and so on. What is common to them all?—Don't say: "There *must* be something common, or they would not be called 'games' "—but *look and see* whether there is anything common to all.—For if you look at them you will not see something that is common to *all*, but similarities, relation-ships, and a whole series of them at that. To repeat: don't think but look!—Look for example at board-games, with their multifarious relationships. Now pass to card-games; here you find many correspon-dences with the first group, but many common features drop out, and others appear. When we pass next to ball-games, much that is common is retained, but much is lost.—Are they all "amusing"? Compare chess with noughts and crosses. Or is there always winning and losing, or competition between players? Think of patience. In

[1] op. cit. p. 367.
[2] On essentialism as such, see PITCHER, THE PHILOSOPHY OF WITTGENSTEIN 215–27 (1964) (Chapter entitled *The Attack on Essentialism*).
[3] See J. L. AUSTIN, PHILOSOPHICAL PAPERS 37–43 (1961).

ball-games there is winning and losing; but when a child throws his ball at the wall and catches it again, this feature has disappeared. Look at the parts played by skill and luck; and at the difference between skill in chess and skill in tennis. Think now of games like ring-a-ring-a-roses; here is the element of amusement, but how many other characteristic features have disappeared! And we can go through the many, many other groups of games in the same way; can see how similarities crop up and disappear.

And the result of this examination is: we see a complicated network of similarities overlapping and criss-crossing: sometimes overall similarities, sometimes similarities of detail.

I can think of no better expression to characterize these similarities than "family resemblances"; for the various resemblances between members of a family: build, features, colour of eyes, gait, temperament, etc. etc. overlap and criss-cross in the same way.—And I shall say: "games" form a family.[1]

Misuse of definition per genus et differentiam

There is evidence that Austin and some of his successors tried to use the technique of definition *per genus et differentiam* to explicate concepts of and about law.[2] Recent legal philosophers recognize, however, that this technique cannot be used illuminatingly on many such concepts, for it presupposes that the concepts to be analyzed are not *sui generis*, that they fall within familiar and well understood genera, and that they can be meaningfully isolated as single words or expressions which can be relatively straight-forwardly correlated with counterparts in the world of fact and then differentiated accordingly from other species of the same genus.[3] These conditions are met in the case of concepts such as 'dog' or 'chair'. These are not *sui generis*; 'animal' is the genus for one and 'furniture' for the other and each genus is itself familiar and well understood. Moreover, the terms 'dog' or 'chair' can be taken in isolation from whole sentences in specific contexts and be more or less straightforwardly correlated with counterparts in the world of fact which can then be differentiated from other species of the same genus. But what of words such as 'corporation',

---

[1] WITTGENSTEIN, PHILOSOPHICAL INVESTIGATIONS 31e–32e (1953).

[2] See AUSTIN, THE PROVINCE OF JURISPRUDENCE DETERMINED (Library of Ideas ed. 1954), and KOCOUREK, AN INTRODUCTION TO THE SCIENCE OF LAW 215–16 (1927).

[3] cf. Hart, *Analytical Jurisprudence in Mid-Twentieth Century: A Reply to Professor Bodenheimer* 105 U. PA. L. REV. 953, 960–3 (1957).

Robert S. Summers

'ownership', 'right', or 'discretion'? The conditions for use of the
technique of definition *per genus et differentiam* to explicate the
uses of terms such as these are simply not present. Even if not
sui generis, they cannot be assigned to a general and well understood
genus. Moreover, it is not possible to take these words singly and
correlate them straightforwardly with counterparts in the world of
fact. They are far more 'context dependent'—far more bound up
with the whole contexts of their particular uses in sentences in
specific cases—than are words such as 'dog' or 'chair'. To explicate
their uses, the analyst can invoke other techniques, one of which
may be called 'contextual explication'.[1] Pursuant to this method
he assembles examples of the relevant uses of the term within
whole sentences in specific contexts.[2] He thus exhibits what these
words do—the concepts they convey in the context of their use
within specific sentences.

The conversion of conceptual questions into straightforward
questions of empirical fact, the process that we have called 'axe
grinding', the use of irrelevant and misleading models, reductionism, essentialism, and misuse of definition *per genus et differentiam*,
are, then, all basic errors or sources of error in legal philosophy.
Today, many thinkers working in this field are cognizant of these,
and of still others of perhaps equal significance, including such
common assumptions as that all concepts have general positive
content;[3] that all dichotomies are truly dichotomies;[4] that an
object of inquiry can, without distortion, be analyzed from only
one point of view;[5] that the object of study is static rather than
dynamic;[6] that related concepts must inevitably 'fit into place in

---

[1] cf. Hart, *Definition and Theory in Jurisprudence* 70 L. Q. REV. 37 (1954).

[2] Lawyers must be cautioned that this is quite different from *inferring from
context* what some particular person most likely meant by the use of a term or
expression on a particular occasion. See generally, BENTHAM, FRAGMENT ON
GOVERNMENT 232–6 (Montague ed. 1891).

[3] Not all do. For example, some function as 'excluders'—terms which have no
general positive content of their own, but are used to rule out a heterogeneous
range of cases. See Hall, *Excluders*, 20 ANALYSIS 1 (1959).

[4] Often they are not. See generally, J. L. AUSTIN, PHILOSOPHICAL PAPERS 138–41
(1961).

[5] For illustrative discussion of the influence of adopting a restricted point of
view, see Summers, *Professor Fuller on Morality and Law* 18 J. LEGAL ED. 1, 19–21
(1966).

[6] Many objects of study are continually changing, some in significant
ways. See generally, Rescher, *Revolt Against Process* 59 J. PHILOSOPHY 410
(1962).

some single, interlocking, consistent conceptual scheme',[1] and that doctrines current in general philosophy are always directly applicable, *mutatis mutandis*, in its special branches.[2]

Though the general scope and methodology of much recent legal philosophy can be set forth rather straightforwardly in the foregoing rough and ready fashion, misconceptions of it abound, particularly in law faculties. Several call for comment. First of all, this work does not constitute a *school*, in any of the usual senses of that word. The thinkers involved owe no *allegiance* to any one thinker. Indeed, it is hard to discern much agreement, *doctrinally*, even on those problems on which they have so far worked in common. In this regard, they are very different, say, from the legal philosophers of the 19th century and early 20th who adopted and followed John Austin's 'imperative theory' that law consists essentially of sovereign commands of an uncommanded commander.[3]

It is sometimes said that most legal philosophers of the type represented here form a school of 'legal positivists'. When this is said, it is usually necessary to dig more deeply to find what is meant, for the phrase 'legal positivist' is today used to cover a wide variety of views, including: (1) that law as it is can be clearly differentiated from law as it ought to be, (2) that only the concepts of existing positive law are fit for analytical study, (3) that force or power is the essence of law, (4) that law is a self-sufficient closed system which does not draw on other disciplines for any of its premises, (5) that laws and legal decisions cannot, in any ultimate sense, be rationally defended, (6) that a logically self-consistent Utopia exists to which positive law ought to be made to conform, (7) that, in interpreting statutes, considerations of what the law ought to be have no place, (8) that judicial decisions are logical deductions from preexisting premises, (9) that certainty is the 'chief end of law', (10) that there is an absolute duty to obey evil laws, (11) that there can be no 'higher law' in any significant sense, and (12) that law consists exclusively of hard and fast rules. No legal philosopher today holds *all* of these views. Some do hold the first—that the law as it is can, in principle, always be clearly differentiated from the law as it ought to be.[4] Otherwise, there is little warrant for labelling anyone

---

[1] J. L. AUSTIN, PHILOSOPHICAL PAPERS 151 n. 1 (1961).

[2] For general discussion of an example, see Hart, *Scandinavian Realism* 1959 CAMB. L. J. 233.   [3] See generally, BROWN, THE AUSTINIAN THEORY OF LAW (1906).

[4] For a comprehensive statement, see Hart, *Positivism and the Separation of Law and Morals* 71 HARV. L. REV. 593 (1958).

a legal positivist. At least we know of no one who plainly holds *any* of the other foregoing views. It would be best, in legal philosophy anyhow, to drop the term 'positivist', for it is now radically ambiguous and dominantly pejorative.

It is also sometimes said that the legal philosophy illustrated here consists of 'linguistic analysis of common usage'. This has been a popular characterization within some law faculties, especially American ones. Several things need to be said. First, a great deal of recent legal philosophy consists of rational justification rather than conceptual analysis. Second, the subject matter even of conceptual analysis in legal philosophy commonly consists not of *common* usage, but of concepts of, about, and within law[1] entertained by lawyers, judges, and others *professionally concerned* with law in some way. Third, while it is easy to see why some of the methods of legal philosophers may seem 'linguistic', in view of the close attention they pay to uses of *words*, this characterization both misleads and trivializes. In actual fact, these methods have to do with *concepts* and conceptual frameworks—with *uses* of words and not with words as such.

Law teachers not infrequently compare recent legal philosophy with the 'analytical jurisprudence' of John Austin and his followers in Britain and America. This philosophy does have more in common with 'analytical jurisprudence' than say, with 'sociological' or 'historical' jurisprudence, but this fact should not be allowed to obscure substantial differences.[2] Recent work is broader in scope in two respects: It encompasses much rational justification as well as conceptual analysis and revision, and its conceptual studies are addressed to a much wider range of topics, especially compared to American Neo-Austinians who, by the 1930s, had become almost exclusively preoccupied with the topic of 'jural relations', e.g.,

[1] 'Common usage' obviously has no 'theories' on many matters of interest to the legal philosopher. But on some matters it is a vital resource. For example, idioms may be highly useful as 'pointers' to important distinctions and ideas. See generally, WARNOCK, ENGLISH PHILOSOPHY SINCE 1900 149–52 (1958).

[2] Somehow a strange terminology worked its way into earlier 'legal philosophy' according to which 'jurisprudence' (as it was called) came to be divided into branches called 'analytical', 'sociological', 'historical', and 'normative'. See URMSON, A CONCISE ENCYCLOPEDIA OF WESTERN PHILOSOPHY AND PHILOSOPHERS 199–200 (1960). This 'schools' scheme of classification is an unhappy one today because (1) few, if any, thinkers are exclusively interested in one type of inquiry (2) such a scheme invites lumping quite different thinkers into the same category, and (3) it encourages some thinkers to 'take sides'. On the latter, see Ryle, *Taking Sides in Philosophy* 12 PHILOSOPHY 317 (1937).

right, duty, power.[1] The new legal philosophy is also more sophisticated in methodology, and less doctrinaire.

While it is obviously too early to tell whether recent legal philosophy will make lasting contributions to our understanding of law, one thing does seem certain. Legal philosophy is rapidly becoming professionalized.[2] Gone are the days when just *any* lawyer or law teacher could venture into the field and hold forth *merely* by virtue of being a lawyer or a law teacher. Gone, too, are the days when legal philosophy could be considered 'just another subject in law, like property, or torts, or tax'. It is not another substantive *law subject* at all, but a *philosophical discipline* with its own distinctive types of problems and methodology.

A NOTE ON ORIGINS

How is this flourish of intellectual activity to be explained? Any answer must inevitably be speculative and incomplete. We may try first to account for the recent outburst of conceptual studies in legal philosophy. During the relevant period, a number of lawyers and a number of philosophers took up such studies. Most of the philosophers practiced that brand of philosophy originating in Britain in this century known as 'analytic philosophy', and it was also to this work that most of the lawyers involved turned for stimulus and example. To give a full account of origins, it would therefore be necessary to go into antecedents of modern analytic philosophy, and this cannot be done here.[3] But several things can be said to help explain why lawyers interested in conceptual studies were drawn to analytic philosophy, and why analytic philosophers were drawn to perform some of their work on concepts dealing with law. First, the lawyers. Much recent analytic philosophy already dealt with concepts of *special* interest to lawyers, e.g., intention, motives, responsibility, obligation, rules, justice. This work naturally attracted their attention, once known.[4] Analytic philosophy also included much work of a methodological

---

[1] See Kocourek, *The Century of Analytic Jurisprudence Since John Austin* in 2 LAW, A CENTURY OF PROGRESS: 1835–1935 195, 216 (1937).

[2] See also Hughes, *Jurisprudence* 1965 ANNUAL SURVEY OF AMERICAN LAW 639 (1966).

[3] See generally, URMSON, PHILOSOPHICAL ANALYSIS, ITS DEVELOPMENT BETWEEN THE TWO WARS (1956).

[4] See the discussion in Hart, *Philosophy of Law and Jurisprudence in Britain* (1945–1952), 2 AMER. J. OF COMP. L. 355, 364 (1953).

nature in which, among other things, it was explicitly held that difficulties in doing philosophy often arose from lack of sophistication about language. This, too, was bound to intrigue theoretically minded lawyers preoccupied with the difficulties of harnessing language for purposes of social control.[1] In the same vein, some modern analytic philosophers openly proclaimed that they had something *new* going which bore on all branches of philosophy.[2] This alerted some of the lawyers involved, especially American ones peculiarly open to stimulus and example after the demise in the 1930s of 'analytical jurisprudence', the only branch of legal philosophy in America in which conceptual studies had figured prominently. One further thought for now: the lawyers, and partly by training, were accustomed to paying careful attention to problems of meaning—to the detailed *uses* of language. Analytic philosophy was *congenial* to them because of this, and also because it was presented in clear, non-technical, ordinary language. Modern philosophy has seldom appeared in quite this form. Compare Hegel. Or even Locke. And particularly the typographical jargon of the many 'formalist' philosophers of the present century.

Why did analytic philosophers turn to conceptual studies of relevance to law? As we have noted, some of them were already at work on notions of special interest to lawyers. That lawyers were drawn to analytic philosophy for stimulus and example therefore involved more of a shift than the shift of some analytic philosophers to concepts of and about law. Still, a perceptible shift of the latter sort did occur. The framework of legal thought and action held special attractions for philosophers, especially in an Age of Activism in Academe. Many analytic philosophers were interested in what might be called the 'philosophy of human action', e.g., the various 'mental elements' that figure in human action, the various 'excuses' for untoward conduct, and so on. The law deals with action, intrinsically so. In describing sources

---

[1] Indeed, the thinker who first contributed to the revival of legal philosophy following World War II was much interested in the possible relevance of philosophy largely for this very reason. See Williams, *Language and the Law* 61 L. Q. REV. 71 *et seq.* (1946).

[2] '. . . recent developments in philosophy have provided [legal philosophy] . . . with a means of getting off to a fruitful new start.' Hart, *Analytical Jurisprudence in Mid-Twentieth Century: A Reply to Professor Bodenheimer* 105 U. PA. L. REV. 953 (1957). See also THE NATURE OF METAPHYSICS 162 (Pears ed. 1957).

relevant to the study of 'excuses' for untoward conduct, one leading philosopher put it this way:

> One source book will naturally be the law. This will provide us with an immense miscellany of untoward cases, and also with a useful list of recognized pleas, together with a good deal of acute analysis of both. . . . It is a perpetual and salutary surprise to discover how much is to be learned from the law; and it is to be added that if a distinction drawn is a sound one, even though not yet recognized in law, a lawyer can be relied upon to take note of it, for it may be dangerous not to—if he does not, his opponent may.[1]

In addition to offering a rich quarry of examples and even some 'acute analysis' of philosophical interest, it is also true, especially in a rapidly changing and reform-minded era, that 'the law is where the action is'. In such a time, law is seen as organized society's chief means of social control, and the relevance of philosophy generally to human concerns is dramatically evident in philosophical studies of the framework of legal thought and action.

Much of what has been said also helps explain why rational justification figures prominently in recent legal philosophy. But more can be added. Conscious of the fantastic abuses of state power in the name of law during this century,[2] many thinkers, philosophers included, were not content to leave the law to the lawyers. Rather, they insisted that its basic premises, structures, and processes should be explicitly tested against general standards of rationality. This implied, too, that these thinkers—and here we may also add the lawyers—rejected, if not the ideologies themselves, at least the irrationalist implications of such ideologies as logical positivism, behavioral determinism, and pseudo-Freudianism.[3] During this period, the outlines of a developing faith in the role of reason in social ordering appeared in some quarters which was quite unlike anything since Bentham.[4] But it should have surprised no one that lawyers should look to philosophy and philosophers to law in formulating and reflecting on[5] general justifying

---

[1] J. L. AUSTIN, PHILOSOPHICAL PAPERS 135–6 (1961).

[2] Of which Nazi Germany is only the most glaring instance.

[3] See above p. 7 for still others.

[4] It should be noted that there is, too, a great revival of interest in Bentham. See, e.g., Hart, *Bentham* 48 PROCEEDINGS OF THE BRITISH ACADEMY 297 (1962).

[5] What analytic philosophers have written about methods and criteria of justification generally is likely to have, *mutatis mutandis*, important applications to legal justification.

arguments for or against basic modes of social ordering. From Plato's utopias[1] to the more piecemeal justificatory analysis characteristic of more recent thought, philosophy had always concerned itself with broad problems of social justification. In like fashion, it might have been said that this was really what law was *supposed* to be all about. Constitutional conventions, occasional though they were, were to decide only after hearing reasons. Legislators were to decide after hearing reasons. Judges after hearing reasons. So, too, administrators at many levels. Of course, justificatory analysis of philosophical interest transcended such particulars, but it nonetheless had to retain relevance for 'men of action', if it was to have value.

This brief account of the origins of recent legal philosophy cannot close without reference to the role of H. L. A. Hart, for his impact has been large.[2] Since 1953, when he became Professor of Jurisprudence in the University of Oxford, he has maintained a steady flow of articles and books, many of which have been read widely. He has also lectured extensively in Britain, in the United States, and on the Continent. In Oxford, he has continuously supervised a growing stream of graduate students many of whom have themselves contributed to the literature. Trained as a lawyer and as a philosopher, Hart's own work has seemed to have a peculiar relevance and authenticity.[3] Much of it is original and innovative, but his feats of critical analysis have probably attracted more attention to his discipline. In particular, two controversies with other social theorists which we may designate *Hart* v. *Fuller*[4] and *Hart* v. *Devlin*[5] have now become *causes célèbres* and have

[1] See both THE REPUBLIC and THE LAWS.

[2] See generally, Pannam, *Professor Hart and Analytical Jurisprudence* 16 J. LEGAL ED. 379 (1964); Summers, *Professor H. L. A. Hart's Concept of Law* 1963 DUKE L. J. 629. For his most recent views on the nature of legal philosophy, see *Philosophy of Law, Problems of* in ENCYCLOPEDIA OF PHILOSOPHY (Edwards ed. 1967).

[3] Several others working in this field are similarly professional philosophers as well as lawyers.

[4] See Hart, *Positivism and the Separation of Law and Morals* 71 HARV. L. REV. 593 (1958); Fuller, *Positivism and Fidelity to Law—A Reply to Professor Hart* 71 HARV. L. REV. 630 (1958); HART, THE CONCEPT OF LAW 198–207 (1961); FULLER, THE MORALITY OF LAW Ch. 3 (1964); Hart, *Book Review* 78 HARV. L. REV. 1281 (1965).

[5] Devlin, *The Enforcement of Morals* 45 PROCEEDINGS OF THE BRITISH ACADEMY 3 (1959); Hart, *Immorality and Treason* 62 THE LISTENER 162 (1959); Devlin, *Law, Democracy and Morality* 110 U. PA. L. REV. 635 (1962); HART, LAW, LIBERTY AND MORALITY (1963); DEVLIN, THE ENFORCEMENT OF MORALS (1965); Hart, *Social Solidarity and the Enforcement of Morality* 35 U. CHI. L. REV. 1 (1967).

inspired a spate of articles by others. Interestingly enough, the first of these controversies is concerned more with conceptual studies than rational justification as such, whereas with the latter the reverse is true. Much of Hart's work is now readily available, and parts of it which were relatively inaccessible in specialist journals have now appeared in a volume of essays edited by himself.[1]

[1] PUNISHMENT AND RESPONSIBILITY, ESSAYS IN THE PHILOSOPHY OF LAW (1968).

PART ONE

Conceptual Studies

Is Law a System of Rules?

RONALD M. DWORKIN[1]

EMBARRASSING QUESTIONS

Lawyers lean heavily on the connected concepts of legal right and legal obligation. We say that someone has a legal right or duty, and we take that statement as a sound basis for making claims and demands, and for criticizing the acts of public officials. But our understanding of these concepts is remarkably fragile, and we fall into trouble when we try to say what legal rights and obligations are. We say glibly that whether someone has a legal obligation is determined by applying 'the law' to the particular facts of his case, but this is not a helpful answer, because we have the same difficulties with the concept of law.

We are used to summing up our troubles in the classic questions of jurisprudence: What is 'the law'? When two sides disagree, as often happens, about a proposition 'of law', what are they disagreeing about, and how shall we decide which side is right? Why do we call what 'the law' says a matter of legal 'obligation'? Is 'obligation' here just a term of art, meaning only 'what the law says'? Or does legal obligation have something to do with moral obligation? Can we say that we have, in principle at least, the same reasons for meeting our legal obligations that we have for meeting our moral obligations?

These are not puzzles for the cupboard, to be taken down on

[1] Ronald M. Dworkin, B.A. 1953 Harvard Univ., B.A. 1955 Oxon., LL.B. 1957 Harvard Law School, is Professor of Law at Yale Law School. The article here reprinted is adapted from a chapter in a forthcoming book. It first appeared in 35 U. CHI. L. REV. 14 (1967); copyright retained by the author. Mr. Dworkin's other writings in legal philosophy include: *Judicial Discretion* 60 J. PHILOSOPHY 624 (1963); *Wasserstrom: The Judicial Decision* 75 ETHICS 47 (1964); *Philosophy, Morality and Law—Observations Prompted by Professor Fuller's Novel Claim* 113 U. PA. L. REV. 668 (1965); *Lord Devlin and the Enforcement of Morals* 75 YALE L. J. 986 (1966). (Footnote by editor.)

rainy days for fun. They are sources of continuing embarrassment, and they nag at our attention. They embarrass us in dealing with particular problems that we must solve, one way or another. Suppose a novel right-of-privacy case comes to court, and there is no statute or precedent either granting or denying the particular right of anonymity claimed by the plaintiff. What role in the court's decision should be played by the fact that most people in the community think that private individuals are 'morally' entitled to that particular privacy? Suppose the Supreme Court orders some prisoner freed because the police used procedures that the Court now says are constitutionally forbidden, although the Court's earlier decisions upheld these procedures. Must the Court, to be consistent, free all other prisoners previously convicted through these same procedures?[1] Conceptual puzzles about 'the law' and 'legal obligation' become acute when a court is confronted with a problem like this.

These eruptions signal a chronic disease. Day in and day out we send people to jail, or take money away from them, or make them do things they do not want to do, under coercion of force, and we justify all of this by speaking of such persons as having broken the law or having failed to meet their legal obligations, or having interfered with other people's legal rights. Even in clear cases (a bank robber or a willful breach of contract), when we are confident that someone had a legal obligation and broke it, we are not able to give a satisfactory account of what that means, or why that entitles the state to punish or coerce him. We may feel confident that what we are doing is proper, but until we can identify the principles we are following we cannot be sure that they are sufficient, or whether we are applying them consistently. In less clear cases, when the issue whether an obligation has been broken is for some reason controversial, the pitch of these nagging questions rises, and our responsibility to find answers deepens.

Certain lawyers (we may call them 'nominalists') urge that we solve these problems by ignoring them. In their view the concepts of 'legal obligation' and 'the law' are myths, invented and sustained by lawyers for a dismal mix of conscious and subconscious motives. The puzzles we find in these concepts are merely symptoms that they are myths. They are unsolvable because unreal, and our concern with them is just one feature of our enslavement. We would do

[1] See *Linkletter* v. *Walker*, 381 U.S. 618 (1965).

better to flush away the puzzles and the concepts altogether, and pursue our important social objectives without this excess baggage.

This is a tempting suggestion, but it has fatal drawbacks. Before we can decide that our concepts of law and of legal obligation are myths, we must decide what they are. We must be able to state, at least roughly, what it is we all believe that is wrong. But the nerve of our problem is that we have great difficulty in doing just that. Indeed, when we ask what law is and what legal obligations are, we are asking for a theory of how we use those concepts and of the conceptual commitments our use entails. We cannot conclude, before we have such a general theory, that our practices are stupid or superstitious.

Of course, the nominalists think they know how the rest of us use these concepts. They think that when we speak of 'the law', we mean a set of timeless rules stocked in some conceptual warehouse awaiting discovery by judges, and that when we speak of legal obligation we mean the invisible chains these mysterious rules somehow drape around us. The theory that there are such rules and chains they call 'mechanical jurisprudence,' and they are right in ridiculing its practitioners. Their difficulty, however, lies in finding practitioners to ridicule. So far they have had little luck in caging and exhibiting mechanical jurisprudents (all specimens captured—even Blackstone and Joseph Beale—have had to be released after careful reading of their texts).

In any event, it is clear that most lawyers have nothing like this in mind when they speak of the law and of legal obligation. A superficial examination of our practices is enough to show this, for we speak of laws changing and evolving, and of legal obligation sometimes being problematical. In these and other ways we show that we are not addicted to mechanical jurisprudence.

Nevertheless, we do use the concepts of law and legal obligation, and we do suppose that society's warrant to punish and coerce is written in that currency. It may be that when the details of this practice are laid bare, the concepts we do use will be shown to be as silly and as thick with illusion as those the nominalists invented. If so, then we shall have to find other ways to describe what we do, and either provide other justifications or change our practices. But until we have discovered this and made these adjustments, we cannot accept the nominalists' premature invitation to turn our backs on the problems our present concepts provide.

Of course the suggestion that we stop talking about 'the law' and 'legal obligation' is mostly bluff. These concepts are too deeply cemented into the structure of our political practices—they cannot be given up like cigarettes or hats. Some of the nominalists have half-admitted this and said that the myths they condemn should be thought of as Platonic myths and retained to seduce the masses into order. This is perhaps not so cynical a suggestion as it seems; perhaps it is a covert hedging of a dubious bet.

If we boil away the bluff, the nominalist attack reduces to an attack on mechanical jurisprudence. Through the lines of the attack, and in spite of the heroic calls for the death of law, the nominalists themselves have offered an analysis of how the terms 'law' and 'legal obligation' should be used which is not very different from that of more classical philosophers. Nominalists present their analysis as a model of how legal institutions (particularly courts) "really operate". But their model differs mainly in emphasis from the theory first made popular by the nineteenth century philosopher John Austin, and now accepted in one form or another by most working and academic lawyers who hold views on jurisprudence. I shall call this theory, with some historical looseness, 'positivism'. I want to examine the soundness of positivism, particularly in the powerful form that Professor H. L. A. Hart of Oxford has given to it. I choose to focus on his position, not only because of its clarity and elegance, but because here, as almost everywhere else in legal philosophy, constructive thought must start with a consideration of his views.

POSITIVISM

Positivism has a few central and organizing propositions as its skeleton and though not every philosopher who is called a positivist would subscribe to these in the way I present them, they do define the general position I want to examine. These key tenets may be stated as follows:

(a) The law of a community is a set of special rules used by the community directly or indirectly for the purpose of determining which behavior will be punished or coerced by the public power. These special rules can be identified and distinguished by specific criteria, by tests having to do not with their content but with their *pedigree* or the manner in which they were adopted or developed. These tests of pedigree can be used to distinguish valid legal rules from spurious legal rules (rules which lawyers and litigants wrongly argue are rules of law) and also from other sorts of social rules (generally lumped together as 'moral rules') that the community follows but does not enforce through public power.

(b) The set of these valid legal rules is exhaustive of 'the law', so that if someone's case is not clearly covered by such a rule (because there is none that seems appropriate, or those that seem appropriate are vague, or for some other reason) then that case cannot be decided by 'applying the law'. It must be decided by some official, like a judge, 'exercising his discretion', which means reaching beyond the law for some other sort of standard to guide him in manufacturing a fresh legal rule or supplementing an old one.

(c) To say that someone has a 'legal obligation' is to say that his case falls under a valid legal rule that requires him to do or to forbear from doing something. (To say he has a legal right, or has a legal power of some sort, or a legal privilege or immunity, is to assert, in a shorthand way, that others have actual or hypothetical legal obligations to act or not to act in certain ways touching him.) In the absence of such a valid legal rule there is no legal obligation; it follows that when the judge decides an issue by exercising his discretion, he is not enforcing a legal obligation as to that issue.

This is only the skeleton of positivism. The flesh is arranged differently by different positivists, and some even tinker with the bones. Different versions differ chiefly in their description of the fundamental test of pedigree a rule must meet to count as a rule of law.

Austin, for example, framed his version of the fundamental test as a series of interlocking definitions and distinctions.[1] He defined having an obligation as lying under a rule, a rule as a general command, and a command as an expression of desire that others behave in a particular way, backed by the power and will to enforce that expression in the event of disobedience. He distinguished classes of rules (legal, moral or religious) according to which person or group is the author of the general command the rule represents. In each political community, he thought, one will find a sovereign—a person or a determinate group whom the rest obey habitually, but who is not in the habit of obeying anyone else. The legal rules of a community are the general commands its sovereign has deployed. Austin's definition of legal obligation followed from this definition

[1] J. AUSTIN, THE PROVINCE OF JURISPRUDENCE DETERMINED (1832).

of law. One has a legal obligation, he thought, if one is among the
addressees of some general order of the sovereign, and is in danger
of suffering a sanction unless he obeys that order.

Of course, the sovereign cannot provide for all contingencies
through any scheme of orders, and some of his orders will inevitably be vague or have furry edges. Therefore (according to Austin)
the sovereign grants those who enforce the law (judges) discretion
to make fresh orders when novel or troublesome cases are presented. The judges then make new rules or adapt old rules, and the
sovereign either overturns their creations, or tacitly confirms them
by failing to do so.

Austin's model is quite beautiful in its simplicity. It asserts the
first tenet of positivism, that the law is a set of rules specially
selected to govern public order, and offers a simple factual test—
what has the sovereign commanded?—as the sole criterion for
identifying those special rules. In time, however, those who studied
and tried to apply Austin's model found it too simple. Many
objections were raised, among which were two that seemed fundamental. First, Austin's key assumption that in each community a
determinate group or institution can be found, which is in ultimate
control of all other groups, seemed not to hold in a complex society.
Political control in a modern nation is pluralistic and shifting, a
matter of more or less, of compromise and cooperation and alli-
ance, so that it is often impossible to say that any person or group
has that dramatic control necessary to qualify as an Austinian
sovereign. One wants to say, in the United States for example,
that the 'people' are sovereign. But this means almost nothing,
and in itself provides no test for determining what the 'people'
have commanded, or distinguishing their legal from their social or
moral commands.

Second, critics began to realize that Austin's analysis fails
entirely to account for, even to recognize, certain striking facts
about the attitudes we take toward 'the law'. We make an important distinction between law and even the general orders of a
gangster. We feel that the law's strictures—and its sanctions—are
different in that they are obligatory in a way that the outlaw's
commands are not. Austin's analysis has no place for any such
distinction, because it defines an obligation as subjection to the
threat of force, and so founds the authority of law entirely on
the sovereign's ability and will to harm those who disobey. Perhaps

the distinction we make is illusory—perhaps our feeling of some special authority attaching to the law is based on religious hangover or another sort of mass self-deception. But Austin does not demonstrate this, and we are entitled to insist that an analysis of our concept of law either acknowledge and explain our attitudes, or show why they are mistaken.

H. L. A. Hart's version of positivism is more complex than Austin's, in two ways. First, he recognizes, as Austin did not, that rules are of different logical kinds (Hart distinguishes two kinds, which he calls 'primary' and 'secondary' rules). Second, he rejects Austin's theory that a rule is a kind of command, and substitutes a more elaborate general analysis of what rules are. We must pause over each of these points, and then note how they merge in Hart's concept of law.

Hart's distinction between primary and secondary rules is of great importance.[1] Primary rules are those that grant rights or impose obligations upon members of the community. The rules of the criminal law that forbid us to rob, murder or drive too fast are good examples of primary rules. Secondary rules are those that stipulate how, and by whom, such primary rules may be formed, recognized, modified or extinguished. The rules that stipulate how Congress is composed, and how it enacts legislation, are examples of secondary rules. Rules about forming contracts and executing wills are also secondary rules because they stipulate how very particular rules governing particular legal obligations (i.e., the terms of a contract or the provisions of a will), come into existence and are changed.

His general analysis of rules is also of great importance.[2] Austin had said that every rule is a general command, and that a person is obligated under a rule if he is liable to be hurt should he disobey it. Hart points out that this obliterates the distinction between being *obliged* to do something and being *obligated* to do it. If one is bound by a rule he is obligated, not merely obliged, to do what it provides, and therefore being bound by a rule must be different from being subject to an injury if one disobeys an order. A rule differs from an order, among other ways, by being *normative*, by setting a standard of behavior that has a call on its subject beyond the threat that may enforce it. A rule can never be binding just because some person

[1] See HART, THE CONCEPT OF LAW 89–96 (1961).
[2] op. cit., pp. 79–88.

with physical power wants it to be so. He must have *authority* to issue the rule or it is no rule, and such authority can only come from another rule which is already binding on those to whom he speaks. That is the difference between a valid law and the orders of a gunman.

So Hart offers a general theory of rules that does not make their authority depend upon the physical power of their authors. If we examine the way different rules come into being, he tells us, and attend to the distinction between primary and secondary rules, we see that there are two possible sources of a rule's authority.[1]

(a) A rule may become binding upon a group of people because that group through its practices *accepts* the rule as a standard for its conduct. It is not enough that the group simply conforms to a pattern of behavior: even though most Englishmen may go to the movies on Saturday evening, they have not accepted a rule requiring that they do so. A practice constitutes the acceptance of a rule only when those who follow the practice regard the rule as binding, and recognize the rule as a reason or justification for their own behavior and as a reason for criticizing the behavior of others who do not obey it.

(b) A rule may also become binding in quite a different way, namely by being enacted in conformity with some *secondary* rule that stipulates that rules so enacted shall be binding. If the constitution of a club stipulates, for example, that by-laws may be adopted by a majority of the members, then particular by-laws so voted are binding upon all the members, not because of any practice of acceptance of these particular by-laws, but because the constitution says so. We use the concept of *validity* in this connection: rules binding because they have been created in a manner stipulated by some secondary rule are called 'valid' rules. Thus we can record Hart's fundamental distinction this way: a rule may be binding (a) because it is accepted or (b) because it is valid.

Hart's concept of law is a construction of these various distinctions.[2] Primitive communities have only primary rules, and these are binding entirely because of practices of acceptance. Such communities cannot be said to have 'law', because there is no way to distinguish a set of legal rules from amongst other social rules, as the first tenet of positivism requires. But when a particular community has developed a fundamental secondary rule that

---

[1] op. cit., pp. 97–107.   [2] op. cit., *passim*, particularly Ch. VI.

stipulates how legal rules are to be identified, the idea of a distinct set of legal rules, and thus of law, is born.

Hart calls such a fundamental secondary rule a 'rule of recognition'. The rule of recognition of a given community may be relatively simple ('What the king enacts is law') or it may be very complex (the United States Constitution, with all its difficulties of interpretation, may be considered a single rule of recognition). The demonstration that a particular rule is valid may therefore require tracing a complicated chain of validity back from that particular rule ultimately to the fundamental rule. Thus a parking ordinance of the city of New Haven is valid because it is adopted by a city council, pursuant to the procedures and within the competence specified by the municipal law adopted by the state of Connecticut, in conformity with the procedures and within the competence specified by the constitution of the state of Connecticut, which was in turn adopted consistently with the requirements of the United States Constitution.

Of course, a rule of recognition cannot itself be valid, because by hypothesis it is ultimate, and so cannot meet tests stipulated by a more fundamental rule. The rule of recognition is the sole rule in a legal system whose binding force depends upon its acceptance. If we wish to know what rule of recognition a particular community has adopted or follows, we must observe how its citizens, and particularly its officials, behave. We must observe what ultimate arguments they accept as showing the validity of a particular rule, and what ultimate arguments they use to criticize other officials or institutions. We can apply no mechanical test, but there is no danger of our confusing the rule of recognition of a community with its rules of morality. The rule of recognition is identified by the fact that its province is the operation of the governmental apparatus of legislatures, courts, agencies, policemen, and the rest.

In this way Hart rescues the fundamentals of positivism from Austin's mistakes. Hart agrees with Austin that valid rules of law may be created through the acts of officials and public institutions. But Austin thought that the authority of these institutions lay only in their monopoly of power. Hart finds their authority in the background of constitutional standards against which they act, constitutional standards that have been accepted, in the form of a fundamental rule of recognition, by the community which they govern. This background legitimates the decisions of government

and gives them the cast and call of obligation that the naked commands of Austin's sovereign lacked. Hart's theory differs from
Austin's also, in recognizing that different communities use
different ultimate tests of law, and that some allow other means of
creating law than the deliberate act of a legislative institution. Hart
mentions 'long customary practice' and 'the relation [of a rule] to
judicial decisions' as other criteria that are often used, though
generally along with and subordinate to the test of legislation.

So Hart's version of positivism is more complex than Austin's,
and his test for valid rules of law is more sophisticated. In one
respect, however, the two models are very similar. Hart, like
Austin, recognizes that legal rules have furry edges (he speaks of
them as having 'open texture') and, again like Austin, he accounts
for troublesome cases by saying that judges have and exercise
discretion to decide these cases by fresh legislation.[1] (I shall later
try to show why one who thinks of law as a special set of rules is
almost inevitably drawn to account for difficult cases in terms of
someone's exercise of discretion.)

RULES, PRINCIPLES, AND POLICIES

I want to make a general attack on positivism, and I shall use
H. L. A. Hart's version as a target, when a particular target is
needed. My strategy will be organized around the fact that when
lawyers reason or dispute about legal rights and obligations, particularly in those hard cases when our problems with these concepts
seem most acute, they make use of standards that do not function
as rules, but operate differently as principles, policies, and other
sorts of standards. Positivism, I shall argue, is a model of and for a
system of rules, and its central notion of a single fundamental test
for law forces us to miss the important roles of these standards
that are not rules.

I just spoke of 'principles, policies, and other sorts of standards'.
Most often I shall use the term 'principle' generically, to refer to
the whole set of these standards other than rules; occasionally,
however, I shall be more precise, and distinguish between principles and policies. Although nothing in the present argument will
turn on the distinction, I should state how I draw it. I call a
'policy' that kind of standard that sets out a goal to be reached,
generally an improvement in some economic, political, or social

[1] op. cit., Ch. VII.

feature of the community (though some goals are negative, in that they stipulate that some present feature is to be protected from adverse change). I call a 'principle' a standard that is to be observed, not because it will advance or secure an economic, political, or social situation deemed desirable, but because it is a requirement of justice or fairness or some other dimension of morality. Thus the standard that automobile accidents are to be decreased is a policy, and the standard that no man may profit by his own wrong a principle. The distinction can be collapsed by construing a principle as stating a social goal (i.e., the goal of a society in which no man profits by his own wrong), or by construing a policy as stating a principle (i.e., the principle that the goal the policy embraces is a worthy one) or by adopting the utilitarian thesis that principles of justice are disguised statements of goals (securing the greatest happiness of the greatest number). In some contexts the distinction has uses which are lost if it is thus collapsed.[1]

My immediate purpose, however, is to distinguish principles in the generic sense from rules, and I shall start by collecting some examples of the former. The examples I offer are chosen haphazardly; almost any case in a law school casebook would provide examples that would serve as well. In 1889 a New York court, in the famous case of *Riggs* v. *Palmer*,[2] had to decide whether an heir named in the will of his grandfather could inherit under that will, even though he had murdered his grandfather to do so. The court began its reasoning with this admission: 'It is quite true that statutes regulating the making, proof and effect of wills, and the devolution of property, if literally construed, and if their force and effect can in no way and under no circumstances be controlled or modified, give this property to the murderer.'[3] But the court continued to note that 'all laws as well as all contracts may be controlled in their operation and effect by general, fundamental maxims of the common law. No one shall be permitted to profit by his own fraud, or to take advantage of his own wrong, or to found any claim upon his own iniquity, or to acquire property by his own crime.'[4] The murderer did not receive his inheritance.

In 1960, a New Jersey court was faced, in *Henningsen* v. *Bloomfield Motors, Inc.*,[5] with the important question of whether (or

---

[1] See Dworkin, *Wasserstrom: The Judicial Decision* 75 ETHICS 47 (1964).
[2] 115 N. Y. 506, 22 N. E. 188 (1889).   [3] idem at 509, 22 N. E. at 189.
[4] idem at 511, 22 N. E. at 190.   [5] 32 N. J. 358, 161 A. 2d 69 (1960).

how much) an automobile manufacturer may limit his liability in case the automobile is defective. Henningsen had bought a car, and signed a contract which said that the manufacturer's liability for defects was limited to 'making good' defective parts—'this warranty being expressly in lieu of all other warranties, obligations or liabilities'. Henningsen argued that, at least in the circumstances of his case, the manufacturer ought not to be protected by this limitation, and ought to be liable for the medical and other expenses of persons injured in a crash. He was not able to point to any statute, or to any established rule of law, that prevented the manufacturer from standing on the contract. The court nevertheless agreed with Henningsen. At various points in the court's argument the following appeals to standards are made: (a) '[W]e must keep in mind the general principle that, in the absence of fraud, one who does not choose to read a contract before signing it cannot later relieve himself of its burdens.'[1] (b) 'In applying that principle, the basic tenet of freedom of competent parties to contract is a factor of importance.'[2] (c) 'Freedom of contract is not such an immutable doctrine as to admit of no qualification in the area in which we are concerned'.[3] (d) 'In a society such as ours, where the automobile is a common and necessary adjunct of daily life, and where its use is so fraught with danger to the driver, passengers and the public, the manufacturer is under a special obligation in connection with the construction, promotion and sale of his cars. Consequently, the courts must examine purchase agreements closely to see if consumer and public interests are treated fairly.'[4] (e) ' "[I]s there any principle which is more familiar or more firmly embedded in the history of Anglo-American law than the basic doctrine that the courts will not permit themselves to be used as instruments of inequity and injustice?" '[5] (f) ' "More specifically, the courts generally refuse to lend themselves to the enforcement of a 'bargain' in which one party has unjustly taken advantage of the economic necessities of other . . .".'[6]

The standards set out in these quotations are not the sort we think of as legal rules. They seem very different from propositions

---

[1] idem at 386, 161 A. 2d at 84.   [2] idem.
[3] idem at 388, 161 A. 2d at 86.   [4] idem at 387, 161 A. 2d at 85.
[5] idem at 389, 161 A. 2d at 86 (quoting Frankfurter, J., in *United States* v. *Bethlehem Steel* 315 U.S. 289, 326 (1942)).   [6] idem.

like 'The maximum legal speed on the turnpike is sixty miles an hour' or 'A will is invalid unless signed by three witnesses'. They are different because they are legal principles rather than legal rules.

The difference between legal principles and legal rules is a logical distinction. Both sets of standards point to particular decisions about legal obligation in particular circumstances, but they differ in the character of the direction they give. Rules are applicable in an all-or-nothing fashion. If the facts a rule stipulates are given, then either the rule is valid, in which case the answer it supplies must be accepted, or it is not, in which case it contributes nothing to the decision.

This all-or-nothing is seen most plainly if we look at the way rules operate, not in law, but in some enterprise they dominate—a game, for example. In baseball a rule provides that if the batter has had three strikes, he is out. An official cannot consistently acknowledge that this is an accurate statement of a baseball rule, and decide that a batter who has had three strikes is not out. Of course, a rule may have exceptions (the batter who has taken three strikes is not out if the catcher drops the third strike). However, an accurate statement of the rule would take this exception into account, and any that did not would be incomplete. If the list of exceptions is very large, it would be too clumsy to repeat them each time the rule is cited; there is, however, no reason in theory why they could not all be added on, and the more that are, the more accurate is the statement of the rule.

If we take baseball rules as a model, we find that rules of law, like the rule that a will is invalid unless signed by three witnesses, fit the model well. If the requirement of three witnesses is a valid legal rule, then it cannot be that a will has been signed by only two witnesses and is valid. The rule might have exceptions, but if it does it is inaccurate and incomplete to state the rule so simply, without enumerating the exceptions. In theory, at least, the exceptions could all be listed, and the more of them that are, the more complete is the statement of the rule.

But this is not the way the sample principles in the quotations operate. Even those which look most like rules do not set out legal consequences that follow automatically when the conditions provided are met. We say that our law respects the principle that no man may profit from his own wrong, but we do not mean that the law never permits a man to profit from wrongs he commits. In fact, people often profit, perfectly legally, from their legal wrongs. The most notorious case is adverse possession—if I trespass on your land long enough, some day I will gain a right to cross your land whenever I please. There are many less dramatic examples. If a man leaves one job, breaking a contract, to take a much higher paying job, he may have to pay damages to his first employer, but he is usually entitled to keep his new salary. If a man jumps bail and crosses state lines to make a brilliant investment in another state, he may be sent back to jail, but he will keep his profits.

We do not treat these—and countless other counter-instances that can easily be imagined—as showing that the principle about profiting from one's wrongs is not a principle of our legal system, or that it is incomplete and needs qualifying exceptions. We do not treat counter-instances as exceptions (at least not exceptions in the way in which a catcher's dropping the third strike is an exception) because we could not hope to capture these counter-instances simply by a more extended statement of the principle. They are not, even in theory, subject to enumeration, because we would have to include not only these cases (like adverse possession) in which some institution has already provided that profit can be gained through a wrong, but also those numberless imaginary cases in which we know in advance that the principle would not hold. Listing some of these might sharpen our sense of the principle's weight (I shall mention that dimension in a moment), but it would not make for a more accurate or complete statement of the principle.

A principle like 'No man may profit from his own wrong' does not even purport to set out conditions that make its application necessary. Rather, it states a reason that argues in one direction, but does not necessitate a particular decision. If a man has or is about to receive something, as a direct result of something illegal he did to get it, then that is a reason which the law will take into account in deciding whether he should keep it. There may be other principles or policies arguing in the other direction—a policy of securing title, for example, or a principle limiting punishment to what the legislature has stipulated. If so, our principle may not prevail, but that does not mean that it is not a principle of our legal system, because in the next case, when these contravening considerations are absent or less weighty, the principle may be decisive. All that is meant, when we say that a particular principle is a principle of our law, is that the principle is one which officials must take into account, if it is relevant, as a consideration inclining in one direction or another.

The logical distinction between rules and principles appears more clearly when we consider principles that do not even look like rules. Consider the proposition, set out under '(d)' in the excerpts from the *Henningsen* opinion, that 'the manufacturer is under a special obligation in connection with the construction, promotion and sale of his cars.' This does not even purport to define the specific duties such a special obligation entails, or to tell us what rights automobile consumers acquire as a result. It merely states—and this is an essential link in the *Henningsen* argument— that automobile manufacturers must be held to higher standards than other manufacturers, and are less entitled to rely on the competing principle of freedom of contract. It does not mean that they may never rely on that principle, or that courts may rewrite automobile purchase contracts at will; it means only that if a particular clause seems unfair or burdensome, courts have less reason to enforce the clause than if it were for the purchase of neckties. The 'special obligation' counts in favor, but does not in itself necessitate, a decision refusing to enforce the terms of an automobile purchase contract.

This first difference between rules and principles entails another. Principles have a dimension that rules do not—the dimension of weight or importance. When principles intersect (the policy of pro- tecting automobile consumers intersecting with principles of freedom of contract, for example), one who must resolve the conflict has to take into account the relative weight of each. This cannot be, of course, an exact measurement, and the judgment that a particular principle or policy is more important than another will often be a controversial one. Nevertheless, it is an integral part of the concept of a principle that it has this dimension, that it makes sense to ask how important or how weighty it is.

Rules do not have this dimension. We can speak of rules as being *functionally* important or unimportant (the baseball rule that three strikes are out is more important than the rule that runners may advance on a balk, because the game would be much more changed with the first rule altered than the second). In this sense, one legal rule may be more important than another because it has a greater or more important role in regulating behavior. But we cannot say that one rule is more important than another within the system of rules, so that when two rules conflict one supersedes the other by virtue of its greater weight. If two rules conflict, one of them cannot be a valid rule. The decision as to which is valid, and which must be abandoned or recast, must be made by appealing to considerations beyond the rules themselves. A legal system might regulate such conflicts by other rules, which prefer the rule enacted by the higher authority, or the rule enacted later, or the more specific rule, or something of that sort. A legal system may also prefer the rule supported by the more important principles. (Our own legal system uses both of these techniques.)

It is not always clear from the form of a standard whether it is a rule or a principle. 'A will is invalid unless signed by three witnesses' is not very different in form from 'A man may not profit from his own wrong', but one who knows something of American law knows that he must take the first as stating a rule and the second as stating a principle. In many cases the distinction is difficult to make—it may not have been settled how the standard should operate, and this issue may itself be a focus of controversy. The first amendment to the United States Constitution contains the provision that Congress shall not abridge freedom of speech. Is this a rule, so that if a particular law does abridge freedom of speech, it follows that it is unconstitutional? Those who claim that the first amendment is 'an absolute' say that it must be taken in this way, that is, as a rule. Or does it merely state a principle, so that when an abridgement of speech is discovered, it is unconstitutional unless the context presents some other policy or principle which in the circumstances is weighty enough to permit the abridgement? That is the position of those who argue for what is called the 'clear and present danger' test or some other form of 'balancing'.

Sometimes a rule and a principle can play much the same role, and the difference between them is almost a matter of form alone. The first section of the Sherman Act states that every contract in restraint of trade shall be void. The Supreme Court had to make the decision whether this provision should be treated as a rule in its own terms (striking down every contract 'which restrains trade', which almost any contract does) or as a principle, providing a reason for striking down a contract in the absence of effective contrary policies. The Court construed the provision as a rule, but treated that rule as containing the word 'unreasonable', and as prohibiting only 'unreasonable' restraints of trade.[1] This allowed the provision to function logically as a rule (whenever a court finds that the restraint is 'unreasonable' it is bound to hold the contract invalid) and substantially as a principle (a court must take into account a variety of other principles and policies in determining whether a particular restraint in particular economic circumstances is 'unreasonable').

Words like 'reasonable', 'negligent', 'unjust', and 'significant' often perform just this function. Each of these terms makes the application of the rule which contains it depend to some extent upon principles or policies lying beyond the rule, and in this way makes that rule itself more like a principle. But they do not quite turn the rule into a principle, because even the least confining of these terms restricts the *kind* of other principles and policies on which the rule depends. If we are bound by a rule that says that 'unreasonable' contracts are void, or that grossly 'unfair' contracts will not be enforced, much more judgment is required than if the quoted terms were omitted. But suppose a case in which some consideration of policy or principle suggests that a contract should be enforced even though its restraint is not reasonable, or even though it is grossly unfair. Enforcing these contracts would be forbidden by our rules, and thus permitted only if these rules were abandoned or modified. If we were dealing, however, not with a rule but with a policy against enforcing unreasonable contracts, or a principle that unfair contracts ought not to be enforced, the contracts could be enforced without alteration of the law.

PRINCIPLES AND THE CONCEPT OF LAW

Once we identify legal principles as separate sorts of standards, different from legal rules, we are suddenly aware of them all around us. Law teachers teach them, lawbooks cite them, legal historians celebrate them. But they seem most energetically at work, carrying most weight, in difficult lawsuits like *Riggs* and *Henningsen*. In cases like these, principles play an essential part in arguments supporting judgments about particular legal rights and obligations. After the case is decided, we may say that the case stands for a particular rule (e.g., the rule that one who murders is not eligible

---

[1] *Standard Oil* v. *United States*, 221 U.S. 1, 60 (1911); *United States* v. *American Tobacco Co.*, 221 U.S. 106, 180 (1911).

D

to take under the will of his victim). But the rule does not exist before the case is decided; the court cites principles as its justification for adopting and applying a new rule. In *Riggs*, the court cited the principle that no man may profit from his own wrong as a background standard against which to read the statute of wills and in this way justified a new interpretation of that statute. In *Henningsen*, the court cited a variety of intersecting principles and policies as authority for a new rule respecting manufacturer's liability for automobile defects.

An analysis of the concept of legal obligation must therefore account for the important role of principles in reaching particular decisions of law. There are two very different tacks we might take.

(a) We might treat legal principles the way we treat legal rules and say that some principles are binding as law and must be taken into account by judges and lawyers who make decisions of legal obligation. If we took this tack, we should say that in the United States, at least, the 'law' includes principles as well as rules.

(b) We might, on the other hand, deny that principles can be binding the way some rules are. We would say, instead, that in cases like *Riggs* or *Henningsen* the judge reaches beyond the rules that he is bound to apply (reaches, that is, beyond the 'law') for extra-legal principles he is free to follow if he wishes.

One might think that there is not very much difference between these two lines of attack, that it is only a verbal question of how one wants to use the word 'law'. But that is a mistake, because the choice between these two accounts has the greatest consequences for an analysis of legal obligation. It is a choice between two *concepts* of a legal principle, a choice we can clarify by comparing it to a choice we might make between two concepts of a legal rule. We sometimes say of someone that he 'makes it a rule' to do something, when we mean that he has chosen to follow a certain practice. We might say that someone has made it a rule, for example, to run a mile before breakfast because he wants to be healthy and believes in a regimen. We do not mean, when we say this, that he is *bound* by the rule that he must run a mile before breakfast, or even that he regards it as binding upon him. Accepting a rule as binding is something different from making it a rule to do something. If we use Hart's example again, there is a difference between saying that Englishmen make it a rule to see a movie once a week, and saying that the English have a rule that one must see a movie once a week. The second implies that if an Englishman does not follow the rule, he is subject to criticism or censure, but the first does not. The first does not exclude the possibility of a *sort* of criticism—we can say that one who does not see movies is neglecting his education—but we do not suggest that he is doing something wrong *just* in not following the rule.[1]

If we think of the judges of a community as a group, we could describe the rules of law they follow in these two different ways. We could say, for instance, that in a certain state the judges make it a rule not to enforce wills unless there are three witnesses. This would not imply that the rare judge who enforces such a rule is doing anything wrong just for that reason. On the other hand we can say that in that state a rule of law requires judges not to enforce such wills; this does imply that a judge who enforces them is doing something wrong. Hart, Austin and other positivists, of course, would insist on this latter account of legal rules; they would not at all be satisfied with the 'make it a rule' account. It is not a verbal question of which account is right. It is a question of which describes the social situation more accurately. Other important issues turn on which description we accept. If judges simply 'make it a rule' not to enforce certain contracts, for example, then we cannot say, before the decision, that anyone is 'entitled' to that result, and that proposition cannot enter into any justification we might offer for the decision.

The two lines of attack on principles parallel these two accounts of rules. The first tack treats principles as binding upon judges, so that they are wrong not to apply the principles when they are pertinent. The second tack treats principles as summaries of what most judges 'make it a principle' to do when forced to go beyond the standards that bind them. The choice between these approaches will affect, perhaps even determine, the answer we can give to the question whether the judge in a hard case like *Riggs* or *Henningsen* is attempting to enforce pre-existing legal rights and obligations. If we take the first tack, we are still free to argue that because such judges are applying binding legal standards they are enforcing legal rights and obligations. But if we take the second, we are out of court on that issue, and we must acknowledge that the murderer's family in *Riggs* and the manufacturer in *Henningsen* were

[1] The distinction is in substance the same as that made by Rawls, *Two Concepts of Rules* 64 PHILOSOPHICAL REVIEW 3 (1955).

deprived of their property by an act of judicial discretion applied *ex post facto*. This may not shock many readers—the notion of judicial discretion has percolated through the legal community—but it does illustrate one of the most nettlesome of the puzzles that drive philosophers to worry about legal obligation. If taking property away in cases like these cannot be justified by appealing to an established obligation, another justification must be found, and nothing satisfactory has yet been supplied.

In my skeleton diagram of positivism, previously set out, I listed the doctrine of judicial discretion as the second tenet. Positivists hold that when a case is not covered by a clear rule, a judge must exercise his discretion to decide that case by what amounts to a fresh piece of legislation. There may be an important connection between this doctrine and the question of which of the two approaches to legal principles we must take. We shall therefore want to ask whether the doctrine is correct, and whether it implies the second approach, as it seems on its face to do. En route to these issues, however, we shall have to polish our understanding of the concept of discretion. I shall try to show how certain confusions about that concept, and in particular a failure to discriminate different senses in which it is used, account for the popularity of the doctrine of discretion. I shall argue that in the sense in which the doctrine does have a bearing on our treatment of principles, it is entirely unsupported by the arguments the positivists use to defend it.

DISCRETION

The concept of discretion was lifted by the positivists from ordinary language, and to understand it we must put it back *in habitat* for a moment. What does it mean, in ordinary life, to say that someone 'has discretion'? The first thing to notice is that the concept is out of place in all but very special contexts. For example, you would not say that I either do or do not have discretion to choose a house for my family. It is not true that I have 'no discretion' in making that choice, and yet it would be almost equally misleading to say that I do have discretion. The concept of discretion is at home in only one sort of context: when someone is in general charged with making decisions subject to standards set by a particular authority. It makes sense to speak of the discretion of a sergeant who is subject to orders of superiors, or the discretion of a sports official or contest judge who is governed by a rule book or the terms of the contest. Discretion, like the hole in a doughnut, does not exist except as an area left open by a surrounding belt of restriction. It is therefore a relative concept. It always makes sense to ask, 'Discretion under which standards?' or 'Discretion as to which authority?' Generally the context will make the answer to this plain, but in some cases the official may have discretion from one standpoint though not from another.

Like almost all terms, the precise meaning of 'discretion' is affected by features of the context. The term is always colored by the background of understood information against which it is used. Although the shadings are many, it will be helpful for us to recognize some gross distinctions.

Sometimes we use 'discretion' in a weak sense, simply to say that for some reason the standards an official must apply cannot be applied mechanically but demand the use of judgment. We use this weak sense when the context does not already make that clear, when the background our audience assumes does not contain that piece of information. Thus we might say, 'The sergeant's orders left him a great deal of discretion', to those who do not know what the sergeant's orders were or who do not know something that made those orders vague or hard to carry out. It would make perfect sense to add, by way of amplification, that the lieutenant had ordered the sergeant to take his five most experienced men on patrol but that it was hard to determine which were the most experienced.

Sometimes we use the term in a different weak sense, to say only that some official has final authority to make a decision and cannot be reviewed and reversed by any other official. We speak this way when the official is part of a hierarchy of officials structured so that some have higher authority but in which the patterns of authority are different for different classes of decision. Thus we might say that in baseball certain decisions, like the decision whether the ball or the runner reached second base first, are left to the discretion of the second base umpire, if we mean that on this issue the head umpire has no power to substitute his own judgment if he disagrees.

I call both of these senses weak to distinguish them from a stronger sense. We use 'discretion' sometimes not merely to say that an official must use judgment in applying the standards set him by authority, or that no one will review that exercise of judgment, but to say that on some issue he is simply not bound by standards set by the authority in question. In this sense we say that a sergeant has discretion who has been told to pick any five men for patrol he chooses or that a judge in a dog show has discretion to judge airedales before boxers if the rules do not stipulate an order of events. We use this sense not to comment on the vagueness or difficulty of the standards, or on who has the final word in applying them, but on their range and the decisions they purport to control. If the sergeant is told to take the five most experienced men, he does not have discretion in this strong sense because that order purports to govern his decision. The boxing referee who must decide which fighter has been the more aggressive does not have discretion, in the strong sense for the same reason.[1]

If anyone said that the sergeant or the referee had discretion in these cases, we should have to understand him, if the context permitted, as using the term in one of the weak senses. Suppose, for example, the lieutenant ordered the sergeant to select the five men he deemed most experienced, and then added that the sergeant had discretion to choose them. Or the rules provided that the referee should award the round to the more aggressive fighter, with discretion in selecting him. We should have to understand these statements in the second weak sense, as speaking to the question of review of the decision. The first weak sense—that the decisions take judgment—would be otiose, and the third, strong sense is excluded by the statements themselves.

We must avoid one tempting confusion. The strong sense of discretion is not tantamount to license, and does not exclude criticism. Almost any situation in which a person acts (including those in which there is no question of decision under special authority, and so no question of discretion) makes relevant certain standards of rationality, fairness, and effectiveness. We criticize each other's acts in terms of these standards, and there is no reason not to do so when the acts are within the center rather than beyond the perimeter of the doughnut of special authority. So we can say that the sergeant who was given discretion (in the strong sense) to pick

---

[1] I have not spoken of that jurisprudential favorite, 'limited' discretion, because that concept presents no special difficulties if we remember the relativity of discretion. Suppose the sergeant is told to choose from 'amongst' experienced men, or to 'take experience into account'. We might say either that he has (limited) discretion in picking his patrol, or (full) discretion to either pick amongst experienced men or decide what else to take into account.

a patrol did so stupidly or maliciously or carelessly, or that the judge who had discretion in the order of viewing dogs made a mistake because he took boxers first although there were only three airedales and many more boxers. An official's discretion means not that he is free to decide without recourse to standards of sense and fairness, but only that his decision is not controlled by a standard furnished by the particular authority we have in mind when we raise the question of discretion. Of course this latter sort of freedom is important; that is why we have the strong sense of discretion. Someone who has discretion in this third sense can be criticized, but not for being disobedient, as in the case of the soldier. He can be said to have made a mistake, but not to have deprived a participant of a decision to which he was entitled, as in the case of a sports official or contest judge.

We may now return, with these observations in hand, to the positivists' doctrine of judicial discretion. That doctrine argues that if a case is not controlled by an established rule, the judge must decide it by exercising discretion. We want to examine this doctrine and to test its bearing on our treatment of principles; but first we must ask in which sense of discretion we are to understand it.

Some nominalists argue that judges always have discretion, even when a clear rule is in point, because judges are ultimately the final arbiters of the law. This doctrine of discretion uses the second weak sense of that term, because it makes the point that no higher authority reviews the decisions of the highest court. It therefore has no bearing on the issue of how we account for principles, any more than it bears on how we account for rules.

The positivists do not mean their doctrine this way, because they say that a judge has no discretion when a clear and established rule is available. If we attend to the positivists' arguments for the doctrine we may suspect that they use discretion in the first weak sense to mean only that judges must sometimes exercise judgment in applying legal standards. Their arguments call attention to the fact that some rules of law are vague (Professor Hart, for example, says that all rules of law have 'open texture'), and that some cases arise (like *Henningsen*) in which no established rule seems to be suitable. They emphasize that judges must sometimes agonize over points of law, and that two equally trained and intelligent judges will often disagree.

These points are easily made; they are commonplace to anyone

who has any familiarity with law. Indeed, that is the difficulty with
assuming that positivists mean to use 'discretion' in this weak
sense. The proposition that when no clear rule is available discretion in the sense of judgment must be used is a tautology. It has no
bearing, moreover, on the problem of how to account for legal
principles. It is perfectly consistent to say that the judge in *Riggs*,
for example, had to use judgment, and that he was bound to follow
the principle that no man may profit from his own wrong. The
positivists speak as if their doctrine of judicial discretion is an
insight rather than a tautology, and as if it does have a bearing on
the treatment of principles. Hart, for example, says that when the
judge's discretion is in play, we can no longer speak of his being
bound by standards, but must speak rather of what standards he
'characteristically uses'.[1] Hart thinks that when judges have
discretion, the principles they cite must be treated on our second
approach, as what courts 'make it a principle' to do.

It therefore seems that positivists, at least sometimes, take their
doctrine in the third, strong sense of discretion. In that sense it
does bear on the treatment of principles; indeed, in that sense it is
nothing less than a restatement of our second approach. It is the
same thing to say that when a judge runs out of rules he has discretion, in the sense that he is not bound by any standards from the
authority of law, as to say that the legal standards judges cite other
than rules are not binding on them.

So we must examine the doctrine of judicial discretion in the
strong sense. (I shall henceforth use the term 'discretion' in that
sense.) Do the principles judges cite in cases like *Riggs* or
Henningsen control their decisions, as the sergeant's orders to take
the most experienced men or the referee's duty to choose the more
aggressive fighter control the decisions of these officials? What
arguments could a positivist supply to show that they do not?

(1) A positivist might argue that principles cannot be binding or
obligatory. That would be a mistake. It is always a question, of
course, whether any particular principle is *in fact* binding upon
some legal official. But there is nothing in the logical character of a
principle that renders it incapable of binding him. Suppose that
the judge in *Henningsen* had failed to take any account of the
principle that automobile manufacturers have a special obligation
to their consumers, or the principle that the courts seek to protect

---

[1] HART, THE CONCEPT OF LAW 144 (1961).

those whose bargaining position is weak, but had simply decided for the defendant by citing the principle of freedom of contract without more. His critics would not have been content to point out that he had not taken account of considerations that other judges have been attending to for some time. Most would have said that it was his duty to take the measure of these principles and that the plaintiff was entitled to have him do so. We mean no more, when we say that a *rule* is binding upon a judge, than that he must follow it if it applies, and that if he does not he will on that account have made a mistake.

It will not do to say that in a case like *Henningsen* the court is only 'morally' obligated to take particular principles into account, or that it is 'institutionally' obligated, or obligated as a matter of judicial 'craft', or something of that sort. The question will still remain why this type of obligation (whatever we call it) is different from the obligation that rules impose upon judges, and why it entitles us to say that principles and policies are not part of the law but are merely extra-legal standards 'courts characteristically use'.

(2) A positivist might argue that even though some principles are binding, in the sense that the judge must take them into account, they cannot determine a particular result. This is a harder argument to assess because it is not clear what it means for a standard to 'determine' a result. Perhaps it means that the standard *dictates* the result whenever it applies so that nothing else counts. If so, then it is certainly true that individual principles do not determine results, but that is only another way of saying that principles are not rules. Only rules dictate results, come what may. When a contrary result has been reached, the rule has been abandoned or changed. Principles do not work that way; they incline a decision one way, though not conclusively, and they survive intact when they do not prevail. This seems no reason for concluding that judges who must reckon with principles have discretion because a set of principles *can* dictate a result. If a judge believes that principles he is bound to recognize point in one direction and that principles pointing in the other direction, if any, are not of equal weight, then he must decide accordingly, just as he must follow what he believes to be a binding rule. He may, of course, be wrong in his assessment of the principles, but he may also be wrong in his judgment that the rule is binding. The sergeant and the referee, we might add, are often in the same boat. No one

factor dictates which soldiers are the most experienced or which fighter the more aggressive. These officials must make judgments of the relative weights of these various factors; they do not on that account have discretion.

(3) A positivist might argue that principles cannot count as law because their authority, and even more so their weight, are congenitally *controversial*. It is true that generally we cannot *demonstrate* the authority or weight of a particular principle as we can sometimes demonstrate the validity of a rule by locating it in an act of Congress or in the opinion of an authoritative court. Instead, we make a case for a principle, and for its weight, by appealing to an amalgam of practice and other principles in which the implications of legislative and judicial history figure along with appeals to community practices and understandings. There is no litmus paper for testing the soundness of such a case—it is a matter of judgment, and reasonable men may disagree. But again this does not distinguish the judge from other officials who do not have discretion. The sergeant has no litmus paper for experience, the referee none for aggressiveness. Neither of these has discretion, because he is bound to reach an understanding, controversial or not, of what his orders or the rules require, and to act on that understanding. That is the judge's duty as well.

Of course, if the positivists are right in another of their doctrines —the theory that in each legal system there is an ultimate *test* for binding law like Professor Hart's rule of recognition—it follows that principles are not binding law. But the incompatibility of principles with the positivists' theory can hardly be taken as an argument that principles must be treated any particular way. That begs the question; we are interested in the status of principles because we want to evaluate the positivists' model. The positivist cannot defend his theory of a rule of recognition by fiat; if principles are not amenable to a test he must show some other reason why they cannot count as law. Since principles seem to play a role in arguments about legal obligation (witness, again, *Riggs* and *Henningsen*), a model that provides for that role has some initial advantage over one that excludes it, and the latter cannot properly be inveighed in its own support.

These are the most obvious of the arguments a positivist might use for the doctrine of discretion in the strong sense, and for the second approach to principles. I shall mention one strong counter-argument against that doctrine and in favor of the first approach. Unless at least some principles are acknowledged to be binding upon judges, requiring them as a set to reach particular decisions, then no rules, or very few rules, can be said to be binding upon them either.

In most American jurisdictions, and now in England also, the higher courts not infrequently reject established rules. Common law rules—those developed by earlier court decisions—are sometimes overruled directly, and sometimes radically altered by further development. Statutory rules are subjected to interpretation and reinterpretation, sometimes even when the result is not to carry out what is called the 'legislative intent'.[1] If courts had discretion to change established rules, then these rules would of course not be binding upon them, and so would not be law on the positivists' model. The positivist must therefore argue that there are standards, themselves binding upon judges, that determine when a judge may overrule or alter an established rule, and when he may not.

When, then, is a judge permitted to change an existing rule of law? Principles figure in the answer in two ways. First, it is necessary, though not sufficient, that the judge find that the change would advance some policy or serve some principle, which policy or principle thus justifies the change. In *Riggs* the change (a new interpretation of the statute of wills) was justified by the principle that no man should profit from his own wrong; in *Henningsen* certain rules about automobile manufacturer's liability were altered on the basis of the principles and policies I quoted from the opinion of the court.

But not any principle will do to justify a change, or no rule would ever be safe. There must be some principles that count and others that do not, and there must be some principles that count for more than others. It could not depend on the judge's own preferences amongst a sea of respectable extra-legal standards, any one in principle eligible, because if that were the case we could not say that any rules were binding. We could always imagine a judge whose preferences amongst extra-legal standards were such as would justify a shift or radical re-interpretation of even the most entrenched rule.

Second, any judge who proposes to change existing doctrine

[1] See Wellington & Albert, *Statutory Interpretation and the Political Process: A Comment on Sinclair* v. *Atkinson* 72 YALE L. J. 1547 (1963).

must take account of some important standards that argue against departures from established doctrine, and these standards are also for the most part principles. They include the doctrine of 'legislative supremacy', a set of principles and policies that require the courts to pay a qualified deference to the acts of the legislature. They also include the doctrine of precedent, another set of principles and policies reflecting the equities and efficiencies of consistency. The doctrines of legislative supremacy and precedent incline toward the *status quo*, each within its sphere, but they do not command it. Judges are not free, however, to pick and choose amongst the principles and policies that make up these doctrines— if they were, again, no rule could be said to be binding.

Consider, therefore, what someone implies who says that a particular rule is binding. He may imply that the rule is affirmatively supported by principles the court is not free to disregard, and which are collectively more weighty than other principles that argue for a change. If not, he implies that any change would be condemned by a combination of conservative principles of legislative supremacy and precedent that the court is not free to ignore. Very often, he will imply both, for the conservative principles, being principles and not rules, are usually not powerful enough to save a common law rule or an aging statute that is entirely unsupported by substantive principles the court is bound to respect. Either of these implications, of course, treats a body of principles and policies as law in the sense that rules are; it treats them as standards binding upon the officials of a community, controlling their decisions of legal right and obligation.

We are left with this issue. If the positivists' theory of judicial discretion is either trivial because it uses 'discretion' in a weak sense, or unsupported because the various arguments we can supply in its defense fall short, why have so many careful and intelligent lawyers embraced it? We can have no confidence in our treatment of that theory unless we can deal with that question. It is not enough to note (although perhaps it contributes to the explanation) that 'discretion' has different senses that may be confused. We do not confuse these senses when we are not thinking about law.

Part of the explanation, at least, lies in a lawyer's natural tendency to associate laws and rules, and to think of 'the law' as a collection or system of rules. Roscoe Pound, who diagnosed this tendency long ago, thought that English-speaking lawyers were tricked into it by the fact that English uses the same word, changing only the article, for 'a law' and 'the law'.[1] (Other languages, on the contrary, use two words: 'loi' and 'droit', for example, and 'Gesetz' and 'Recht'.) This may have had its effect, with the English speaking positivists, because the expression 'a law' certainly does suggest a rule. But the principal reason for associating law with rules runs deeper, and lies, I think, in the fact that legal education has for a long time consisted of teaching and examining those established rules that form the cutting edge of law.

In any event, if a lawyer thinks of law as a system of rules, and yet recognizes, as he must, that judges change old rules and introduce new ones, he will come naturally to the theory of judicial discretion in the strong sense. In those other systems of rules with which he has experience (like games), the rules are the only special authority that govern official decisions, so that if an umpire could change a rule, he would have discretion as to the subject matter of that rule. Any principles umpires might mention when changing the rules would represent only their 'characteristic' preferences. Positivists treat law like baseball revised in this way.

There is another, more subtle consequence of this initial assumption that law is a system of rules. When the positivists do attend to principles and policies, they treat them as rules *manqué*. They assume that *if* they are standards of law they must be rules, and so they read them as standards that are trying to be rules. When a positivist hears someone argue that legal principles are part of the law, he understands this to be an argument for what he calls the 'higher law' theory, that these principles are the rules of a law above the law.[2] He refutes this theory by pointing out that these 'rules' are sometimes followed and sometimes not, that for every 'rule' like 'no man shall profit from his own wrong' there is another competing 'rule' like 'the law favors security of title', and that there is no way to test the validity of 'rules' like these. He concludes that these principles and policies are not valid rules of a law above the law, which is true, because they are not rules at all. He also concludes that they are extra-legal standards which each

---

[1] R. POUND, AN INTRODUCTION TO THE PHILOSOPHY OF LAW 56 (rev. ed. 1954).
[2] See e.g., Dickinson, *The Law Behind Law* (pts. 1 and 2) 29 COLUM. L. REV. 112, 254 (1929).

judge selects according to his own lights in the exercise of his
discretion, which is false. It is as if a zoologist had proved that fish
are not mammals, and then concluded that they are really only
plants.

THE RULE OF RECOGNITION

This discussion was provoked by our two competing accounts of
legal principles. We have been exploring the second account,
which the positivists seem to adopt through their doctrine of
judicial discretion, and we have discovered grave difficulties. It is
time to return to the fork in the road. What if we adopt the first
approach? What would the consequences of this be for the skeletal
structure of positivism? Of course we should have to drop the
second tenet, the doctrine of judicial discretion (or, in the alternative, to make plain that the doctrine is to be read merely to say that
judges must often exercise judgment). Would we also have to
abandon or modify the first tenet, the proposition that law is
distinguished by tests of the sort that can be set out in a master
rule like Professor Hart's rule of recognition? If principles of the
Riggs and *Henningsen* sort are to count as law, and we are nevertheless to preserve the notion of a master rule for law, then we must
be able to deploy some test that all (and only) the principles that do
count as law meet. Let us begin with the test Hart suggests for
identifying valid *rules* of law, to see whether these can be made to
work for principles as well.

Most rules of law, according to Hart, are valid because some
competent institution enacted them. Some were created by a
legislature, in the form of statutory enactments. Others were
created by judges who formulated them to decide particular cases,
and thus established them as precedents for the future. But this test
of pedigree will not work for the *Riggs* and *Henningsen* principles.
The origin of these as legal principles lies not in a particular decision of some legislature or court, but in a sense of appropriateness developed in the profession and the public over time. Their
continued power depends upon this sense of appropriateness being
sustained. If it no longer seemed unfair to allow people to profit
by their wrongs, or fair to place special burdens upon oligopolies
that manufacture potentially dangerous machines, these principles
would no longer play much of a role in new cases, even if they had
never been overruled or repealed. (Indeed, it hardly makes sense

to speak of principles like these as being 'overruled' or 'repealed'. When they decline they are eroded, not torpedoed.)

True, if we were challenged to back up our claim that some principle is a principle of law, we would mention any prior cases in which that principle was cited, or figured in the argument. We would also mention any statute that seemed to exemplify that principle (even better if the principle was cited in the preamble of the statute, or in the committee reports or other legislative documents that accompanied it). Unless we could find some such institutional support, we would probably fail to make out our case, and the more support we found, the more weight we could claim for the principle.

Yet we could not devise any formula for testing how much and what kind of institutional support is necessary to make a principle a legal principle, still less to fix its weight at a particular order of magnitude. We argue for a particular principle by grappling with a whole set of shifting, developing and interacting standards (themselves principles rather than rules) about institutional responsibility, statutory interpretation, the persuasive force of various sorts of precedent, the relation of all these to contemporary moral practices, and hosts of other such standards. We could not bolt all of these together into a single 'rule', even a complex one, and if we could the result would bear little relation to Hart's picture of a rule of recognition, which is the picture of a fairly stable master rule specifying 'some feature or features possession of which by a suggested rule is taken as a conclusive affirmative indication that it is a rule. . . .'[1]

Moreover, the techniques we apply in arguing for another principle do not stand (as Hart's rule of recognition is designed to) on an entirely different level from the principles they support. Hart's sharp distinction between acceptance and validity does not hold. If we are arguing for the principle that a man should not profit from his own wrong, we could cite the acts of courts and legislatures that exemplify it, but this speaks as much to the principle's acceptance as its validity. (It seems odd to speak of a principle as being valid at all, perhaps because validity is an all-or-nothing concept, appropriate for rules, but inconsistent with a principle's dimension of weight.) If we are asked (as we might well be) to defend the particular doctrine of precedent, or the particular

[1] HART, THE CONCEPT OF LAW 92 (1961).

technique of statutory interpretation, that we used in this argument, we should certainly cite the practice of others in using that doctrine or technique. But we should also cite other general principles that we believe support that practice, and this introduces a note of validity into the chord of acceptance. We might argue, for example, that the use we make of earlier cases and statutes is supported by a particular analysis of the point of the practice of legislation or the doctrine of precedent, or by the principles of democratic theory, or by a particular position on the proper division of authority between national and local institutions, or something else of that sort. Nor is this path of support a one-way street leading to some ultimate principle resting on acceptance alone. Our principles of legislation, precedent, democracy, or federalism might be challenged too; and if they were we should argue for them, not only in terms of practice, but in terms of each other and in terms of the implications of trends of judicial and legislative decisions, even though this last would involve appealing to those same doctrines of interpretation we justified through the principles we are now trying to support. At this level of abstraction, in other words, principles rather hang together than link together.

So even though principles draw support from the official acts of legal institutions, they do not have a simple or direct enough connection with these acts to frame that connection in terms of criteria specified by some ultimate master rule of recognition. Is there any other route by which principles might be brought under such a rule?

Hart does say that a master rule might designate as law not only rules enacted by particular legal institutions, but rules established by *custom* as well. He has in mind a problem that bothered other positivists, including Austin. Many of our most ancient legal rules were never explicitly created by a legislature or a court. When they made their first appearance in legal opinions and texts, they were treated as already being part of the law because they represented the customary practice of the community, or some specialized part of it, like the business community. (The examples ordinarily given are rules of mercantile practice, like the rules governing what rights arise under a standard form of commercial paper.)[1] Since

[1] See Note, *Custom and Trade Usage: Its Application to Commercial Dealings and the Common Law* 55 COLUM. L. REV. 1192 (1955), and materials cited therein at 1193 n. 1. As that note makes plain, the actual practices of courts in recognizing trade customs follow the pattern of applying a set of general principles and policies rather than a test that could be captured as part of a rule of recognition.

Austin thought that all law was the command of a determinate sovereign, he held that these customary practices were not law until the courts (as agents of the sovereign) recognized them, and that the courts were indulging in a fiction in pretending otherwise. But that seemed arbitrary. If everyone thought custom might in itself be law, the fact that Austin's theory said otherwise was not persuasive.

Hart reversed Austin on this point. The master rule, he says, might stipulate that some custom counts as law even before the courts recognize it. But he does not face the difficulty this raises for his general theory because he does not attempt to set out the criteria a master rule might use for this purpose. It cannot use, as its only criterion, the provision that the community regard the practice as *morally* binding, for this would not distinguish legal customary rules from moral customary rules, and of course not all of the community's long-standing customary moral obligations are enforced at law. If, on the other hand, the test is whether the community regards the customary practice as *legally* binding, the whole point of the master rule is undercut, at least for this class of legal rules. The master rule, says Hart, marks the transformation from a primitive society to one with law, because it provides a test for determining social rules of law other than by measuring their acceptance. But if the master rule says merely that whatever other rules the community accepts as legally binding are legally binding, then it provides no such test at all, beyond the test we should use were there no master rule. The master rule becomes (for these cases) a non-rule of recognition; we might as well say that every primitive society has a secondary rule of recognition, namely the rule that whatever is accepted as binding is binding. Hart himself, in discussing international law, ridicules the idea that such a rule could be a rule of recognition, by describing the proposed rule as 'an empty repetition of the mere fact that the society concerned . . . observes certain standards of conduct as obligatory rules.'[1]

Hart's treatment of custom amounts, indeed, to a confession that there are at least some rules of law that are not binding because they are valid under standards laid down by a master rule but are binding—like the master rule—because they are accepted as binding by the community. This chips at the neat pyramidal architecture we admired in Hart's theory: we can no longer say that

[1] HART, THE CONCEPT OF LAW 230 (1961).

E

only the master rule is binding because of its acceptance, all other rules being valid under its terms.

This is perhaps only a chip, because the customary rules Hart has in mind are no longer a very significant part of the law. But it does suggest that Hart would be reluctant to widen the damage by bringing under the head of 'custom' all those crucial principles and policies we have been discussing. If he were to call these part of the law and yet admit that the only test of their force lies in the degree to which they are accepted as law by the community or some part thereof, he would very sharply reduce that area of the law over which his master rule held any dominion. It is not just that all the principles and policies would escape its sway, though that would be bad enough. Once these principles and policies are accepted as law, and thus as standards judges must follow in determining legal obligations, it would follow that *rules* like those announced for the first time in *Riggs* and *Henningsen* owe their force at least in part to the authority of principles and policies, and so not entirely to the master rule of recognition.

So we cannot adapt Hart's version of positivism by modifying his rule of recognition to embrace principles. No tests of pedigree, relating principles to acts of legislation, can be formulated, nor can his concept of customary law, itself an exception to the first tenet of positivism, be made to serve without abandoning that tenet altogether. One more possibility must be considered, however. If no rule of recognition can provide a test for identifying principles, why not say that principles are ultimate, and *form* the rule of recognition of our law? The answer to the general question 'What is valid law in an American jurisdiction?' would then require us to state all the principles (as well as ultimate constitutional rules) in force in that jurisdiction at the time, together with appropriate assignments of weight. A positivist might then regard the complete set of these standards as the rule of recognition of the jurisdiction. This solution has the attraction of paradox, but of course it is an unconditional surrender. If we simply designate our rule of recognition by the phrase 'the complete set of principles in force', we achieve only the tautology that law is law. If, instead, we tried actually to list all the principles in force we would fail. They are controversial, their weight is all important, they are numberless, and they shift and change so fast that the start of our list would be obsolete before we reached the middle. Even if we succeeded, we would not have a key for law because there would be nothing left for our key to unlock.

I conclude that if we treat principles as law we must reject the positivists' first tenet, that the law of a community is distinguished from other social standards by some test in the form of a master rule. We have already decided that we must then abandon the second tenet—the doctrine of judicial discretion—or clarify it into triviality. What of the third tenet, the positivists' theory of legal obligation?

This theory holds that a legal obligation exists when (and only when) an established rule of law imposes such an obligation. It follows from this that in a hard case—when no such established rule can be found—there is no legal obligation until the judge creates a new rule for the future. The judge may apply that new rule to the parties in the case, but this is *ex post facto* legislation, not the enforcement of an existing obligation.

The positivists' doctrine of discretion (in the strong sense) required this view of legal obligation, because if a judge has discretion there can be no legal right or obligation—no entitlement—that he must enforce. Once we abandon that doctrine, however, and treat principles as law, we raise the possibility that a legal obligation might be imposed by a constellation of principles as well as by an established rule. We might want to say that a legal obligation exists whenever the case supporting such an obligation, in terms of binding legal principles of different sorts, is stronger than the case against it.

Of course, many questions would have to be answered before we could accept that view of legal obligation. If there is no rule of recognition, no test for law in that sense, how do we decide which principles are to count, and how much, in making such a case? How do we decide whether one case is better than another? If legal obligation rests on an undemonstrable judgment of that sort, how can it provide a justification for a judicial decision that one party had a legal obligation? Does this view of obligation square with the way lawyers, judges and laymen speak, and is it consistent with our attitudes about moral obligation? Does this analysis help us to deal with the classical jurisprudential puzzles about the nature of law?

These questions must be faced, but even the questions promise more than positivism provides. Positivism, on its own thesis, stops short of just those puzzling, hard cases that send us to look for theories of law. When we reach these cases, the positivist remits us to a doctrine of discretion that leads nowhere and tells nothing. His picture of law as a system of rules has exercised a tenacious hold on our imagination, perhaps through its very simplicity. If we shake ourselves loose from this model of rules, we may be able to build a model truer to the complexity and sophistication of our own practices.

Social Justice

A. M. HONORÉ[1]

This article re-examines the concept of social justice. Some justification may be desirable for writing on a topic which has been so luxuriantly treated in the past. Professor Del Vecchio's work,[2] translated by Professor Campbell, contains a very full account of the history of the literature. A number of reasons may however be adduced for a fresh attempt to analyze this concept.

During the last century the emphasis has shifted from analysis of justice *tout court* to that of social justice. Indeed justice by itself no longer arouses the responses it once did. Perhaps this is because modern social and economic developments have made it clear that individual justice, justice between wrongdoer and victim is only a partial and incomplete form of justice. We find that in this century the notion of social justice has everwhere received attention. For instance, the development of the welfare state is generally thought of as an application of the notion. The interest of the Catholic Church in social justice is borne out in many passages of the recent encyclical *Mater et Magistra* of Pope John XXIII.[3] The cry for equality of opportunity for the underprivileged is increasingly heard, and underdeveloped countries are increasingly

---

[1] A. M. Honoré, B.A. (South Africa) 1946, B.A. 1946, B.C.L. 1948, D.C.L. 1967, Oxon., is Rhodes Reader in Roman–Dutch Law in the University of Oxford and a Fellow of New College. The essay here is a revised version of *Social Justice*, 8 MCGILL L. J. 78 (1962). Other writing in legal philosophy by the author: HART & HONORÉ, CAUSATION IN THE LAW (1959); *Ownership* in OXFORD ESSAYS IN JURISPRUDENCE 107 (Guest ed. 1961); *Rights of Exclusion and Immunities Against Divesting* 34 TULANE L. REV. 453 (1960); *Can and Can't* 73 MIND 463 (1964). (Footnote by editor.)

[2] DEL VECCHIO, JUSTICE, translated by A. H. Campbell (Edinburgh, 1952), to which I am greatly indebted (hereinafter cited as DEL VECCHIO). Cf. SIDGWICK, THE METHOD OF ETHICS Ch. 6 (1874) and PERELMAN, DE LA JUSTICE. ROSS, ON LAW AND JUSTICE Ch. 12 (1959).

[3] L'ENCYCLIQUE MATER ET MAGISTRA 52, 57, 69, 95. (Intro. by C. Ryan, Montreal, 1961.)

thought to have claims on more developed economies for the capital and technique necessary to develop them. All these phenomena, it would generally be agreed, illustrate the importance of the notion of social justice in the modern consciousness.

Another reason for undertaking the investigation is that, despite these modern developments, much of the literature about justice continues to be influenced by the approach which, from Aristotle's time onwards, has been considered orthodox. By this I mean that approach which looks at justice from the point of view of the just man, the person who is bound to act justly. It would seem more consistent with modern notions, or at any rate more refreshing, to look at the matter rather from the point of view of the citizen to whom just treatment is due. In other words, it may be revealing to consider not primarily the duty to act justly but the demand for just treatment. Again, it may often be more illuminating to ask not what would amount to 'just treatment' or 'just action' but in what circumstances we would describe treatment or actions as 'unjust'. In this, as in many spheres, the negative concept is easier to grasp and illustrate than the positive.[1] Finally in the English language the words 'just' and 'unjust' have a somewhat heavy and even pompous connotation. I have preferred in many places to use the words 'fair' and 'unfair' instead. These mean the same or very nearly the same as just and unjust.[2] Their connotation is lighter and by the use of them the temperature of the discussion can be lowered.

But the most important reason for reopening old controversies is that I believe that it is possible to make some progress in the inquiry and to reach a conclusion which is not a purely skeptical one.[3] The thesis I shall argue is that the notion of social justice represents something more than merely the opinion of a group as to what demands they think should be conceded. It represents something more than merely a formal notion. It is not merely a question of conforming to the rules whatever they may be. The view I shall advocate is that the principle of social justice consists in two propositions. The first is the contention that *all men considered merely as men and apart from their conduct or choice have a claim to an equal share in all those things, here called advantages, which*

---

[1] On this, see CAHN, THE SENSE OF INJUSTICE (1949).

[2] See HART, THE CONCEPT OF LAW 154 (1961) (hereafter cited as HART). Contrast RAWLS., NOMOS—JUSTICE VI 98–117 (1963).

[3] For a skeptical conclusion, see VERMEERSCH in IL XL ANNIVERSARIO DELLA ENCICLICA 'RERUM NOVARUM' 556 (1931). HART 162–3. DEL VECCHIO 123, No. 2.

are generally desired and are in fact conducive to their well-being.
By this I mean such things as life, health, food, shelter, clothing,
places to move in, opportunities for acquiring knowledge and skill,
for sharing in the process of making decisions,[1] for recreation,
travel, etc.

Men not only have a claim to these things but to an equal share
in them. It would be misleading to advance the first half of this
proposition without the second or *vice versa.* If we say that men
have a claim to equal shares in all advantages without saying that
they have a claim to them irrespective of shares, then this claim
might be satisfied by a system which distributed misery equally
and gave men no share or an infinitesimal share in the advantages
generally desired. Conversely if we say that men have a claim to
these advantages without adding that their claim is to an equal
share, then the proposition might be satisfied by a system which
allots or distributes advantages in an arbitrary way. The word
'claim' is used rather than the words 'opportunity'[2] or 'privilege'.
Following Hohfeld's usage[3] it seems appropriate to use the word
'claim'[4] in this context to mark the point that we are here concerned not, as we are in the analysis of liberty, with the question
'What are men permitted to do', but with the question 'What are
men entitled to demand?'

The second proposition that I shall advance is that *there is a
limited set of factors which can justify departure from the principle
embodied in the first proposition.* This is to say that there are a
limited number of *principles of discrimination* and that the claim of
men to an equal share in all advantages can fairly be modified,
restricted or limited by only two main factors. These are the
choice of the claimant or the citizen on the one hand and his
conduct on the other; there are also certain principles of individual
justice dealt with under the rubrics of 'the justice of transactions'
and of 'special relations'.

From this it will be evident that, while I do not believe that any

---

[1] Emphasized by Lasswell and McDougal, *Legal Education* 52 YALE L. J. 203
(1943) and McDougal, *Comparative Study of Law for Policy Purposes* 61 YALE
L. J. 915 (1952) with, however, a careful avoidance of the term 'Social Justice'.
[2] On equality of opportunity, see below.
[3] W. N. HOHFELD, FUNDAMENTAL LEGAL CONCEPTIONS Ch. 1 (1964).
[4] Also adopted by D. D. Raphael, *Equality and Equity* 21 PHILOSOPHY 118,
119–20 (1946) and *Justice and Liberty* 51 PROCEEDINGS OF THE ARISTOTELIAN
SOCIETY 167, 179 (1951).

single formula such as distribution according to desert, or according to need, can adequately express the concept of social justice, I believe it is possible to state the basic principles underlying the concept in a way which makes it more than an empty form. Perhaps the greatest single obstacle to the analysis of the notion of justice is, indeed, the belief that a single formula can and must be found which will express a principle applicable to those various circumstances in which the allocation of advantages is in question. This is an illusion; but the opposite belief, that the various formulae represent nothing more substantial than the preference of those who advocate them, is equally mistaken.

The inquiry will take the following form. The different principles of justice which have been advocated in the past or are generally accepted at the present day will be examined one by one in order to discover which, if any, of them forms a part of the notion of social justice. After they have been dealt with I shall end by considering briefly what, if any, explanation of and justification for the advocacy for social justice can be found.

THE LEADING PRINCIPLES OF JUSTICE

It would seem that if we are to be guided by ordinary usage, that is by the circumstances in which people commonly complain of being treated unfairly, or put forward a claim to fair treatment, there are at least six principles of justice to be distinguished.

1. *The justice of transactions: restoration of the status quo or its equivalent*

The first type may be called the justice of transactions. This corresponds to some extent with Aristotle's notion of rectificatory justice, but not entirely. Aristotle's rectificatory[1] or diorthotic justice is thought of as a principle by virtue of which matters which are crooked must be put straight. Thus if A lends B a book, the balance is restored if B returns the book to A. Again, if B steals A's book the balance between A and B is restored when B returns the book to A, and this, again, is what rectificatory justice requires. On the other hand if A sells B a house, this form of justice requires that the equivalent of the value of the house should

---

[1] Various translations of 'diorthotic' have been proposed. See DEL VECCHIO 59: e.g. commutative (the commonest suggestion), directive, regulative, corrective, reparative, remedial. Ross' *rectificatory* (used in his translation of the NICOMACHAEAN, ETHICS) is the most satisfactory term so far proposed.

be paid by way of price. In this case rectificatory justice requires not the return of the identical thing which had previously been transferred but an equivalent. Thus this form of justice may require either restoration *in specie* or alternatively compensation in the form of the giving of an equivalent for what has been received. It covers therefore the notions of *restitution* and *compensation*.

According to Aristotle this form of justice can be applied to assess the punishment due when a wrongdoer has committed an offence and not merely the compensation or restitution due in civil transactions. Thus Aristotle draws no distinction between rectificatory justice between citizen and state. The distinction between crime and delict was not in the fourth century B.C. a very distinct one and in consequence he seems not to have marked it clearly. From a modern point of view it is desirable to make this distinction and accordingly what is here called the justice of transactions is not identical with Aristotle's rectificatory justice, but is confined to those situations where it is fair that one citizen should restore something to another citizen, compensate him for a wrong or pay him for goods or services rendered. This form of justice, unlike justice between citizen and state, presupposes that some transaction has taken place between the claimant and the person against whom the claim or complainant is made. Such a transaction may be a direct one, as when there is a contract between parties, or where the claimant is the victim of a delict committed by the other party, or again when the dealings between the parties have given rise to a claim for unjust enrichment. On the other hand the transaction may be indirect, as in certain cases of contract in favor of or binding third parties, of unjust enrichment by or against third parties and of delicts affecting third parties. This does not affect the description of the form of justice involved, namely the justice of transactions, because the claim is one by an individual citizen against another individual citizen without reference to the remaining members of society, and always arises from a particular transaction.

The object of this form of justice is, then, the restoration of the original position or its equivalent. It seems proper to call this a form of individual, not of social justice,[1] since the claim to which

---

[1] On the definition of TAPARELLI, SAGGIO TEORETICO DI DIRITTO NATURATE APPOGGIATO SUL FATTO I, 158 (social justice is justice between man and man) this is a form of social justice.

it gives rise is directed solely toward other individual citizens and cannot be conceived as a claim against other members of society as a whole. Nor does it involve a comparison of the treatment received by the claimant with the treatment accorded to others. From a social point of view the restoration of the *status quo* or of a state of affairs that approximates to it, although in itself a fair objective, does not necessarily produce a situation which would be described as a completely fair one.[1] This is because the *status quo* is not necessarily itself regarded as representing a fair allocation of advantages among members of society. This form of justice therefore possesses a conservative tendency[2] and, while it would be unfair not to give effect to it, we cannot conclude that the state of affairs produced, when effect has been given to it, is a fair state of affairs.

2. *The justice of special relations*

Another individual type of justice is exemplified by the claims which members of the same family and others who stand in some special relation to one another are considered to have against each other. These claims may be independent of merit or need; it would be unfair of a father to disinherit his child even if the child was not in need and, conversely, fair to leave him property by will though he had done nothing to earn it, perhaps because his studies had only recently been completed. But this, again, is not a type of social justice because it upholds not the claims of man as man but only of man as standing in a special relation to some particular fellow-man.

3. *The justice of conformity to rule*[3]

The third form of justice here considered is one which is sometimes regarded, but I think mistakenly, as possessing a merely formal character. This is the justice of conformity to rule.[4] Each member of society is thought to have a claim that the rules by which society is regulated, whatever they may be, should be

---

[1] DEL VECCHIO 67, No. 13.

[2] On 'conservative' justice, see SIDGWICK, THE METHOD OF ETHICS 273, 293 (1874).

[3] Also called 'legal justice'—but this is really a species of the genus 'the justice of conformity to rule'. On legal justice see DEL VECCHIO 33–37, 115.

[4] I omit to consider the subsidiary aspects of this principle, such as the rules of 'natural justice': these are designed to secure that the rules are in fact impartially and objectively applied. HART 156.

observed. Thus it is unfair to *A* to apply to him a rule unfavorable to him if this rule is not also applied to *B*, who is also covered by the conditions prescribed by the rule. Conversely it is unfair to *B* to refuse to apply to him a rule favorable to him that is applied in the case of *A*, again on the assumption that the conditions prescribed by the rule apply equally to both. Thus if a rule forbids parking in a certain area it is unfair to *A* who has parked in that area that he should be fined for doing so, whilst *B*, who has done the same thing, is not prosecuted, Again if a rule prescribes a tax remission for those whose children are under a certain age, it is unfair to *B* to refuse him the tax remission, when his children are under the stated age, whilst a remission is granted to *A* who is in the same position. Hence we can state as a general principle that every man has a claim that the rules should be interpreted and adhered to *at least as favorably* in his own case as in the case of his fellow-man, assuming that both fall within the categories prescribed by the rules and conditions mentioned in them.

The notion of conformity to rule can be made to yield the notion that like cases should be treated alike. If we think of those species of rule that prescribe that certain people be treated in a certain way when certain conditions are fulfilled, the demand that such rules should be observed entails the demand that cases falling within the conditions mentioned should be treated in the way prescribed in the rule, that is that people who are alike in the relevant respect should be treated alike. This, then, involves the principle *treat like cases alike*.[1]

But, so far, this only means that cases alike in the respect prescribed by the rules should be treated alike, not that cases alike in some other respect should be so treated. Thus, if the rules prescribe that every adult citizen shall have the right to vote, this means merely that cases alike in that they are cases of adult male citizens shall be treated in that way, namely by being allowed to vote. Where human beings are concerned there are always similarities and differences between any two members of the class

[1] This in turn yields the principle 'give each man his due', at least on one interpretation of 'due', namely, what the rules allot to each man. But it seems that 'due' is often interpreted more widely as in the Encyclical *Quadragesimo Anno of Pius* XI (*1931*): '*Sua igitur cuique pars bonorum adtribuenda est, efficiendumque, ut ad boni communis seu socialis justitiae normas revocetur et conformetur partitio bonorum creatorum.*' On *suum cuique tribuere*, see DEL VECCHIO 74, No. 27, 112.

in question. The principle of treating like cases alike is therefore an empty, though as we shall see not a merely formal, one, until we know in what respect the cases are supposed to be like or unlike. If the rules prescribed that those of a certain height or religious belief should alone be allowed to vote, this would be condemned as constituting an unfair discrimination against those not of the right height or religion. Yet a judge or official, who applied these rules impartially, though he would be discriminating unfairly, from one point of view, against the underprivileged category, would in doing so conform to the rules laid down; and in that case his conduct could not be called unfair or unjust, so far as the principle of conformity to rule is concerned. Thus persons not of the prescribed height or religious belief, who were denied the right to vote, could not complain of unfair treatment *in relation to other persons* falling within the same category.

It is perhaps worth noting that, contrary to what is sometimes asserted,[1] the principle of conformity to rule cannot be made to yield the principle *treat unlike cases unlike*. Thus if a rule prescribes that adult male citizens shall have the right to vote, this means that those men who are alike in possessing the characteristics of being adult male and citizens should be treated alike in respect of the right to vote. But we cannot conclude, and it may be quite false to assert, that those who do not fall into this category are to be denied the right to vote, for instance that adult women who are citizens have no right to vote. It is a merely contingent matter whether such a rule should be interpreted *e contrario* so as to exclude the right to vote in the case of all those who do not fall into the category mentioned. Nor does the fact that a certain category of men are forbidden to act in a certain way, for instance, hotelkeepers to operate without a liquor license, imply that the conduct in question is permissible in the case of persons not falling within the category mentioned. It does not follow from the fact that hotelkeepers may not operate without a liquor license that all other members of society may do so.

The principle *treat unlike cases unlike* is in fact not part of the notion of justice, or of social justice in particular, and represents rather an inaccurate way of stating the following idea. There are certain principles of discrimination, such as the principle of justice according to desert, of justice according to choice and of justice

---

[1] e.g. HART 155.

according to need,[1] and, according to these, it is not unfair to treat cases which are dissimilar *in respect of the criteria listed* in a dissimilar way. But this does not carry with it the conclusion that it is right so to treat them, because the fairness of the treatment depends not merely on the presence or absence of factors justifying discrimination, but on the principles of social justice, of which the demand for conformity to rule is only one. It does not follow from the fact that discrimination is sometimes excusable (and is not unfair) that whenever it is excusable fairness positively requires it.

Furthermore the maxim *treat unlike cases unlike,* even if it represented the truth, would only apply when the conditions, subject to which the rules prescribed unlike treatment, actually obtained. In the case of the justice of conformity to rule it must be stressed that the existence of a rule, prescribing certain treatment for persons in a certain category, does not necessarily entail the existence of a rule prescribing different treatment for persons not in that category.

The claim of each man to be treated no less favourably than his fellow-man, if both fall within the category prescribed by the rule and both fulfill the conditions mentioned in it, is not the empty generality which at first sight it appears to be. Thus, it is not confined to cases where the rule involved is a legal one. It would be regarded as unfair for a father, who had a habit of giving his married children $100 each for Christmas and his unmarried children $50 each, to abandon this practice without warning and to give his unmarried children $100 each, his married children $50 each. The reason why this would be condemned as unfair is that the claim that our fellow-men should conform to rule is not based merely on the fact that the rules under consideration are legally or morally binding, that is, are prescriptive rules. The principle of conformity is not merely regarded as giving each member of society a legal or moral right to equal treatment, but is partly based on the fact that failures to conform to rules, whether binding or not, disappoint known expectations reasonably entertained, infringe human dignity and so are unfair from a second point of view.[2] What is involved when rules are jettisoned is not merely

---

[1] See below, pp. 72, 81 and 78.

[2] The expectations must be known, otherwise Kant's neighbors who set their watches by his daily walk can't justly have complained on the occasion when he failed to take it.

discrimination when there is an obligation, moral or legal, not to discriminate; discrimination is objectionable whenever it disappoints or defies expectations known to be reasonably entertained.

The demand for conformity to rule is therefore partly based on a claim for consistent treatment, whether obligatory or not. Nor does it matter whether the course of conduct, which consistency has demanded, is itself rational or not. In the case of the father and the Christmas present, the father has changed from a rational mode of distribution, namely one based on the need of his children, to an irrational mode which disregards their needs. But it would also have been unfair to the unmarried children, if the father had previously given the unmarried children $100 for Christmas and the married ones $50, to change without warning and thereafter to give the unmarried children $50, the married children $100. This is true despite the fact that the father would then have changed from an irrational mode of distribution to a rational one based on need. The reason why the change would be unfair is that it would disappoint the known expectations which the unmarried children have reasonably formed, and affront their dignity.

The demand for conformity to rule prevails in practice even when the rule in question is a mere habit and not morally or legally binding. Of course it does not operate unless some advantage or disadvantage to the claimant, the individual citizen, is involved. Thus, it may be immaterial to A whether B follows the usual habit of taking off his hat when he meets a lady. A is not entitled to demand conformity to habit or rule in this case, because he derives no advantage from it. But it is otherwise if we consider the point of view of the lady whom we may call C. She has in the past had the advantage of B's courtesy and so is entitled to complain if B without warning abandons his former habit and keeps his hat on when he meets her. What is more, she can complain of unfair treatment if B continues to take off his hat when he meets another lady, E, since this, besides disappointing her expectations, infringes her dignity. The demand for conformity to rule does not therefore essentially depend on the character of the habit or obligation involved, but on the existence of a regular practice which gives rise or may reasonably give rise to a known expectation on the part of the citizen affected, to his advantage, that the rule will be adhered to. The citizen is entitled to protection against irregular or unusual discrimination.

Now such a principle cannot be described as one of a merely formal character. The protection of reasonable expectations and of human dignity is the protection of a substantial interest and illustrates a form of social justice. Of course it is not the whole of social justice but it constitutes a necessary element in that notion. It is in fact one part of what man as man is entitled to demand of his fellow man: equal treatment in so far as the fulfillment of known reasonable expectations is concerned.

It remains true, however, that the rules to which conformity has been demanded may be of an oppressive or iniquitous sort. They may, for instance, involve unfair discrimination on the basis of race or religion, as in the case of the Nuremberg anti-Jewish laws and the apartheid laws in South Africa. The rigorous and impartial enforcement of such laws may well be called, in a certain sense, not unfair. Harsh though they may be, impartial enforcement will be held less unfair to the person against whom they are enforced than if their application was partial or capricious. On the other hand, it would be wrong to describe the rigorous and impartial enforcement of rules or laws which are in themselves unfair as being itself a fair or just action, or as producing a fair result.[1] The way to describe this situation is rather to say that provided the rules are followed, the enforcement of them against A and B indiscriminately is not unfair to either, whereas the enforcement of them in the case of A would be unfair to A if B, who fell within the same rules, because he fulfilled the conditions laid down for their application, was not treated as prescribed by the rules. Conformity to an unfair rule does not create a fair or just result but rather one which is not unfair relatively to any individual person falling within the rules who receives the treatment prescribed by it. Such a situation is not unfair as violating the subject's dignity in relation to others in the same category, but is unfair *vis-à-vis* his relation to persons outside the category. We may conclude that conformity to rule is a necessary element in the notion of social justice but is not conclusive of the fairness of the result produced when it is applied. It is an element in the notion of social justice because it expresses a demand properly voiced by men as members of society against their fellow men: but it is not the whole of what they may properly and fairly demand.

---

[1] An extreme form of the view that (legal) rules cannot be unjust is stated by HOBBES, LEVIATHAN Ch. 30.

4. *The justice of allocation according to desert*
(*for short:* '*justice according to desert*')

The fourth variety of justice corresponds approximately to
Aristotle's distributive justice.[1] This rests on the principle that
it is fair to reward others according to their merits or deserts. The
first thing to ask in this connection is: how is merit to be assessed?
A very clear example of reward according to merit would be a case
in which payment is made to someone according to the quality or
value of the work he has done. In this simple case at least merit
depends on performance; in other words, on the claimant's
actual conduct.

By a corollary it may be said that desert can equally depend on
demerit, on bad conduct, in that the principle of justice according
to desert includes also the principle that those who have behaved
badly or harmfully should be punished according with the extent
and character of their wrongdoing. If this is accepted, the core of
the desert principle is the notion that men are responsible for
their actions and that it is fair for society to reward them according
to their responsibility. It is not unfair to penalize persons in
certain circumstances for what they have done, the notion of
penalty here straddling civil and criminal law.

If we take these two aspects of the desert principle together,
the principle seems to amount to this: that it is fair to reward
citizens according to what they have done, the reward being
favorable or advantageous if the action is beneficial and disadvantageous if the action is harmful. By a further development of
the same principle it is often asserted that the reward should in
both cases be *proportional*[2] to the conduct in question. Wages,
for instance, should be proportional to the work done and punishment to the seriousness of the offense. A citizen is entitled to more
or less according to whether he has made a positive or a negative
contribution to the welfare of the community.

It must be conceded that this principle represents an important
part of the notion of justice. In a sense one might say that it forms
part of the notion of social justice, because it represents a claim
made by the citizen on his fellow-men as a whole, and not one

---

[1] DEL VECCHIO Ch. VI. ARISTOTLE, ETH. NIC. V. ii (5) 1130b 31–33; V. iii (6)
1131a 20–27; V. iii (7) 1131b 11–20.

[2] On proportion see DEL VECCHIO 51. ARISTOTLE, ETH. NIC. V. iv (7) 1131b 25,
1132a 10.

merely made on those with whom he has entered into a particular transaction. But though in a broad sense the principle of desert is a principle of social justice, in a narrower and more precise sense it is not. The reason is that it does not provide any answer to the question, 'What is it that men are entitled to demand of their fellow-men considered simply as such?' It is a principle that allocates advantages or disadvantages to men according to the particular conduct of each and not according to their mere character as human beings. An example will make this clear. Suppose that A has done twice as much work as B, but both receive the same wage. A is entitled to complain that he has been unfairly treated in comparison with B. This unfairness disappears if A is paid twice as much as B. But this is not the only type of problem that can arise when men are allocating advantages. Suppose that the problem is whether a surplus of production should be distributed or dumped in the sea. On the principles of distributive justice here considered—distribution according to desert—B has no right to complain if the latter solution is adopted and neither has A. Of course the principle of distribution according to need may be prayed in aid, if B is in fact in need. But this, as we shall see,[1] is a part of the notion of social justice itself. If B is not actually in need, there is so far no principle by virtue of which either he or A can complain of the dumping of the surplus in the sea, unless we can discover a principle of justice independent of the particular conduct or choice of the individual. It would seem, therefore, that the principle of justice according to desert explains only how the fair demands of men as men on their fellow-men may be modified by their conduct, not what those demands are apart from their conduct.

There are several points in the principle of justice according to desert which need to be elucidated. The first concerns the notion of desert or merit itself. So far it has been assumed that the criterion of desert is conduct, that is, what the citizen who claims to be treated according to desert has actually done. But in fact this is only part of the notion of desert. Thus it would be fair to appoint to a vacant post the person best qualified for it, even if the assumption of the claimant's qualifications was based not on his past performance but on his ability and promise. The candidate who failed to secure the appointment could not complain of unfair

---

[1] Below, p. 78.

A. M. Honoré

treatment in such a case, and the best qualified candidate would properly be said to deserve the appointment. It seems clear however that where, as here, performance is not the basis of desert, potential performance is.[1] The reason why it is fair to appoint the best qualified, i.e. the most promising, candidate is that, although this cannot be regarded as a reward for past work, it can be based on the promise of future work. *A*, who is likely to achieve more than the other candidate *B*, is therefore the right person to appoint. It seems then that the principle of desert can be applied either when advantages or disadvantages are allotted according to actual performance or when they are allotted on the basis of potential performance.

Similarly, it may sometimes be fair to punish an offender who is potentially very dangerous more severely than one who is less dangerous, though their past conduct has been similar; so that in this type of case too, potential performance may be taken into account. The principle however is one to be applied with caution: potential performance is a criterion of desert primarily when there is no adequate evidence of actual performance.

A second point requiring elucidation is this. The principle of distribution according to desert seems to depend on the notion of proportion.[2] According to some, this is a key notion in the analysis of the concept of justice as a whole. But it seems that the notion of proportion, though important, can easily be overstressed. For one thing, there are situations where this notion does not apply, even when the principle of justice according to desert is in question. Suppose that one theatre ticket or one school place is available for distribution. *A* and *B* are the claimants. A distribution proportional to desert or proportional to any other factor, such as need, is here impossible, since the ticket or school place is indivisible. What is here regarded as fair is that priority should be assigned to the claimant with the greatest merit or desert, not that the thing available for distribution should be distributed in proportion to the merits of the various claimants. The notion of proportion therefore

---

[1] Alternatively, allocation according to capacity might be regarded as a separate principle of (discriminatory) justice. HART 159. Raphael, *Equality and Equity* 21 PHILOSOPHY 125 (1946). Although the latter plausibly argues that allocation on the basis of capacity does not involve inequality, though it does involve differentiation, I think it safer to assume that it does or may involve inequality sometimes.

[2] ARISTOTLE, ETH. NIC. V. i–iii.

must be supplemented by that of priority, in order to cater to those cases in which the distribution of indivisible advantages is in question. The citizen with the greater desert has the *prior and greater claim*, not just the greater claim to those goods which are to be allocated.

Thirdly, the notion of distribution can itself be criticized as apt to mislead in some contexts. The picture apt to be conjured up by it is that of material goods being allocated to different members of society. No rational distinction however can be drawn between the following categories of 'advantage', using that word in a wide sense: (A) material goods, (B) incorporeal things such as copyrights, contractual rights, etc., (C) interests which are not legally regarded as property but which are legally protected, such as life, health, honor, reputation, and (D) opportunities or facilities such as the right to vote, to have free education, to leave property by will, travel, etc. These latter are not protected primarily by legal claims but involve the exercise of legal powers coupled with privileges. It seems that interests such as life, health, etc., can with difficulty be thought of as *distributed* by society to its members. We can all agree that, if it were necessary to choose between saving the life of *A* or *B*, it would be proper to consider the merits or deserts of them both before making a decision. It would not be unfair to select the more deserving, if such a painful choice had to be made. Similarly as regards health, if there were time and opportunity to operate on one of two persons *A* and *B* in order to save his eyesight, it would not be unfair to select the more deserving of the two. But it would not be natural to speak of such a choice as involving the 'distribution' of life or health between the two. It is for this reason that the terminology of Aristotle, namely that of distributive justice, hardly seems adequate to express the principle of justice according to desert.[1] It is more accurate to think of this form of justice as one according to which claims, whether to property in the legal sense or not, are to depend upon the relative merits of the claimants.

Finally there is the question whether, as I have so far assumed, punishment is rightly thought of as illustrating a form of justice according to desert. Clearly there is no complete parallel between

---

[1] Aristotle's position could however be improved by adding to the notion of distributive justice that of *redistributive justice*. But even this is not quite adequate for cases such as those mentioned in the text.

reward according to desert and punishment according to desert. This is best seen by considering the claim of the citizen who is entitled to demand fair treatment and complain of unfair treatment. The citizen who deserves a greater reward is entitled to claim it and to complain if he does not receive it. But the citizen who deserves a greater punishment is not entitled to nor would he in fact claim it. No unfairness to him is involved in failing to assign to him the appropriate or indeed any punishment. The failure to see this stems from a failure to think of justice as involving claims.[1]

Nevertheless a person who has committed a wrong may be unfairly treated by being punished in circumstances such as the following. Suppose that *A* and *B* have each committed a crime of similar magnitude and type; for instance, that each has stolen an automobile. *Prima facie* it is unfair to *B* to punish him by sentencing him to a year's imprisonment for a crime similar to that for which *A* receives only six months' imprisonment.[2] That is to say, *B* has a claim not to be punished more severely than a person who has committed a crime similar in magnitude and type. In the same way when rewards are being considered, a person who has done the same amount and quality of work as another has a claim not to be rewarded less than the other. This does not entail that a person punished no more severely than a person who has committed an equally serious offense has been fairly punished. It means only that he is not unfairly punished so far as his relation with the other offender is concerned.[3] In order that he should be said to be fairly punished, it would be necessary to show that the level of punishment is itself fair, a point to which I advert later. It would also be necessary to show that the rule for the breach of which he has been punished is itself a fair one. Even then, it is necessary to point out

---

[1] Claims are psychologically primary, as Rousseau noted: 'le premier sentiment de la justice ne nous vient pas de celle que nous devons, mais de celle que nous est due'. ÉMILE II, 87.

[2] As I am concerned to analyze the modern concept of justice it seems immaterial that Aristotle thought it unjust that a free man and a slave should be punished equally for the same offense. See MAGNA MORALIA I. xxxiv 1194a 31. Usually such discrimination is nowadays openly based on utility, not justice, or on the spurious reasoning that some persons, e.g. negroes, are less sensitive to suffering than others.

[3] 'The idea of demerit . . . signifies the removal of a claim normally present . . . justice stands aside, for it is satisfied that its claims raise no obstruction'. Raphael, *Justice and Liberty* 51 PROCEEDINGS OF THE ARISTOTELIAN SOCIETY 178 (1951).

that justice and fairness are not the only factors involved in punishment and indeed, on one view, ought not to be taken into consideration at all. Regard for the protection of society and for the perfection of the individual also have their necessary and perhaps predominant place among the objectives that those who legislate or judge should bear in mind.

There is another respect in which the parallel between earning a reward and earning a punishment breaks down. We have seen that besides the question of allocation of rewards in a certain proportion and according to a certain priority, there is or may be a residuary problem about the allocation of surpluses, that is, of benefits surplus to those which the principle of justice based upon desert requires to be allocated. But there is no similar question whether the whole of all possible or available punishments should be allocated to wrongdoers, that is to say there is no question about the distribution of surplus disadvantages. It is immaterial from the point of view of justice whether prisons are kept full and hangmen busy.

This perhaps teaches us something about the scope of the principle of justice according to desert. As already mentioned, this principle involves the notion of proportion and priority, of greater or lesser rewards or punishments. But these are relative notions, and there remains a further problem, namely a problem of the *level of rewards and punishments.* How are we to fix the appropriate level of each? It seems natural to say that the levels of rewards and punishments should be fixed in such a way as to maximize rewards for advantages and to minimize punishments or disadvantages. In other words the level of rewards should be as high as possible, or at any rate should be at the highest level compatible with the demands of other values such as preservation of society and individual liberty. Again the level of punishment should be as low as possible, that is to say should be set at the lowest level compatible with the protection of society from the depredations of wrongdoers. But neither of these principles bearing on the level of reward and punishment can be derived from the principle of justice according to desert, unless we say, what is highly implausible, that everyone deserves as much advantage and as little disadvantage as can be safely managed. I do not think this will be seriously maintained. The principle of justice according to desert therefore seems to require to be completed by some further principle which will

enable us to determine the fair claims of men as men, that is, as
members of society.

5. *The justice of allocation according to need*
(for short, 'justice according to need')

The principle here involved is one by which it is fair to allocate
advantages, and to recognize the claims of citizens according to
their needs.[1] The notion of need is here to be taken in an objective
not a subjective sense. That is to say the criterion of need is taken
to be not whether the citizen thinks he needs something but whether
in fact he does so. For it would be extravagant to argue that every
person has a proportional or prior claim to all those things which
he thinks he needs. The concept of need is a somewhat complex
one. What it presupposes is that there are certain advantages such
that, if they are not satisfied, no existence at all or at any rate no
decent or complete existence is possible. Without life no existence
at all is possible and without adequate food, shelter and clothing
no decent existence is possible. Nor is this the limit of the
advantages which people may be said to need. The boundaries
of need shift from time to time with changes in the social and
economic conditions of society and in the exigencies which
a decent or complete existence is thought to postulate. What
is at one time a luxury becomes at another time a necessity and
need.

It is clear that the needs of different people vary and this might
be thought to entail that the principle of justice according to need
is not part of the concept of social justice. But this would be a
mistake. The principle of social justice as formulated earlier lays
down that men have a claim to advantages and not merely to an
equal share in advantages. From the point of view of this principle,
those who are in need are entitled to point to the fact that they lack
advantages which the principle of social justice entitles them.
Therefore the principle of justice according to need may be regarded as one aspect, or one corollary, of the principle of social
justice.[2] The fact that men's needs vary does not mean that the
satisfaction of needs is not something which they are entitled to

---

[1] cf. HART 159. DEL VECCHIO 142, 147.

[2] Raphael, *Justice and Liberty* 51 PROCEEDINGS OF THE ARISTOTELIAN SOCIETY
167, 189 (1951): 'thus the basis of the claim of social need is really a recognition of the claim to equality'. This is so despite the fact that men's needs differ
in detail; all need health equally, but some need more sleep.

claim as members of society rather than by virtue of their choice or conduct.

The principle of justice according to need is one which would generally be recognized at least in appropriate cases. Thus if a gift of $100 is to be distributed between *A* and *B*, the fact that *A*'s need is greater than *B*'s would be a factor fairly taken into consideration and would justify giving *A* a greater share. Nor is the notion confined to the distribution of gifts. A person in need, for instance, a person who is unemployed or ill, is regarded as having a claim, derived from his need, to a contribution by his fellow-men, to help to relieve his lack of earnings and his ill health respectively.[1] In fixing salaries and wages the need of citizens is often taken into account. Thus where one employee is married and has a family he is often awarded more than an employee doing similar work who is unmarried. A comparable principle is often observed in the imposition of burdens. Thus progressive taxation according to income or, in the case of estate duties, to capital, rests on the principle that the need of those who have a higher income or have greater capital assets is less than that of the persons who have a lower income or capital assets. The need principle like the merit principle therefore applies not merely to the allocation of advantages but to the allocation of disadvantages. Again however the parallel is not complete, since it would be wrong to assert that the person whose need is less, because he is wealthy, has a claim to be taxed more heavily than a person whose need is greater. The position would be more correctly stated if we said that a person whose need is less is not unfairly treated in relation to other taxpayers if he is taxed more than a person whose need is greater. But it is not true to say that the tax imposed on him is necessarily fair since this in turn is dependent upon whether the total level of taxation is itself fair.

It is plain that the principles of justice according to desert and justice according to need can and often do conflict.[2] The analysis of these notions does not in itself enable us to say how such conflicts are to be resolved. Nevertheless there would I think be agreement on a general approach to the resolution of these conflicts. The different advantages which citizens claim and of the

---

[1] 'So distribution should undo excess, and each man have enough.' (SHAKESPEARE, KING LEAR Act IV sc. 1: cited by DEL VECCHIO 148.)

[2] DEL VECCHIO loc. cit. ARAMBURO, FILOSOFIA DEL DERECHO I 388.

deprivation of which they complain may be arranged in an order of importance. Thus life may be regarded as more important than health, health than recreation and so on, although all three are properly described as needs and as advantages which men generally desire. The order of importance depends partly on the choice which most men would make if confronted with the alternative of selecting one or the other. The hierarchy of importance will depend, then, partly on the extent which the advantages in question are in fact desired, and partly on the extent which they actually conduce to well-being, that is to a happy and complete existence.

Now the natural solution of the problem that arises when there is a conflict between the principles of justice according to need and justice according to desert will be somewhat as follows: the more important the advantage in question the more weight will be given to the principle of justice according to need. Conversely the less important the advantage in question the less weight will be given to the principle of justice according to need and the greater weight to the principle of justice according to desert. Thus if A's life is in danger his need would generally be held to prevail over his lack of desert, no matter how extreme. It would be thought that he had a claim to be rescued or to receive the appropriate medical treatment even if he had done nothing especially deserving during his life or had been guilty of serious misconduct. It is of course a matter of controversy where the point comes at which demerit outweighs the claim to life which every member of society normally is thought to possess. The controversy about capital punishment illustrates this very clearly. On the other hand if the question was whether an opportunity of recreation, such as a place in a football team, should be afforded to A or B, and A was a better footballer than B, A's deserts would normally be held to outweigh the greater need which B could adduce on the ground that he had fewer opportunities for recreation. This is because recreation is a less important need than health or life. There will be intermediate cases where the weight of the conflicting principles is more nearly equal and then it will be a delicate question to strike a balance.

If this analysis is correct, the principle of justice according to need is regarded, at least by our modern consciousness, as a more fundamental one than the principle of justice according to desert. It is more fundamental in the sense that it is held to outweigh the latter principle when those advantages which are of fundamental importance, that is, those which are most generally esteemed and are most conducive to a full existence, are concerned. However, just as in the case of justice according to desert, it would be found that there are problems falling outside its scope: for instance the problem of the relative claims of those citizens whose needs have been satisfied. Such cases might be covered by the desert principle but, again, we have seen that this has itself a limited scope and in principle does not solve the problem of the appropriate level of reward and punishment.

6. *The justice of allocation according to choice*
(for short: 'justice according to choice')

This principle of justice is perhaps so obvious that it is generally overlooked. Clearly a person may choose not to claim that to which he would be fairly entitled. In that case it may or may not still be fair to give him the thing in question; the precise bearing of choice on the principles of justice is complex and cannot be properly considered here, despite its evident importance.

7. *The principle of social justice*[1]

We are now in a better position to elucidate the notion of social justice. We have to ask, first, whether there is such a principle; that is, whether, men are entitled merely as members of society and apart from their choice or conduct to claim any advantages from their fellow-men. If they are so entitled, what is it which they are entitled to claim?

It is already clear that men are entitled merely as such to claim something from their fellow-men, namely conformity to rules whatever they may be. This claim is based in part on the notion that known reasonable expectations should not be disappointed, in part on the notion that that form of discrimination is objectionable, as an affront to B's dignity, which fulfills the expectations of A but disappoints those of B. This, as we have seen, is a form of social justice because it expresses a claim that belongs to man as man apart from his conduct or choice. Again, we have seen that, when

---

[1] DEL VECCHIO 37. The identification of social justice with the pursuit of the common good hardly advances the inquiry because the 'common good' (a) is a vague conception; (b) on one interpretation at least comprises values other than justice, e.g. the preservation of society. Encyclical DIVINI REDEMPTORIS (19.3.1937) 'Socialis justitiae est id omne ab singulis exigere, quod ad commune bonum necessarium sit.'

the notion of justice according to need was examined, another form of social justice emerged, namely that according to which men have a claim as men to those advantages which are necessary in order that a decent and full life may be made possible.

It would be surprising if the principle of social justice protected the single types of interest already examined, namely the interest in conformity to rule and the interest of those who are in need, and not other human interests. Once it is admitted, indeed, that reasonable expectations are the subject of fair claims by men as men, there seems no principle by which we can deny the existence of similar claims, not only in the case of bodily health, shelter, food, clothing and other advantages which would rank as necessities, but also of recreation, travel, opportunities for amusement and education and those other advantages which might not be classified, at least in all societies, as human needs.

Again, it would be surprising if one particular form of discrimination, namely discrimination between persons in respect of their known reasonable expectations, were regarded as objectionable and other forms of discrimination regarded as acceptable. Can any rational distinction be drawn between discrimination in respect of known reasonable expectations and discrimination in respect of other interests whether falling within the notion of necessary advantages or not? Clearly a wider principle is involved and we must ask in what this principle consists.

A number of arguments tend to show that the wider principle of social justice consists simply in the claims of all men to all advantages and to an equal share in all advantages which are commonly regarded as desirable and which are in fact conducive to human well being. The first is an argument based on the analogy of the principle of the justice of conformity to rules. The principle of conformity to rule involves not merely that discrimination is objectionable but that any failure to conform to rule which disappoints reasonable expectations can be criticized as unfair. Thus, if the principle that all men have a right that their reasonable expectations should not be disappointed is extended to other advantages, we arrive at the proposition that all men have a claim to an equal share in all such advantages, and this is the principle of social justice for which I am contending.

The second argument is of an empirical character. We observe in practice that the claim to equal treatment naturally commends itself at least at the present day to most people. In fact children begin from an early age to advance this claim *vis-à-vis* other members of the family. Parents notice that the basic demand made by their children is for equal treatment in all respects; the exceptions which are made to this on the ground of desert or choice are of a sophisticated character and come to be accepted only when children attain a certain degree of understanding. They are modifications of the basic demand for equal treatment in all respects.

This demand is not confined to food, toys or material things but extends to opportunities for entertainment, recreation, education, travel, etc., and is indeed of a quite general character. The family being the basic unit of society or at least the unit to which we are all introduced first, it seems likely that the demand voiced by adults for equal treatment is modeled perhaps unconsciously on the habits they have acquired as children of demanding equal treatment from their parents. In other words the demand for fair treatment is not identical with the equal claim of all men to all advantages and to an equal share in all advantages. 'Treatment' covers a wide spectrum but not the whole field of vision. However the step by which this becomes generalized to cover those advantages which do not strictly speaking consist in treatment by our fellow-men is a natural one.

A third argument is as follows: there exists a general conviction in modern society that all unjustifiable or irrational discrimination is objectionable. Irrational or inconsistent behavior is open to criticism even when human beings are not involved or affected by it. Thus a person who gives one rose bush twice as much water as another apparently similar bush may readily be called upon to explain his action and to justify it, though he cannot be accused of unfairness.

It is arguable that our judgment would be different even when a non-human but conscious being such as an animal is involved.[1] Thus if a man gives one cat twice as much milk as a cat of a similar size and appetite, it will be thought that his conduct not merely calls for explanation and justification, but is open to the criticism that he is acting unfairly toward the cat who receives less. This criticism clearly depends upon the assumption that the less-privileged cat is capable of knowing that he is receiving less than his fellow. The notion involved seems to be that the consciousness

[1] On justice among animals see DEL VECCHIO 99 ff.

that a creature is subject to discrimination is itself an evil or disadvantage to be avoided as far as possible. This is true in particular if the notions of justice according to merit or need do not modify our assessment of the situation. Thus suppose two cats are equally deserving and suppose that neither needs more milk in order to live happily. It still remains true that it is objectionable to discriminate between them.

The point can be made more forcibly in relation to children, of whose consciousness of discrimination we are in no doubt. When adult human beings are in question, the discrimination is still more keenly felt to be unfair, since they have a fuller appreciation than children of what it involves. It is true that discrimination appears objectionable chiefly to those who think of themselves as belonging to the same category as those against whom the discrimination operates (cats, children in the same family), or as belonging to a superior category, namely one which in the opinion of the person in question is entitled to more than the category against which discrimination operates. Thus if white men think that white men belong to a category superior to negroes they will not find discrimination against negroes and in favor of white men objectionable though they will find discrimination of the opposite type objectionable. But such belief in superior and inferior categories is not innate; it has to be learned. We naturally and unreflectively think of ourselves as belonging to the same category as our fellow-men. A child does not naturally entertain notions of separate social, racial, religious or economic categories, but has to be taught them.

It is perhaps not easy at first sight to state what exactly the notion of discrimination means.[1] Discrimination must mean discrimination between classes which have something in common, in this case between human beings who clearly have many characteristics in common. It most naturally applies to the denial of opportunities to A which are accorded to B, e.g. opportunities of education, travel, using public transport, etc. Similarly the refusal to distribute to A goods that are distributed to B would be regarded as a form of discrimination. But are we to describe as

---

[1] In one sense 'discrimination' is consistent with equal treatment. Thus, if A likes whisky and B likes beer, it is consistent with the principle of equal claims to give each what he likes; yet, in a certain sense to do so is to discriminate, i.e. to differentiate between the two. But 'discrimination' is here used of those differentiations which produce unequal satisfactions.

discrimination the inaction of a person or government who does not intervene in the affairs of society, for instance, does not provide free education for anyone and leaves each family to fend for itself so far as education is concerned? Strictly speaking it would seem that no discrimination is involved in such conduct or inaction. All that is done is to give effect to the liberal notions of the last century that each person should fend for himself and that the state should refrain from interfering in the affairs of its citizens. If this distinction between discrimination and non-intervention is made, then the principle of non-discrimination, viz. that discrimination between human beings is objectionable in the absence of some rational justification, is not formally equivalent to the principle of social justice but corresponds only to a limited part of it, namely that part which consists in a demand for equal treatment. However, it is easy to see that the demand for non-discrimination and the demand for intervention in order to secure equal advantages are related rather closely. The former principle, though directed towards securing what is fair, is at the same time directed towards the maintenance of the *status quo* or its equivalent. In other words the non-discrimination principle seeks to retain for the various members of society the resources and assets which they already possess and to equalize opportunities and the distribution of advantages thereafter. Thus while discrimination is certainly open to objection as unfair in the absence of special circumstances, non-discrimination does not necessarily produce a fair result or a just society, but only does so if the initial distribution of resources and assets was itself fair.

It looks therefore as if the principle of non-discrimination, like the principle of conformity to rule and the principle of justice according to need, forms part, but not the whole, of the notion of social justice. To put the matter differently, there is a residuary question whether the initial distribution of skills, resources and assets can itself be regarded as fair or discriminatory. Before we tackle the latter question it will be as well to deal with some objections to the view that the principle that there should be no discrimination between human beings, except on rational grounds, is a part of the notion of social justice. It may be said (1) that in many or most societies discrimination has been accepted in certain cases (2) that even if the general principle of non-discrimination is accepted the wide scope of the factors which rationally justify departures from that principle is such as to empty it of content.

As to the first objections, it is certainly true that discrimination, often on grounds other than those of desert or choice, is accepted in most societies. Discrimination on grounds of the existence of factors such as choice, desert, need and conformity to rule is everywhere admitted and practiced. But it does not follow from this that irrational discrimination, not based on one of the factors listed, is accepted as justifiable. On the contrary it is noticeable that those who seek to justify discrimination which is in fact irrational seek to show that one of the factors listed above which justify departures from the principle of equal claims applies to the form of discrimination which they have in mind.[1]

Thus if racial discrimination is sought to be justified, it will be either on the ground that it is a regular and habitual practice, that it has existed in the past and that members of different races have come to expect it, or that members of different races voluntarily choose to observe it and that the discriminatory laws merely give effect to this choice, or that members of one race have less urgent and compelling needs than those of another; or finally that members of one race are less deserving and meritorious or 'capable' than another. The latter argument was the one which Aristotle adopted in his attempt to justify discrimination between free and slave, Greek and barbarian.[2] He asserted that in principle the capacity, that is to say, the potential achievement of slave and barbarian, was different. It will be seen that the flaw in this argument resides partly in errors of fact, for instance in a false belief in the different capacities of different races, where this is not borne out by the evidence, or in a belief that people prefer discrimination when in fact they do not. Partly the flaw lies in a failure to recognize that these justifications are exceptions to the general principle of equal claims.

Secondly, it may be argued that the list of exceptions is so long and vague as to empty the general principle of any real content. But it would seem that the exceptions are in fact limited to those listed. An apparent further exception occurs in the case of those incapacities which the law imposes on those incapable of managing their own affairs, such as minors and prodigals.

[1] cf., HART 158. We must add to the factors listed discrimination on the basis of individual justice.   [2] POLITICS I, ii, 3–22.

The desirability of imposing these restrictions rests on the fact that, if they are not imposed, the interests of the person concerned may be harmed; but this is not in itself a fair reason for intervening, otherwise one might fairly intervene in the affairs of another in a manner involving discrimination against him whenever it was in his interests to do so. This would certainly not be an acceptable principle.

The restrictions in question rest partly on the principle of justice according to need, partly on that of justice according to choice.[1] Since there is a hierarchy of advantages, it may be fair to restrict or refuse a lesser advantage in order to preserve one of which the person concerned has a greater need. Hence a minor may be prevented from alienating immoveables in order to preserve the greater advantage of his claim to a home and shelter which is more important than the power of alienating property.

But the restrictions rest in part on the principle of justice according to choice, since a minor along with other categories of persons under disability is thought of as incapable of making a free and considered choice. Just as by the principle of justice according to choice those who choose to forgo their claims are entitled to nothing, so those who choose to claim benefits but whose choice is imperfect are entitled to less in certain cases. In some such instances, but not all, the principle of justice according to desert also plays a part.

It has not been shown therefore that any principles of discrimination other than those listed are in fact accepted as forming part of the notion of justice. Although these principles cover a wide field, they are not all of equal importance. Thus, the justice of conformity to rule being based on the idea of protecting reasonable expectations, is consistent with change, since when reasonable notice of changes in rules or habits has been given, then the unfairness of departing from rules previously accepted disappears. Indeed even without such notice, the principle of conformity to rule is, according to the notion of *equity*, subject to some limited modifications in the interest of justice according to merit and need. The notion of equity is not however accepted everywhere. In a conflict between the principles of justice according to choice and the other principles

---

[1] And, still more, on social utility; but the latter is not a principle of justice or equity; it is a political and legal value which often conflicts with justice. Raphael, *Equality and Equity* 21 PHILOSOPHY 131 (1946).

of discrimination the former will prevail, since a citizen may voluntarily forgo that which his desert or need or expectation reasonably entitles him to demand. When there is a conflict between the principles of justice according to desert and justice according to need we have seen that the latter prevails when the more fundamental advantages such as life and health are in jeopardy. From this we can draw a conclusion of some importance for the analysis of social justice.

If we say that the need principle has precedence so far as these fundamental advantages are concerned, and that discrimination is justified in such cases (the man who is most seriously ill is entitled to the one vacant hospital bed, the man with the largest family to the one vacant house in the district) we have in fact discovered a further part of the principle of social justice. For if certain needs are regarded as having priority and as justifying discrimination, this means that a certain principle of redistribution or equalization is regarded as forming part of the notion of social justice. Thus if A is in good health, B in bad health, B's claim to medical treatment based on need prevails over his lack of desert and justifies discrimination in his favor.

The theory underlying this must be that B and A should be placed in the same position, so far as health is concerned, before the principles of non-discrimination and of justice according to desert are applied to both of them. To put the matter slightly differently, each man as man has a prior claim to at least certain essential advantages and this will involve a redistribution or equalization of at least certain such advantages. The word 're-distribution' is perhaps inadequate to describe a claim to preserve one's life or health; it applies more appropriately to those advantages which fall within the legal notion of property; but it is here used in the absence of a better term. Now this claim for equalization or redistribution is something which belongs to man as a member of society and is therefore part of the notion of social justice.

It may be objected that such claims belong to men only by virtue of their particular circumstances, and not as members of society. Thus it may be said that A's prior claim to health arises from the special circumstances that he is ill. But though it is true that the fact that particular circumstances are taken into account distinguishes this type of claim from the claim that rules should be observed or from the principle of non-discrimination, the objects to which the claim is directed, life, health, etc., are not variable and do not depend on individual circumstances. The truth is merely that in many or most cases the demand has already been satisfied and it is not necessary or sensible to voice it.

If however we recognize that such basic claims are entitled to prevail when the most important advantages are in question, are we not bound to say that similar claims exist in relation to other advantages, but may be overridden by principles of discrimination such as the principle of justice according to desert? For on what principle could it be said that justice demands that equal claims be recognized in regard to the most important advantages but not in regard to the less important? Surely such claims must form part of the notion of social justice and must be entitled to prevail in the absence of countervailing factors such as desert. These in turn will explain and justify what was noted in the discussion of justice according to desert, that we naturally think that the level of claims as opposed to their distribution should be maximized. This cannot be explained on the desert principle, but is explained on the view that social justice requires that all men have a claim to, and to an equal share in, all, not merely the more important advantages.

So far a number of arguments have been adduced to show that the principle of social justice requires that all men have a claim to an equal share in all advantages, and that the principles of non-discrimination and conformity to rule are merely subordinate aspects of this basic principle. This is to say that they are subordinate principles applying directly to the principle of social justice in order to preserve particular advantages, namely the fulfillment of reasonable expectations and the preservation of human dignity, which requires equal respect for all and is inconsistent with discrimination. Two objections may now be considered: (1) Is this principle restricted to advantages or does it also extend to disadvantages? (2) Does the principle of social justice consist in equal claims or rather in *equality of opportunity*?

1. It seems clear that the principle of social justice is confined to goods and does not extend to disadvantages. The even spread of misery over the face of society is regarded as neither fair nor desirable. Otherwise social justice might consist in imprisoning all members of society except the jailors. As we have seen before no man has a claim to disadvantageous treatment; at most the

G

infliction of such treatment on him may not be unfair to him in certain circumstances, for instance, when he has chosen to commit a criminal act.

2. On the second point an argument might be adduced as follows. Equality of opportunity is the essence of social justice, because we mostly believe, not that all advantages should be equally distributed to all men, but rather that, provided that all men have equal opportunities, distribution should be made according to desert.[1] Thus we do not generally think that social justice requires that the income of all should be equal. The formula of equal claims should on this view be abandoned in favor of the principle of equal opportunities.

But what exactly is meant by equal opportunities? Those who argue along these lines probably have in mind such facilities as schools, hospitals, etc., that is the provision of opportunities for acquiring knowledge, skill, health, etc. which will conduce to good work and to the enjoyment of life. The equality of opportunity envisaged is an equality of opportunities for acquiring that bodily and mental equipment which, so far as the citizen is capable of acquiring it, will enable him to compete fairly with his fellow-man. But fair competition and fair opportunities in this context can only exist if each citizen has an equal claim to those sources of opportunity, such as instruction, books, medical attention, sport, space, radio and television facilities, etc., which will put him on an equal footing with his fellow-men, so far as he is capable of profiting from them. There is therefore no inconsistency between the assertion that each man has an equal claim to all advantages, subject to discrimination on the basis of desert, and the principle of equality of opportunity, if it is interpreted in the way suggested.

The principle of equality of opportunity is however, on another interpretation, rather wider than this. On this second interpretation it is not necessarily confined to opportunities of acquiring capital, human or inanimate, in order to work and earn and so, if the citizen works better than his fellows, to become entitled to better treatment than they. Equality of opportunity may be taken to apply also to equality of opportunities for enjoyment, that is, for the enjoyment of literature, art, music, sport, recreation, the countryside, and all those other advantages which are not directly

---

[1] Raphael puts the problem thus: Have men a claim to equal happiness or only to an equal chance of pursuing happiness?

relevant to an increase in the quality or quantity of one's work. Now if these opportunities are to be provided the citizen has a corresponding claim to those things which are necessary in order that he may profit from them, such as access to amusements, parks, concerts, playing grounds, television facilities, etc. Whether therefore we take opportunity as meaning opportunities for earnings or opportunities for enjoyment, the idea of equality of opportunity implies the existence of equal claims for all men to the means and facilities necessary in order to seize the opportunities listed. Of course it is senseless to speak of a claim to enjoy something which the citizen is incapable of enjoying or to do work which he is incapable of doing. In this sense the formula of equality of opportunity serves to mark the point that no amount of social justice will do more than extend and develop the capacities of citizens to their limit, whatever those limits may turn out to be. But properly understood, equality of opportunity is not inconsistent with, but on the contrary presupposes the notions of, equal claim.

It will be as well to summarize our conclusions on the notion of social justice. The principle of social justice resides in the idea that all men have equal claims[1] to all advantages which are generally desired and which are in fact conducive to human perfection and human happiness. This has two main aspects: first, the equalization of the human condition as far as capital assets, human and inanimate, that is, the prerequisites of a good life are concerned. This involves equal claims to the necessities of life, to life itself, health, food, shelter, etc., and also equality of opportunity for both work and enjoyment. The second aspect of the principle of social justice consists in the principles of non-discrimination and conformity to rule. These ensure that what has been accorded under the first heading will not be taken away subsequently. There are some exceptions to the principle of social justice, in particular to the principle of non-discrimination. These exceptions fall under subordinate principles of justice such as the justice of transactions, justice according to desert, justice according to choice and justice according to need. There are no further exceptions to be found.

[1] I have not explicitly dealt with the relation between justice and equality; but it is obvious that on the analysis here suggested equality is the fundamental notion, whilst inequality, though sometimes fair, is a subsidiary one. On equality see DEL VECCHIO Ch. V; ARISTOTLE, MAGNA MORALIA I. i 1182a 14; METAPHYSICA I. v 985 b 29; XIII. iv 1078 b 23.

It would be wrong to seek to disguise the radical character of the principle I have attempted to describe. According to it, there can be no difference in principle between such generally accepted ideas as that there should be universal free education for all children and other ideas which are not necessarily accepted by everyone: for instance the claim for free medical treatment for all, the claim that victims of road accidents should be indemnified by society irrespective of fault, and the claim that the surface of the earth should be redistributed in proportion to the population of different regions, or that natural resources should be redistributed proportionately to population. It would be easy to multiply the radical conclusions which would follow from the acceptance of the notion of social justice as I have outlined it.

Of course it is true that justice is not the only political, moral or legal value. Liberty is equally important and its demands frequently conflict with those of justice. The preservation of society and of the individual is still more important and may conflict with both.[1] But on a long view, we have every reason to foresee that the consequences inherent in the notion of social justice, as it has been elucidated, will be clearer and will be voiced more widely and more persistently as time goes by. They are indeed beginning to be voiced already: thus the demand for aid for underdeveloped countries is part of the demand of social justice on a world-wide scale. But the full implications of the principle have, I am convinced, by no means yet penetrated the consciousness of our society. Many sober citizens will be startled when they do.

EXPLANATION AND JUSTIFICATION OF THE NOTION OF SOCIAL JUSTICE

Even supposing I have depicted this notion correctly it does not follow that anyone should adopt it or propagate it. I have merely attempted to show that this is a notion which many or perhaps most people give their unconscious suffrage when they approve of such institutions as free universal education, perhaps without realizing what they are doing.

But it can be shown, I think, that the equal claim doctrine is at least a natural one for human beings to hold. If we assume with

[1] On the conflict of justice and utility see Rawls, *Justice as Fairness* 68 PHILOSOPHICAL REVIEW 164–94 (1958).

Hobbes[1] that there is a rough though not precise equality[2] among men in their physical and mental powers, it will be natural for man to hold the equal claims doctrine. Thus A will not be satisfied to claim less than B with whom he is roughly equal in physical and mental strength. On the other hand B for the same reason will not be satisfied to claim less than A with whom he in turn is roughly equal in strength, and A will fear that, unless he concedes equality to B, B will attack him.[3] The equal claim formula will therefore be the only one which in practice has a reasonable chance of securing general acceptance, reconciling the conflicting claims of A and B and thereby producing a stable order of society, acceptable to both and to all. In practice no doubt human equality is far from exact and in some cases human variation and inequality seems the more striking phenomenon.[4] To assert that the equal claims principle is a natural one is to assert that on the whole and over a greater area of human experience, the similarity of human powers, mental and physical, is a more obvious and striking phenomenon than any variations that may exist: or, to put it another way, that natural inequalities are not great enough to make it sensible to abandon the formula which is most likely to win general acceptance.

The notion of 'nature' is, of course, one which notoriously straddles explanation and justification. In saying that the equal claims principle is a natural one, I do not think it possible to distinguish between its power to explain and its power to justify. If this thought is inadequate, and some further justification is sought for the principle of social justice, we will be compelled to analyse the notion of human brotherhood, a notion the empirical and logical status of which lies beyond the limits of this article.

[1] Followed e.g. by HUME, AN INQUIRY CONCERNING THE PRINCIPLES OF MORALS, sect. iii and appx. iii.

[2] Equality of personality, emphasized by DEL VECCHIO 150, No. 5, is inadequate as a justification of the idea of justice. Why should we respect the personality of others, except that we fear their claims?

[3] The idea is expressed by Sully-Prudhomme, *La Justice*, in OEUVRES vol. IV, cited by DEL VECCHIO 96, as follows:

> L'égoisme entre égaux veille à la paix commune:
> L'être le plus féroce épargne alors autrui,
> Parce qu'il reconnaît sa propre vie en lui,
> Et fait sur lui l'essai de sa propre fortune.

[4] DEL VECCHIO 96; BROWN, W. J., THE UNDERLYING PRINCIPLES OF MODERN LEGISLATION 226 (1920).

SUMMARY

1. The principle of social justice requires that all men should have a claim to an equal share in all those advantages which are commonly desired and which conduce to human well-being.
2. This principle is not identical with the demand for equal treatment for all men; it rather requires preferential treatment for the underprivileged, who lack advantages possessed by others.
3. The principle of allocation according to need is a subordinate aspect of social justice.
4. The principle of conformity to rule is also a subordinate aspect of social justice. This principle is designed to secure to all men two advantages: that their reasonable expectations will be fulfilled and their dignity respected.
5. Discrimination is justified only: (1) to give effect to the principle stated in 2 above; (2) on the basis of the conduct, actual or potential or choice of the person to be subjected to discrimination; (3) so far as the justice of transactions and special relations requires it.
6. It is arguable that, given the rough equality of human beings, the equal claim principle is the only principle likely in the long run to lead to social stability.

Punishment for Thoughts

HERBERT MORRIS[1]

Those who attempt to answer either the question 'what is the nature of law?' or the question 'what is the nature of morality?' often also consider how law and morality are related. When they do this, they tend to give answers that emphasize differences rather than likenesses. They are interested, however, in not just any differences but in those that are 'essential'. Most believe that there is *one* such difference. They often express this in a 'formula' or 'maxim' that sums up their views both on law and morality and on the essential difference between them.[2]

The most famous and perhaps the most obscure of these formulae is: 'Law is concerned with external conduct; morality with internal conduct'. Short work has sometimes been made of this proposal.[3] If the claim is, as it is sometimes taken to be, that the law is concerned exclusively with conduct and morality exclusively with states of mind, it is only necessary to point out that states of mind are relevant to the law and conduct is relevant to morality. The definitions of burglary and murder, to take two obvious examples, demonstrate that states of mind are relevant to the law. And conduct seems relevant to morality, for we blame people for telling lies, breaking promises, killing people, not just, or perhaps

[1] Herbert Morris, B.A. U.C.L.A. 1951, LL.B. 1954 Yale Law School, D.Phil. 1956 Oxon., is Professor of Philosophy and Law, U.C.L.A. School of Law and Department of Philosophy. The essay here is reprinted from 49 MONIST 342 (1965). Other writings include: *Dean Pound's Jurisprudence* 13 STAN. L. REV. 185 (1960); *Verbal Disputes and the Legal Philosophy of John Austin* 7 U.C.L.A. L. REV. 27 (1960); FREEDOM AND RESPONSIBILITY: READINGS IN PHILOSOPHY AND LAW (Morris ed. 1961); *Imperatives and Orders* 26 THEORIA 183 (1966). (Footnote by editor.)
[2] e.g., Law aims at a minimum; morality at a maximum. Law is prohibitive; morality is injunctive. The aim of law is not to punish sin but to prevent certain external results.
[3] e.g., EDMOND N. CAHN, THE MORAL DECISION 44–46 (1955).

ever, for merely contemplating, desiring, or intending, to do these things. What, then, is left of the view that law is concerned with external conduct and morality with internal conduct?

The ease of this refutation may produce a vague disquiet, a feeling that perhaps the point of the maxim has escaped the critic. Could those philosophers who have thought it true been oblivious to these facts about our moral and legal life to which appeal is made in refuting it? The facts seem too obvious to be overlooked. It is reasonable to suppose that philosophers who have thought in terms of the external–internal distinction were getting at something.

This is the view adopted by other philosophers. They are in agreement that the maxim is obscure, but they think that it contains some important insight into the nature of law and morals. Stammler writes that we are given 'only a suggestion of a difference'.[1] Radbruch writes of 'concealed' meanings.[2] Kantorowicz believes we must maintain the distinction provided that it is 'rightly understood'.[3] Hart believes that 'though it contains a hint of truth it is, as it stands, profoundly misleading'.[4] When the truth hinted at is brought into the open, these critics turn out to be not wholly in agreement on what is hidden. In some cases there are clear differences of opinion as to the truth it contains. In some cases what is proposed as an implication of the maxim seems to have little connection with it; the use of the words 'external' and 'internal' has simply called something to mind.

It seems to me, too, that there may be some truth in the formula. My aims in this paper are (1) to offer an interpretation of the formula; (2) to examine one limited aspect of it that relates to law; and (3) to offer a defense of this limited aspect.

There are at least three points that a philosopher committed to the view that 'law is concerned with external conduct, morality with internal conduct', may wish to make:

a. Law requires external conduct. In morality one may be blamed or praised for one's mental state alone; there are sins and virtues of thought.

---

[1] RUDOLPH STAMMLER, THEORY OF JUSTICE 41 (New York: The Macmillan Company, 1925).

[2] Gustav Radbruch, *Legal Philosophy* in THE LEGAL PHILOSOPHIES OF LASK, RADBRUCH AND DABIN 78 trans. K. Wilk (Cambridge: Harvard University Press, 1950).

[3] HERMANN KANTOROWICZ, THE DEFINITION OF LAW 43 (1958).

[4] H. L. A. HART, THE CONCEPT OF LAW 168 (1961).

b. In law, conduct by itself is sufficient to constitute compliance with rules. In morality conduct alone is never sufficient.

c. In law, conduct alone is (may be) sufficient to create liability. In morality one may never be blamed for conduct alone.

Each of these claims about law and about morality is, as it stands, obscure, suggestive and worth, I think, examining in some detail. That would be a large undertaking. In this paper my goal is relatively modest. I restrict inquiry to the first claim that law requires external conduct. I restrict myself still further by interpreting the claim as one made about the criminal law. When the word 'law' occurs, then, it should be understood as meaning 'the criminal law'.

There are at least two sources of obscurity with respect to the claim. First, if someone says, 'for law there must be external conduct', we may be unsure what would and what would not satisfy this demand. Does the philosopher mean, for example, that punishment for omitting to do something is, in some sense, unacceptable? Second, we may be unsure whether or not the cases that come readily to mind as possible counterinstances have relevance to the claim, not because, as with omissions, we are unsure what class of things would count for or against the claim, but because we are unsure about the status of the claim. By this I mean we may be unsure what procedures, if any, are appropriate for confirming or disconfirming the claim. Is it a factual claim or a moral claim or some other kind of claim? Does it make any difference to its validity, for example, that a statute has been enacted in accord with law that makes it an offense to intend to commit arson? We must look more carefully at each of these sources of obscurity if we are to settle whether or not this limited aspect of the maxim is valid. Let us turn to the first source of obscurity.

I

Among the things a philosopher may mean when he says 'law is concerned with external conduct' is 'for law there must be conduct'. If he means this, he is claiming not, as it is sometimes supposed he is, that law is exclusively concerned with conduct, a position that appears obviously untenable, but rather that law is not concerned with states of mind alone, a position that is not obviously untenable. What, then, would it be like for the law to be concerned with a state of mind alone?

In the remainder of this part of the paper I shall attempt to clarify the relationship between conduct and mental states in a variety of legal situations so that we have a better grasp of the kind of case to be ruled out by the philosopher's claim 'for law there must be conduct'.

1. Suppose that it is made a punishable offense *to disbelieve* the story of creation as recorded in the Old Testament. Suppose, further, that an admission in open court is required for conviction and that such an admission by itself is sufficient for conviction of the offense. Here we have a clear case of a law concerned with a state of mind alone. What are some of its features? First, the offense is defined exclusively in psychological terms. Second, an admission without any accompanying conduct is sufficient to convict a person for the offense. Third, there is no interest the law seeks to protect that is threatened by the admission, thus there is nothing paradoxical in the law's seeking to encourage the admission. Fourth, the law is prohibiting a state of mind. Fifth, in prohibiting a state of mind the object of the law is merely to induce persons not to have a state of mind, and we shall assume that the law's aim is not thereby to prevent some harm related to the state of mind.

A person who understood this law would realize that he had committed an offense when he disbelieved the story of creation. He would understand that to admit disbelief was not to commit an offense but merely to reveal its commission. It is natural to say in such a case that a person punished for committing this offense is being punished for thought alone and hence that the law was concerned with a state of mind alone.[1]

2. Our first case may suggest that one is punished for thought alone if one is punished for committing an offense defined exclusively in psychological terms. I am not sure that this criterion will do. Suppose persons possessed the capacity to arouse fear in other persons merely by thinking in a particular way. Suppose that it were a punishable offense to arouse fear in others by exercising this capacity. It is at least arguable that this is an offense defined exclusively in psychological terms. Punishment for committing the offense, however, would not be for thought alone but for arousing fear by thought. From this it follows: (a) that some

---

[1] I do not discuss in this paper those many difficult problems that arise if the states made punishable by law are ones over which we have no control.

offenses may be defined exclusively in psychological terms and yet there be 'external conduct' and (b) that there may be 'external conduct' even though an offense may be committed without a person's doing anything that involves a bodily movement.

3. There is another reason why it is undesirable to restrict 'external conduct' to conduct that involves a bodily movement. It is, of course, understandable that we should think of external conduct in terms of bodily movements. A philosopher who says 'there must be external conduct' contrasts external conduct with what is misleadingly labeled 'internal conduct', that is, with mental states, such as beliefs, desires, wishes, and intentions. This seems clear enough. If we then ask what is meant by 'external conduct', it seems reasonable to suggest that it means 'a physical act or acts', for we often contrast the physical with the mental. If we then ask 'what is a physical act?' the response, no doubt, will be that it is or involves a bodily movement. If we then turn attention again to the claim, 'there must be external conduct', it looks as if it is being claimed that there cannot be a legal offense or there cannot be punishment unless there is some bodily movement. But now a difficulty presents itself. When we hold a person liable for an omission we do not hold him liable only on condition that he has moved his body. We may, then, wonder how omissions are accommodated by the philosopher's statement and conclude that they are not. Rules which require persons to do things would, in some sense, be unacceptable to the philosopher.

If, when we say, 'there must be external conduct', we intend merely to rule out punishment for thought alone, it is strange to rule out omissions, for this would suggest that a person punished for omitting to pay taxes was being punished for thought alone. And this, of course, is not so. Suppose, however, that we were legally required to have certain thoughts. Punishment for omitting to have the thoughts would be punishment for thought alone. One reaches the conclusion that omissions are not external conduct only by identifying external conduct with bodily movements and interpreting one who claims 'there must be external conduct' as claiming that there is no legal offense without bodily movement whereas the aim behind the remark, I believe, is to preclude punishment merely for having or not having a certain mental state. Omissions then may or may not, depending on whether it is an omission to act or to think, be 'external conduct' within the meaning of this phrase as employed by one who insists that law can't punish for thought alone.

4. Suppose that it were a punishable offense *to intend* to assassinate a public official. Suppose, on analogy with the evidential requirement for conviction of treason,[1] that an evidential rule required, for conviction, that evidence be introduced that the accused took substantial steps toward assassinating a public official. In these circumstances, the class of those who may be convicted of *intending* to assassinate a public official may coincide with the class of those who may be convicted of *attempting* to assassinate a public official, for attempting may be defined as intending to perform some act and taking substantial steps in furtherance of one's intention. Now, if the philosopher would not object to punishment for attempts, would he object to the offense that we have imagined? There are grounds, I think, for believing that he would regard punishment under these circumstances as punishment for thought alone.

Suppose, first, a very unusual situation. The law's *sole* interest in or concern with the substantial steps might be evidential. If this were so, the law might even encourage those steps that reveal the intention. We could, in fact, understand the law providing inducements to persons to do all that they could to realize their intentions, for such behavior would provide the best evidence of one's intending to assassinate a public official. In these circumstances the law would be seeking to prevent what it prohibits and nothing else. If one were punished in such a case it would not be *for* acting any more than it was *for* admitting in our case of disbelief in the story of creation. While conduct is a prerequisite for conviction it is not *for conduct* that the person is being punished.

Clearly, the more realistic case is one in which there is a different attitude toward the conduct insisted upon by the evidential rule. In prohibiting an intention to assassinate a public official we naturally would be aiming at diminishing the number of such assassinations. And if this is so, it would be absurd to encourage the conduct that provides evidence of intention. Two preliminary questions are raised by such an offense where the concern with

---

[1] *U.S. Constitution* Art. III, Sec. 3: 'No person shall be convicted of Treason unless on the Testimony of two witnesses to the same overt Act, or on confession in open Court.'

conduct is not exclusively evidential. First, what is the point of the evidential requirement? Second, why are the substantial steps not a defining element of the offense?

First, it is understandable that there should be such an evidential requirement. A balance is always struck between the aims of convicting the guilty and avoiding the conviction of the innocent. While fewer guilty persons will be convicted if we require substantial steps, rather than a mere confession, there will also be fewer innocent persons convicted. Persons innocent of intending might confess to intending for any number of reasons, but, so the theory might be, fewer of those innocent of intending would take substantial steps toward assassinating a public official.

Second, if in this system one may be punished for the separate crime of 'intending to assassinate a public official and taking substantial steps in furtherance of one's intention', that is, for attempting to assassinate a public official, what is the point of the additional offense of merely intending? To answer this question we must look at this law from the point of view of one seeking to comply with legal rules. The offense of intending to assassinate a public official may operate to disincline persons from forming such intentions. It may lead to an exercise of self-restraint at a stage earlier than a law with respect to attempts. I shall have some more comments on this explanation later on, but for the moment I propose we accept it.

What shall we say about whether or not punishment for such an offense is punishment for thought alone? There are two respects in which conduct is relevant here that it was not in the case of disbelief in the story of creation. Conduct, apart from admissions, is insisted upon by an evidential rule. And it is harmful conduct and not merely an intention that we are, by hypothesis, seeking to diminish by making the intention wrongful. But these differences do not warrant concluding that this is a case in which we are punishing for something apart from thought. First, the status of the conduct in the evidential rule is like that of the admission in our case of disbelief. Conduct simply affords more reliable evidence than a mere admission of the state made illegal. But this is not relevant to what it is that one is being punished for. Second, from the fact that we are interested in prohibiting intentions in order to diminish certain harm it does not follow that we punish, not for intentions, but for conduct or for harm. If we punish a person, for example, for behaving recklessly, in the absence of actual harm, we punish for his reckless conduct although our ultimate aim may be to diminish a type of harm the risk of which is increased by the reckless conduct. We must distinguish between *what* it is we are punishing *for* and *why* it is that we are punishing.

5. Suppose we had a device for detecting sincere confessions. Would we then seek to punish persons who intended to assassinate public officials but who, subsequent to intending and before taking steps, changed their minds? If our purpose is to prevent harm, what, we might wonder, is to be served by punishing such persons? Someone may then suggest that we should be interested not in mere intentions but in firm ones. Let us, then, suppose it is a punishable offense 'to have the *firm intention* to assassinate a public official'. Suppose an evidential requirement similar to the one we have been considering. Would punishment for this offense be for thought alone? What is 'firm intention'?

Perhaps a 'firm intention' is to be contrasted with a state of indecision. If one's mind is made up, one's intention is firm or fixed. But is it, then, clear what 'an intention' that is not firm might be? It may be that 'firm' is to be contrasted with 'weak' rather than with 'not yet definite'. 'Firmness' would be a function of one's belief and feelings with regard to a change of mind. If, for example, a person believes that nothing will dissuade him from seeking to realize his intention and if his feelings are strong on the matter, his intention may be regarded as firm. If he believes that only extraordinary circumstances will make him change his mind and feels rather strongly, then his intention may be considered only relatively firm. If he is prepared to change his mind at any moment and for almost any reason, he may be considered merely to intend. Given the law's aim to strike some balance between preventing harm and not interfering with those who will do no harm, one could understand the law's drawing a distinction between those who intend and those who firmly intend. The latter are more likely to invade interests protected by law. Still, for the reasons offered in the preceding case, a person would be punished for thought alone if punished for this state of mind whatever our ultimate object in punishing such persons.

6. Sometimes firm intention is used interchangeably with another phrase, 'firm resolve' or 'constancy of purpose' and this

suggests another situation.[1] Suppose it were a punishable offense 'to have the *firm resolve* to assassinate a public official'. Suppose, again, the evidential requirement. Now what class of persons interests us here? Some class, by hypothesis, that differs from those who intend and those who firmly intend as we have understood these phrases. This class may be described as the class of those 'who really intend' or the class of those whose 'purpose is constant'. Let us attempt to clarify the notion.

In those cases in which intention and firm intention were made criminal, it did not seem particularly difficult to understand what state it was we were not to have in order to conform to the law. It was assumed that a person could have the state in question, realize that he had it, and realize that his conduct served merely to reveal his inner state to others. Were we to have a machine that could reliably test when one was sincerely reporting his state of mind, such a machine would allow us to determine whether or not one intended or firmly intended even in the absence of conduct in furtherance of intention.[2] What shall we say of 'firm resolve'? The phrase may be introduced to cover the following situation. We may believe that a person was sincere in expressing an intention, sincere in expressing a firm intention and yet not believe that he 'really intended' or that 'his resolve was firm' or that 'his purpose was constant'. We might hold such beliefs if, when the occasion arrived for the person doing what he said he intended to do, he did nothing. When 'the chips are down' he didn't come through as he said he intended to. Now someone may say that law should be restricted to those who firmly resolve, to those who 'really intend'. But what, then, does 'firm resolve' imply?

It seems to me that conduct is related to 'firm resolve' in a way unlike we took it to be related to intending and firmly intending. In those cases we viewed conduct merely as a sign of the intention. With 'firm resolve', however, the conduct is not only a sign of the intention or resolve but part of the meaning of 'firm'. If a person, for whatever reason, does not do what he believes necessary to realize his intention one cannot say his resolve was firm. Lie-

---

[1] See GLANVILLE WILLIAMS, CRIMINAL LAW 485 (London: Stevens & Sons, Ltd., 1953) (hereafter cited as CL).

[2] I do not wish to suggest by this that conduct is in no way connected with the meaning of intention. Certainly in some cases a person can intend to act without acting. Whether this could generally be the case and our concept of intention remain the same, I leave open.

detecting devices might come to be accepted as reliable guides to intention and firm intention, but hardly for 'firm resolve' as I am construing it. For 'firm' implies that the person does what he believes necessary to realize his resolve.[1] To detect 'firm resolve', then, we would need a device that could foretell the future. But now, if 'firm resolve' implies more than merely having a certain mental state, what is it that persons are to avoid doing if they are to comply with the law making it criminal to have a firm resolve to assassinate a public official? What does the law direct persons not to do? It must be to avoid *acting* with a certain state of mind. But if this is so, are we prohibiting a state of mind by itself?

The topic of 'firm resolve' leads to the next major problem in understanding what constitutes 'punishment for thought alone.' Sometimes it is suggested that a person is punished for thought alone despite the fact that the offense he has committed is defined partly in physical terms. Laws, for example, with respect to conspiracy, vagrancy,[2] and possession of burglar's tools may occasion such an observation. It is most often made about the law of attempts.[3]

[1] WILLIAMS, CL 485. In commenting on attempts:

'. . . what of the supposed rule that repentance after the proximate act and before consummation of the full crime comes too late? Such repentance would seem to be the clearest indication that there was never a firm resolve, whatever the accused himself may have thought.'

[2] See *State* v. *Grenz*, 26 Wash. 2d 764, 175 P. 2d 633, 637 (1946).

[3] JOHN AUSTIN, LECTURES ON JURISPRUDENCE 441 (London: John Murray, 5th ed. 1885) (hereafter cited as LJ):

'Where a criminal intention is evidenced by an attempt, the party is punished in respect of the criminal intention. . . . Why the party should be punished in respect of a mere intention, I will try to explain hereafter. The reason for requiring an attempt, is probably the danger of admitting a mere confession. When coupled with an overt act, the confession is illustrated and supported by the latter. When not, it may proceed from insanity, or may be invented by the witness to it.'

J. W. C. Turner, *Attempts to Commit Crimes*, in MODERN APPROACH TO CRIMINAL LAW 277–8 (Leon Radzinowicz and J. W. C. Turner eds. London: The Macmillan Company, 1945):

'The important point is, however, that the *actus reus* in attempt need not be forbidden in itself. It follows, therefore, that whereas in most crimes it is the *actus reus*, the harmful result, which the law desires to prevent, while the *mens rea* is only the necessary condition for the infliction of punishment on the person who produced the harmful result, in attempt the position is reversed, and it is the *mens rea* which the law regards as of primary importance and desires to prevent, while a sufficient *actus reus* is the necessary condition for the infliction of punishment on the person who formed the criminal intent. . . . If then, in attempt, the sole purpose of the *actus reus* is to establish the existence of *mens rea*, it is necessary to decide . . . what will be a sufficient *actus reus*.'

It has been claimed that the sole purpose for requiring conduct in the law of attempts is to establish the *mens rea*. This assimilates the conduct requirement in such laws to the evidential status of conduct in our earlier cases of intention and firm intention. Such claims are misleading. But showing why this is so does not settle the issue whether or not we punish for thoughts alone when we punish for attempts. I want first to suggest three reasons why conduct is an element of the offense.[1]

First, crimes of attempt allow enforcement officials to prevent both those who have set out to commit crimes from consummating them and those who failed to consummate crimes through some accident or mistake from trying again. The law of attempts enables enforcement officials to interfere with individuals before any harm has been done· so that harm may be prevented. This power to interfere, however, is circumscribed. While we wish to protect individuals against theft and murder we also wish to protect individuals against interference by the state if these individuals, whatever their state of mind, would not in fact commit

[1] cf. Wechsler, Jones, and Korn, 572–3.

PATRICK JOHN FITZGERALD, CRIMINAL LAW AND PUNISHMENT 97–98 (Oxford: Clarendon Press, 1962):

'An intention to commit a crime does not by itself suffice to make a person guilty of a crime. . . . Although mere criminal intention is not punishable, punishment is not reserved only for cases where the intention is fulfilled. Midway between the mere intention and the completed crime stands the inchoate crime of Attempt. . . . In some instances statutes provide a lesser punishment for the attempt than for the full offense. The reason is no doubt the fact that less harm results from the former than from the latter. In fact, here the law would seem to be penalizing mere criminal intention, contrary to the general rule.'

WILLIAMS, CL 485–6 (London: Stevens & Sons, Ltd., 1953):

'Austin put forward the interesting view that in attempt the party is really punished for his intention, the act being required as evidence of a *firm* intention. There is much to be said for this. Admitting that intention in general can be proved by a confession, a confession is not sufficient proof in attempt because, standing alone, it gives no assurance that the accused would have had the constancy of purpose to put his plan into execution. The commission of the proximate act proves not merely the purpose but (in considerable degree) the firmness of the purpose.'

Herbert Wechsler, William Kenneth Jones, and Harold L. Korn, *The Treatment of Inchoate Crimes in the Model Penal Code of the American Law Institute: Attempt, Solicitation, and Conspiracy* 61 COLUMBIA LAW REVIEW 573 (1961). (hereafter cited as Wechsler, Jones and Korn):

'. . . the crime becomes essentially one of criminal purpose implemented by an overt act strongly corroborative of such purpose.'

H

crimes. There is a point, an ill-defined one, at which the risk of harm to interests the law seeks to protect becomes so great that it is thought desirable to interfere with individuals who might change their minds. Now at what point does the law decide that that interference is worth the risk of penalizing those who would change their minds? Those who claim the sole purpose of requiring conduct is to establish the *mens rea* seem to imply that the law would, if sufficiently reliable evidence were available, interfere with those who intend or firmly intend to commit crimes. And, indeed, here might be some justification for such a viewpoint, for it is probably the case that individuals with such states of mind are more likely than the general run of persons to act to realize their intentions and invade the interests of others protected by law. But if our ultimate aim is to balance the policy of preventing harm to persons with the policy of minimizing interference with those who would not do all they believe necessary to realize their intentions, then the law may insist upon conduct because, comparing the class of those who firmly intend with the class of those who firmly intend and who take steps to realize their intentions, members of the former class are more likely than those of the latter to change their minds. In drawing the line at 'performing the proximate act' the law assures that fewer of those who would change their minds are convicted although it also thereby, of course, assumes a greater risk that the sphere of protected interests will be invaded.

Second, a person who takes steps in furtherance of his intention to commit a crime may be regarded as more disposed than the general run of persons to criminal activity generally. It is understandable that we may wish to have control over such persons in order to apply whatever corrective measures are thought beneficial. Those who intend to commit crimes, those who firmly intend to commit crimes, those who take steps to realize their intentions are all more disposed to criminal activity than the general run of persons. But it is also the case that those who take steps in furtherance of their intentions are more disposed toward criminal activity than those who do not take any steps to realize their intentions. It is reasonable and compatible with the definition of the offense of attempt that the law draw a line guided by this consideration so that those who take no steps are excluded from liability.

Third, were we to exculpate individuals who attempted to commit crimes but failed, say, through some fortuity, there would be an inequality of treatment of persons who were equally guilty from a moral point of view. Now, if we consider the class of persons who intend, the class of those who firmly intend, the class of those who take steps to realize their intentions, and the class of those who take the last step necessary to realize their intentions, we may regard them all as more morally blameworthy than the general run of persons. But they are not equally so. Those who take the last step are, in general, as blameworthy as those who succeed. Those who take the 'proximate step' may, of course, change their minds before the last step, but as we have seen, they are less likely than the general run of persons who intend to commit crimes to do so. Because of this it is less likely that they differ significantly in blameworthiness from those who actually commit the crime.

It might be admitted that the foregoing was a fairly adequate explanation of why the offense is defined in physical terms and still be maintained that when a person is punished for attempting to commit a crime he is being punished *for* his state of mind alone and not for what he has done. What he has done may be harmless, and it cannot be for what is harmless that we are punishing him.

In assessing this view it is advisable, I think, to distinguish those attempt situations in which the individual has done all he believes necessary to realize his intention and fails for one reason or another and those in which, while he has taken substantial steps in furtherance of his intention, he has not yet taken the last step he believes necessary to realize his intention. Let us consider the first class of attempts.

Here it is surely strange to say that we are punishing for a state of mind alone. If we view the situation as it actually exists, a particular person held liable for an attempt may have done no harm. We can hardly, however, infer from this that we are punishing such a person for his state of mind alone. This would suggest that we are punishing him for precisely what we would be punishing a person for if mere or firm intention were made criminal. The natural thing to say for this class of attempts is that we are punishing the person for doing all that he believes necessary to accomplish his intention. The person has engaged in conduct with a certain state of mind and the law has deemed that that conduct with that state of mind creates risks the law seeks to diminish. From the fact that one who drives recklessly is punished in the absence of harm one cannot, as we have seen, legitimately infer that the person is not being punished for reckless driving. Such conduct creates risks of harm and though it may not in a particular case result in harm the law may seek to diminish the risk. Likewise, persons who perform all they believe necessary to achieve their intentions generally do succeed, which suggests that in conducting themselves as they do, these persons create serious risk of harm.

The more interesting case is that of attempts in which the last step has not been taken. Are we not in such cases punishing for a state of mind alone? It is seriously misleading to say we are. It may suggest that were lie-detecting devices regarded as reliable, admissions of intentions, tested by such devices, would provide precisely what substantial steps now provide us in attempted crimes. And this is mistaken, I think, for several reasons. First, it cannot be disputed that one may intend to commit a crime and provide reliable evidence of one's intention and not be guilty of attempt. In attempt it is those persons with 'firm resolve' that interest us; it is those who 'really intend', those whose purpose will be constant, and this no lie-detecting machine that tests one's mental state before action can reveal. The conduct in attempt is part of the meaning of the state we are concerned with detecting. In order to prevent harm, we believe it desirable to interfere with persons before they do all that they believe necessary to realize their intentions. This does not mean that we are punishing for mere intention. We are punishing such persons in the belief that they are members of the class of those who will not change their minds, the class of those whose purpose is constant. In interfering before the last step we must always feel some doubt that the person had the state that we label 'firm resolve'.

Second, suppose that the state could be defined independently of conduct and that machines could provide what the conduct is now taken to provide. There might still be good reason for distinguishing those persons who take substantial steps in furtherance of their intention from those who do not. First, the person who intends to assassinate a public official and who takes steps may be regarded as *making it* less likely that he will change his mind. The theory would be that the closer one gets to the actual commission of the deed the greater one's psychological commitment to perform the deed and the progressively diminishing probability of a change of mind and the corresponding progressively increased probability that harm will come about. One is, then, by one's acts putting oneself into a state that may be regarded as socially undesirable because it creates the risk that one will be less likely to change one's mind and this creates a greater risk that the harm we seek to prevent will come about. Further, the taking of steps makes it easier for the person to realize his aims. In this respect, too, it may be regarded as socially undesirable because in making it easier for harm to be done, it makes it more probable that harm will be done.

We can now turn to our second source of obscurity in the claim that 'for law there must be external conduct'.

<h2 style="text-align:center">II</h2>

When someone says 'there must be external conduct' we may be troubled not just by what would and what would not be acceptable as external conduct but by the claim that there *must* be such conduct. How shall we take this claim? There are a number of possible interpretations.

First, when people thinking of law say 'there must be external conduct', they may have in mind no more than what is and what is not in fact taken into account by all or most legal systems that have existed. They convey to us information that legal systems explicitly or implicitly preclude punishing persons for having or failing to have a certain state of mind. One who puts forward such a claim, if confronted by a case in which there is such an offense, may simply limit his generalization and admit that there are exceptions. Changes in the actual content of legal systems reflect on the adequacy of the claim and given a sufficiently large number of legal rules addressed to thought alone, one who makes such a claim may say, 'it is no longer true that there must be external conduct'. Such a reaction, of course, gives it away that the remark is not philosophical.

Second, it has been suggested that external conduct is necessary, for without outer signs it is impossible to prove inner states and were we not to insist upon some conduct we should have to rely upon unfounded charges. Blackstone wrote in explanation of the overt act requirement:

... as no temporal tribunal can search the heart, or fathom the intentions of the mind, otherwise than as they are demonstrated by outward actions, it therefore cannot punish for what it cannot know. For which reason in all temporal jurisdictions an overt act, or some open evidence of an intended crime, is necessary in order to demonstrate the depravity of the will before the man is liable to punishment.[1]

Blackstone appears to have believed that the overt requirement is justified by the limited access we have to the minds of others. This view differs from that of philosophers who have defended the view that 'there must be external conduct' in at least two respects. First, there are situations in which by appropriate evidentiary requirements we might take into account our limited access to the minds of others and nevertheless be 'punishing for thought alone'. Second, were we to enact rules making certain mental states criminal and accept confessions as reliable evidence for conviction, Blackstone would not be troubled by the character of such enactments as laws. But it would be precisely their character as laws that would trouble the philosopher.

Third, someone may think that conduct is necessary in another respect. The law, it might be argued, aims at promoting peace in the community. To this end there are rules that prohibit violence, theft, and deception and which set up institutions to interpret rules and to determine guilt. A legal system is a refined substitute, so it may be suggested, for private wars. Now if we were to imagine a society in which all the rules were such that what people did to others was irrelevant for the applicability of the rules, then those rules could not possibly realize peace in the community. There must, then, be external conduct in precisely the same sense as a carpenter must use certain materials if he desires a chair to withstand pressure.[2]

First, it is not clear that such a system would totally fail to effectuate the aims of law. Suppose offenses were defined in terms of intentions to kill and in terms of those states of mind associated with reckless and negligent conduct. In principle many more persons would be guilty of legal wrongs within such a system than now are within our own. Those who intend to kill but who do not yet do anything would have committed a legal offense. But we

---

[1] WILLIAM BLACKSTONE, COMMENTARIES Bk. IV, Ch. II.

[2] cf. LON FULLER, THE MORALITY OF LAW 96 (New Haven: Yale University Press, 1964). With respect to such features as the generality of legal rules, their promulgation, their clarity, etc., and the relation of such features to law he writes: 'They are like the natural laws of carpentry, or at least those laws respected by a carpenter who wants the house he builds to remain standing and serve the purpose of those who live in it.'

might then accomplish what we now do and something besides. Those who now kill, steal, etc. would under this imagined system be punished as under our own. Their conduct would stand to their thoughts in precisely the relation that confessions stand to thoughts except that we might regard the conduct as more reliable evidence. When it was established that a person killed we should be able to infer the criminal state of mind. Thus, a failure to have the overt act requirement would not entirely defeat the aim of diminishing external harm. There are, however, two cautionary remarks needed here. Were the system to address itself to states of mind unrelated to harm, the system would presumably fail to effectuate these aims associated with law. And if all offenses consisted in the having of a state of mind and none in the doing of certain things, the system would be irrational in not rewarding restraint from harm. Persons who merely intend and those who do all that they believe necessary to realize their intentions would be treated alike. But, as we remarked above, this peculiarity, which we shall examine more carefully in a moment, does not mean that there would be a total lack of effectiveness to the system.

Suppose, however, that it were necessary to prohibit conduct in order to preserve peace in the community. The test of the philosophical character of the claim that 'there must be external conduct' would be brought out in this way. If the system did not insist upon conduct for violation of the law, would this occasion the remark, 'it's merely an ineffectual legal system', or the remark, 'it's not a legal system at all or if it is, it is a very atypical one'? Is there an inclination to say that a legal rule prohibiting thought is not a legal rule or is there merely an inclination to say that it is impractical and ineffectual? The philosopher is inclined to make the former type of comment.

Fourth, in saying that 'there must be external conduct', one may put forward a moral demand. The claim might be construed as 'it is morally undesirable to make psychological states by themselves legally wrongful'. The person who holds this view reacts to instances where thought is prohibited or required by law in this way: (1) he resembles the philosopher, for he doesn't withdraw his statement or claim, however many instances there are of legal rules that prohibit thought; (2) he differs from the philosopher because he isn't necessarily inclined to say such things as 'it is not really law' or 'it is a strange kind of law'. He places a demand upon the content of legal rules which, if unsatisfied, reflects not on the enactment's being a law but on its being a moral law.

III

The claim that law insists upon external conduct may be unlike the claim that in fact legal systems do not punish for thought alone, unlike the claim that given our limited access to the minds of others legal systems must insist upon conduct, unlike the claim that in order to be effective legal systems must insist upon conduct, and unlike the claim that to be moral legal systems must insist upon a person's doing something wrong. What, then, is the character of the claim? It is, of course, a conceptual remark. Something is being said about the concept of law. We have now to look more closely at the character of the conceptual observation.

First, some philosophers believe that law is essentially linked to morality. For them a necessary condition for a rule to be a legal rule is that it not be immoral. Such philosophers may also believe that it is immoral to prohibit thought. They might, then, conclude that a rule making thought alone criminal was not a legal rule. They would reach this conclusion because they believe there exists some necessary connection between law and morality. This is one possible line of argument, but it has all the limitations associated with the view that an immoral law is not a law.

Second, a philosopher may believe that the connection between a legal rule and external conduct is more like the connection between being a legal rule and simply being a rule than it is like the connection between being a legal rule and being enforced by men rather than women. It is more like the connection between being a widow and being a woman than it is like the connection between being a woman and dying before one reaches the age of 120 years. Such a philosopher may argue that it is not only more like the former types of cases than the latter but that it is precisely the same. He might recognize his divergence from ordinary usage by remarking about rules making thought alone criminal, 'such rules aren't really legal rules'. He would be aware that there is a difference between 'if x is a legal rule, then x is a rule', and 'if x is a legal rule, there must be external conduct'. He is aware also that moral criticism of such enactments condemns them as 'immoral laws'.

Now what might account for the philosopher's straying from ordinary language? Let me suggest this possibility. He may be led to his position by an inability to find a comfortable middle-ground between 'if x is a legal rule, then x is a rule' and 'if x is a legal rule, then x is enforced by men'. He compares the relation between a legal rule and external conduct with the relation between a legal rule and enforcement by men rather than women. He believes that were women to enforce the law it would not alter our judgment that it was law. But with respect to external conduct he feels the situation is different. Law seems to him an ordering for the promotion of peace and this seems to imply that regulating the conduct of people is connected with the meaning of law. When concepts are connected in meaning, it is natural to think them connected as a legal rule is connected with simply being rule, for that is so obviously a connection in meaning. But it seems clear that the concepts of legal rule and external conduct are not connected in that way. How, then, are they connected if they aren't connected as legal rules are connected with rules nor as enforcement by men is connected with legal rules?

Third, some may take this line. The connection is more subtle than that suggested by the philosopher who believes that a rule is not a legal rule unless it prohibits or requires conduct. Consider, again, the punishable offense of disbelieving in the story of creation. Is not such a rule a legal rule? There are several grounds for saying that it is. Such an enactment may resemble in a number of relevant particulars typical legal rules. And it may be an element in a system, the purpose of which is to promote values normally associated with law. Admitting this, someone might argue that law was still essentially a matter of preventing men from harming one another and that while this purpose is compatible with an atypical use of legal rules, it is not compatible with the general use of rules that prohibit merely thought. If we imagine a system, no rule of which is concerned with what men do but all of the rules of which are concerned exclusively with what they think, we would not be imagining a legal system. In saying, then, that 'for law there must be external conduct' one may be making the point that it is necessarily the case for a system to be a legal system that some subset of its rules prohibit persons from harming one another. And this is like, someone might say, the connection between rules and a legal system, for while there are elements of legal systems that are not rules, it is necessary that there be at least some rules if there is to be a legal system at all.

This suggestion is bothersome. Suppose a system in which all of the rules defining offenses prohibit thought alone. Is such a system a legal system? The answer to this question is surely not as clear-cut as the answer to the question 'Is a "system" without rules a legal system?' We can surely foresee disputes arising over whether or not a system in which only thought is punished is a legal system. There is clearly something to be said in favor of the view that it is a legal system. It doesn't seem to me a necessary condition for a system to be a legal system that some, at least, of its rules prohibit persons from harming one another.

Fourth, it is possible, however, to claim that external conduct is connected in meaning with law and that it is not connected as the idea of a rule is connected with the idea of a legal system. It seems to me that the alternative I shall now elaborate provides the most defensible position.

Prohibiting harm stands to the idea of law as the legs of a chair stand to the idea of a chair. Neither the absence nor the presence of such a feature is determinative of a thing's being of a certain kind though it is relevant to a thing's being of a certain kind. That there are rules which prohibit harm is not a necessary condition for a system's being a legal system. That there are rules prohibiting harm is a feature that would incline one to classify a system as a legal system. That there are no rules prohibiting harm is relevant to classifying the systems as other than a legal one. Prohibiting harm stands to the idea of law, I believe, as provision for a sanction stands to the idea of law. Not every legal rule need be supported by a sanction for the system of rules to be a legal system. But were a system of rules to have no provision whatsoever for sanctions, the general absence of the feature would weigh against our classifying the system as a legal one. Its absence is not, however, determinative of the system's being a legal system.

Now let us imagine two different types of system: (a) a system in which all of the rules prohibit or require states of mind believed to be unrelated to conduct that harms others, and (b) a system in which all the rules prohibit intentions to do harmful things and where our aim in making intentions criminal is to diminish harmful occurrences.

With respect to the first system there are apparent oddities and divergencies from what would be regarded as a legal system. I want to elaborate on the second system, for the pull to say that it is a legal system seems to me stronger and if one appreciates the oddity of this system, *a fortiori* one will accept it with regard to the first system.

When we ask ourselves what is law or what is a legal system, a defining characteristic that naturally comes to mind is that of organized sanctions for the enforcement of rules. This feature has, of course, been regarded by some as an essential characteristic of law. Putting aside the issue of its essential character, it would be accepted, by most persons, as a feature quite central to our idea of law. The primary role of the sanction is to induce compliance among those who might be inclined to violate the rules. Sanctions, then, are provided for when there is law and these sanctions are, when the system is functioning, generally effective. If there were a system in which no provision were made for sanctions or a system in which it was known that the sanctions provided for were never applied, we would only hesitantly, if at all, apply the label 'legal' to the system.

Now if we turn to our imagined system in which all of the offenses are defined in terms of intentions to act, the following argument may be made. Threats of punishment in such a system play an entirely different role from what they do in most legal systems, for in law such threats generally operate to induce compliance with the rules among those inclined not to obey. In the system we have imagined, however, threats do not generally operate to induce compliance among those inclined to disobey. The threats operate merely to induce individuals to refrain from giving evidence of their criminal state. Thus, we would have a system in which the laws could, in general, be violated with impunity, a system, in other words, in which sanctions exist on paper but in which their characteristic role is absent. We have a system, then, that diverges in a respect relevant to classification from a clear case of a legal system.

I think that there is something wrong with this argument. With respect to some states of mind it has, I think, some validity. With respect to intentions I do not think that, as it stands, it is adequate.

Imagine the order, 'Don't intend to raise your arm!' issued by one who has made it clear that if one does intend, the person will be shot. The foregoing line of argument would lead to the conclusion that this was an absurd type of situation. One could with impunity disobey the order, for the person ordered need only intend to raise his arm and not reveal his intention. We are to imagine a person who thinks to himself, 'I'll intend to raise my arm but not raise my arm'. But an order is not merely a form of words. In general, when one orders, one has the capacity to induce fear in a person that if he does not do what he is ordered to do he will suffer some harm. But here there is no such capacity nor would there generally be in such cases. Thus, one may conclude that it is not really an order or that it is an unusual kind of order.

There is, of course, something strange about this argument. If the person intends to raise his arm, this is no doubt compatible with his changing his mind and not raising his arm. But if one intends to raise one's arm, it is incompatible with one's believing that one will not raise one's arm where this belief derives from one's intending not to raise one's arm. In a word, if the person intends to raise his arm, he hasn't decided not to raise his arm. Thus, in ordering a person not to intend and threatening harm in case of disobedience, one may induce a person not to form an intention. From this it seems to follow that threats may play a role in a system in which one is prohibited from intending similar to the role they play in a system in which persons are prohibited from doing.

Still, there is something strange about ordering a person not to intend to raise his arm.[1] What is it? If one's aim is to induce a person not to intend to raise his arm, one can accomplish what one wishes by ordering him not to raise his arm. And if one's aim is to induce him not to raise his arm, the natural thing is to tell him not to. But more than this, if one were to order a person not to intend to raise his arm, one would be suggesting that one wanted him to refrain from doing something other than not raising his arm, that is, one would be suggesting that it was his intending that interested one and not his raising his arm. But if his raising his arm is what one wishes him not to do then simply ordering him not to raise his arm would accomplish what one wishes.

Nevertheless, there may be a point to framing laws, at least some

[1] cf. JOHN AUSTIN, LJ 460–1:

'We might . . . be obliged to forbear from intentions, which respect future acts, or future forbearances from action; or, at least to forbear from such of those intentions as are settled, deliberate, or frequently recurring to the mind. The fear of punishment might prevent the frequent recurrence; and might, therefore, prevent the pernicious acts or forbearances, to which intentions (when they recur frequently) certainly or probably lead.'

laws, in terms of intentions rather than acts. There will be some persons who form intentions despite the existence of rules prohibiting the acts they intend to perform. By framing offenses in terms of intentions we may be enabled to interfere with such persons at the stage of intending and thus prevent them from doing what they intend to do. It is not, then, that a rule framed in terms of intentions has any greater deterrent value than one framed in terms of acts or harm but it may well have a greater preventative value. We have seen that this was so with respect to attempts.[1] We are to imagine, then, a system the thrust of which is primarily preventative rather than deterrent. Now, I think, that one can see that the implications of such a system are such that it diverges considerably from what we understand by a legal system.

First, the system we are considering is described as one whose aim is the prevention of harm. This emphasis on prevention of harm naturally inclines us toward regarding the system as a legal one, for this is a commonly accepted aim of legal systems. But given that this is the aim of our imagined system, what can account for its restricting its offenses to those that exclusively prohibit intentions? Mustn't a system with such an aim have some prohibitions on persons doing harm so as to encourage self-restraint at some point before commission of the harm that the law aims at preventing? Once the person reaches the stage at which he provides what the law regards as sufficient proof of intention he will have no incentive to restrain himself from continuing. With respect to this point, one may say that the system is irrational or that it is not as effective as it might be and yet argue that its irrationality does not reflect on whether or not it is a legal system.

---

[1] cf. Jerome Michael and Herbert Wechsler, *A Rationale of the Law of Homicide II* 37 COLUMBIA LAW REVIEW 1295–6 (1937), and Wechsler, Jones, and Korn, op. cit. 572:

'Since these offenses always presuppose a purpose to commit another crime, it is doubtful that the threat of punishment for their commission can significantly add to the deterrent efficacy of the sanction—which the actor by hypothesis ignores —that is threatened for the crime that is his object. There may be cases where this may occur, as when the actor thinks the chance of apprehension low if he succeeds but high if he should fail in his attempt, or when reflection that otherwise would be postponed until too late is promoted at any early state—which may be true of some conspiracies. These are, however, special situations. Viewed generally, it seems clear that deterrence is at most a minor function to be served in fashioning provisions of the penal law addressed to inchoate crimes; that burden is discharged by the law dealing with the substantive offenses.'

Second, whatever truth there is in the view that there is an oddity in the idea of a legal system that exclusively prohibits thought must derive from our concept of law. What, then, are the features of this concept relevant to our inquiry?

Law is not merely a system of enforceable rules where the rules might have any content whatsoever.[1] The law establishes an ordering of men so as to reduce certain recognized evils. It involves an accommodation of the interests of human beings that may come into conflict. But there is more to it than this. The general, though not universal, rule is that violations of the law involve interferences with the interests of others. We can understand that there might be some laws—indeed all legal systems have such—whose violation did not occasion interference with others. But that laws might in general be violated and people remain unaffected conflicts with our concept of law. At the core of any legal system is a set of rules, then, general compliance with which provides benefits for all persons. The benefits consist in one's having a sphere of interests immune from interference by others. There is good reason for believing that one has a moral obligation to obey such rules. This obligation derives from the fairness of one's assuming certain burdens that others have assumed and which make these benefits possible. Further, it is reasonable to support such kinds of rules with sanctions, for if there were no sanctions for noncompliance, those who voluntarily complied with the rules would have no protection against those prepared to accept the benefits of the system without assuming the burdens. But the burdens one morally assumes are merely those which are necessary for persons to assume if the benefits of the system are in fact to accrue.

Now, the peculiarity of our imaginary system when compared with such law is that when the rules are violated the interests of others are unaffected. As long as persons restrain themselves from doing what they intend to do interferences with others are avoided. It is never in the forming of an intention, the only thing made illegal, that one harms others. If the world were to change drastically we might harm others merely by forming intentions. But, then, of course, it would not be for mere intention that one was being punished. Under our imagined system, given men as we know

---

[1] That the legal rules regulate conduct and not thought is usually assumed. One need only recall classic definitions of law.

them, harm can only come about from conduct. Still, general compliance with the rules prohibiting intention may be thought, like compliance with rules prohibiting conduct, to confer benefits of precisely the kind that a legal system normally confers and thus to impose upon all, as is the case when legal rules are involved, a moral obligation to obey such rules. No doubt, benefits would accrue if people did not form certain intentions. There would be a diminished risk of harm. But the benefits we associate with a legal system, namely the creation of a sphere of interests immune from interference, would also accrue if, given that persons formed intentions, they changed their minds and did not act in a way harmful to others. To be sure, in accepting the benefits of a system of rules one assumes the burdens necessary to realize those benefits. But one does not morally assume burdens beyond what is necessary. And because restraint from harming others is all that is necessary to achieve the aim of a sphere of interests immune from interference the only obligation derivable from acceptance of the benefits of such a system is not acting in certain ways. One doesn't, then, have an obligation to obey such 'laws' as one has an obligation to obey laws that prohibit conduct. But, then, the system diverges from law as we understand it, for we commonly accept an obligation to obey the law.

Compare, too, the function of sanctions in our imagined system with their function in a legal system. Rules of law are such that those who voluntarily comply with them take on a special risk which becomes acceptable only because of the presence of sanctions which gives some assurance that those who voluntarily comply will not suffer at the hands of those who are not prepared to voluntarily comply.[1] But in a system in which exclusively intentions are prohibited, persons who do not form intentions that the system prohibits are not by such voluntary compliance with the rules, thereby putting themselves in any special way at the mercy of those who don't comply. Thus, the sanctions in such a system do not have their ordinary function, namely to reduce the risks of complying with the rules. Sufficient for protection of persons who voluntarily comply would be sanctions for persons acting in certain ways.

This paper opened with the claim 'law is concerned with external conduct; morality with internal conduct'. We had put aside

---

[1] cf. HART, op. cit. 193.

any consideration of the claim with respect to morality. But have we, ironically, returned to issues of morality and come upon, not some difference, but some connection between law and morality? It has been suggested, with some justification I believe, that it is a principle of a just constitution that 'each person has the equal right to the most extensive liberty compatible with a like liberty for all'.[1] Now if this is so, we can see that the system we have imagined involves a universal rejection of this principle. By merely intending to do harm one does not interfere with the liberty of others. Thus, in prohibiting intentions the law would deny a person a liberty compatible with a like liberty for all. But a system that did this as a general rule would also, I have argued, be a system that diverges from what we conceive of as a legal system. Is a system, then, that fails to give minimal respect to this principle of justice not only an unjust system but a system that diverges from what we understand as a legal system? I think so.

---

[1] John Rawls put forward this claim in *Justice as Fairness* 67 PHILOSOPHICAL REVIEW 164 (1958).

The Concept of Legal Liberty

GLANVILLE WILLIAMS[1]

The concept of legal liberty may be called the *pons asinorum* of analytical jurisprudence; but unlike Euclid's fifth theorem it is a bridge at which not only the beginner but some grave and learned men have been known to stumble. Even among the professional exponents of jurisprudence there is no full agreement upon the answers to what would appear at first sight to be elementary questions.

I. THE DEFINITION OF LEGAL LIBERTY

A liberty, as that word will be used in the following discussion, means any occasion on which an act or omission is not a breach of duty. When I get up in the morning, dress, take breakfast, and so on, I am exercising liberties, because I do not commit legal wrongs. Since the commission of legal wrongs is relatively infrequent, almost every act is the exercise of a liberty.

An example of a liberty appearing in legal works is the defense of privilege in defamation; also the (more or less) general defenses in tort, such as consent, necessity, private defense, and statutory authority. When a person has a substantive defense in law to an action or prosecution, that is to say a legal defense on the merits, he has a liberty, i.e., the conduct of which complaint is made is not a breach of duty. This is not necessarily true of a merely procedural or adjectival defense. The defense under statutes of limitation, for example, generally does not deny the duty, but alleges that the

[1] Glanville Williams, LL.B. 1931 Wales, M.A. 1937, LL.D. 1946 Cantab., is Professor of English Law in the University of Cambridge. The essay here is reprinted from 56 COLUM. L. REV. 1129 (1956). Other work in legal philosophy by Mr. Williams includes: *International Law and the Controversy Concerning the Word 'Law'* 22 BRIT. YB. INT'L L. 146 (1945); *Language and the Law* (pts. 1–5) 61 L. Q. REV. 21, 179, 293, 384 (1945), 62 L. Q. REV. 387 (1946); SALMOND ON JURISPRUDENCE (11th ed. 1957); and *Carelessness, Indifference and Recklessness: Two Replies* 25 MODERN L. REV. 49, 55 (1962). (Footnote by editor.)

duty has become unenforceable through lapse of time. Several other unenforceable duties are known to the law. Except in the case of these unenforceable duties or other procedural objections it is true to say that a successful objection in point of law to a claim involves the assertion of a liberty.[1]

Most legal liberties are not to be found stated in law books, because there is generally no point in making these negative statements. It will not surprise the reader to know that there is no entry of 'breakfast, liberty to eat', in the index to *Corpus Juris*. If the law lays down no duty, it is generally indicated in legal works by making no reference to the subject. When a liberty is stated, it is generally by way of expressing the limits of a legal duty. Thus freedom of speech, which is a liberty, represents the limits of the duty not to utter defamation, blasphemy, obscenity, and sedition. Even so, we should not bother to proclaim liberty of speech unless this were regarded as a special value, to be jealously guarded. We are particularly likely to express a liberty when the law was formerly otherwise, or when the law of foreign countries is otherwise, or when some people want to make our law otherwise. Take as an example the liberty of the press: this is in part a memory of the fact that at one time there were in England press licensing laws, which made it an offense to print without previous license. If no one had ever challenged the liberty of the press, by imposing a certain duty not to print, we should hardly pause to think of it as a freedom. Similarly the so-called right of combination, which is really the liberty of workmen to combine in trade unions, derives its special meaning in England from the historic struggle to repeal the combination laws.

It follows from what has been said that the question, sometimes mooted, whether liberties are conferred by law, is one of words. If law is conceived as a system of rights and duties, liberties lie outside it; they are an 'extra-legal phenomenon', representing what is left of possible conduct after deducting the part regulated

---

[1] The 'trust of imperfect obligation' or 'honorary trust' is in fact a liberty conferred upon the trustees to waste the trust property in a certain way; the tombstone or the animal is not (as is sometimes supposed) the beneficiary. The only beneficiary, because the only person with a right, is the next-of-kin or residuary legatee who can claim if the property is not wasted in the specified manner. Hence a so-called trust of imperfect obligation is in truth a fully enforceable trust for the next-of-kin, subject to a condition precedent which confers on the trustee the liberty stated. It is not a case of unenforceable duty.

by rules of duty. However, it is often convenient to think and speak of liberties as being included in the law. The law, in this sense, includes rules denying duties as well as rules affirming duties. Considerable portions of law books are taken up with the denial of duties, that is to say the affirmation of liberties.

Liberties may be 'given' either by general rules of law (representing in reality the limits of legal duty) or by act of party; in the latter event a particular person has by law the power to dispense with duty that would otherwise exist. Exercising this power, he confers a liberty. Liberties so given by act of party are generally termed licenses. A clear example is the revocable license to enter land. At the moment I am under a duty not to enter your land, but if you give me gratuitous license to enter, my duty will be replaced by a liberty to enter. It is sometimes said to be a 'right' to enter; but since this supposed right may be revoked by the landowner at any time, it is much better called a liberty. Even an irrevocable license is a liberty, though, being irrevocable, it is coupled with the licensee's right against the landowner, during the term of the license, not to be interfered with in its enjoyment.

Whenever a liberty is given for the first time, it involves the abrogation of a previous duty to do the opposite. For example, the abrogation of a duty not to enter land creates a liberty to enter it. These two possibilities (duty to act in a certain way, liberty to act in the opposite way) are mutually exclusive, being contradictory in meaning.

The illustration of the landowner's license may serve to introduce another point. Suppose that, after you have given me the license to enter your land, I made a contract with you that I will enter your land for a specified purpose, say to repair the fence. Now, under my contract, I am under a duty to enter, a contractual duty. What has become of my liberty to enter? Clearly it is still there. Even since the making of the contract, it is true to say that my general duty not to enter the land of others remains abrogated in respect of your land, and consequently it is true to say that I have a liberty to enter. This liberty is not inconsistent with my duty to enter. A liberty and duty *of the same content* may exist together. The statement that I am at liberty to enter means that I commit no tort or other crime or other legal wrong in entering. The statement that I am under a duty to enter means that I shall commit a wrong if I do not enter.

II. THE CHOICE OF THE WORD 'LIBERTY'

In the present discussion, the concept of absence of duty is being
expressed by 'liberty' (the term used by Austin and Salmond)
instead of Hohfeld's 'privilege'. This departure from Hohfeld is
made with reluctance, because the need for an agreed technical
language is so great that it counterbalances any minor difficulties
that may be urged against the choice of this or that particular
word. Moreover, Hohfeld's terminology has been quite generally
accepted in American legal writing, and has been used in the
Restatement of the Law of Torts. For many years, when teaching
Jurisprudence in the University of London, I used Hohfeld's
term, abandoning it only when I had become convinced that it
created an excessive amount of difficulty. The term 'privilege'
carries the strong popular and etymological meaning of a special
favor given to the individual or a narrow class (*privilegium*, a
private law), and the tendency is for this to fight down the general
meaning that Hohfeld chose to assign to it. I found that, however
clearly I tried to explain to students that 'privilege' in jurisprudence was to mean merely what Salmond called a liberty, some
seemed unable to hold this explanation in the mind. Hence I was
constantly faced with the objection to particular illustrations:
'That is not a privilege, because everybody has it.'

Hohfeld's meaning of 'privilege' not only runs counter to the
popular use, but it departs from the technical legal use. As
Spencer Bower observed, except in defamation 'the term [privilege]
is uniformly employed to connote two ideas: (1) the notion of
something in excess of the ordinary law, (2) something which is
conferred by grant, statute, or usage on a particular person, corporation, place, class or profession.'[1] Even in defamation the
defense of privilege implies some restriction by person or circumstance; the defense open to the whole world is called not
privilege but fair comment upon a matter of public interest. Fair
comment is the exercise of a liberty, but is not in ordinary legal
language a privilege. Sociological writers keep a similar distinction
alive when they speak of the privileged as opposed to the deprived
classes; sometimes one hears the somewhat ridiculous phrase 'the

---

[1] BOWER, ACTIONABLE DEFAMATION 315 (2d ed. 1923), and see his long discussion generally. See also MILLER, DATA OF JURISPRUDENCE 103–8 (1903);
5 VINER, ABRIDGEMENT (Supp. 1905), *s.v.* 'Privilege'.

under-privileged classes'. Even the *Restatement* does not wholly adopt Hohfeld, because it denies the term 'privilege' to the situation at common law where the defendant need not pay damages for negligence because of the plaintiff's contributory negligence;[1] according to Hohfeld's definition such conduct would be privileged, because it would not be a breach of duty.

There are other objections to the term privilege, of a minor character. In some contexts it is a eulogistic word, and this is apt to interfere with a strictly scientific use. In other contexts it means something different from liberty. Thus the privilege of a legislature to compel the attendance of witnesses is a power, while the privilege of its members to be free from arrest is an immunity; and diplomatic privilege is an immunity. Occasionally the term 'privilege' is applied in law to things, e.g., the privilege of goods from distress and of documents from production in court, whereas the liberty-privilege is exclusively an attribute of legal persons.

Now the word 'liberty' is free from the principal defect of 'privilege': it is ordinarily used both for liberties common to all (e.g., liberty of speech) and for special privileges. As an example of the latter, a landowner, in permitting another to enter his land, may quite naturally say: 'You are at liberty to use the path.' It is true that the term once had a very narrow meaning in English law: Blackstone said that 'franchise and liberty are used as synonymous terms: and their definition is a royal privilege, or branch of the king's prerogative, subsisting in the hands of the subject'.[2] But liberty now generally has a wider meaning, and sometimes it even includes a power (as in the phrase 'liberty of contract'). For the purpose of analytical jurisprudence a liberty and power are, of course, distinguished from each other. Another disadvantage of the word 'liberty' is that it is used in a variety of meanings differing from the meaning it bears in jurisprudence. Political philosophers use it to mean liberty of choice, liberty to choose the good, political liberty, economic liberty, etc. None of these represents the meaning of liberty when this word is placed in the table of jural relations.

The unreliable nature of our present legal dictionary may be illustrated by an English case[3] turning on the words in section 62

---

[1] RESTATEMENT, TORTS § 10, comment *a* (1934).
[2] 2 BLACKSTONE, COMMENTARIES *37; cf. MILLER, op. cit. *supra* note 2, at 96–100, 102; WHARTON, LAW LEXICON (14th ed. 1938), *s.v.* 'Liberty'.
[3] *LeStrange* v. *Pettefar*, 161 T.L.R. 300 (Ch. 1939).

of the Law of Property Act, 1925: 'liberties, privileges, easements, rights and advantages'. Luxmoore, L. J., said:

A 'liberty' must, I think, be something which results from a permission given to, or something enjoyed under sufferance by, a particular person or body of persons, as distinguished from something enjoyed by sufferance by all and sundry, while a 'privilege' describes some advantage to an individual or group of individuals, a right enjoyed by a few as opposed to a right enjoyed by all. 'Easement' and 'right' are obviously words not appropriate to universal enjoyment nor is the word 'advantage', for it necessarily connotes the enjoyment of something which is denied to others.

As general definitions these remarks are open to doubt. To seize upon the most obvious error, 'right' is clearly a word appropriate to universal as well as to particular enjoyment (e.g., the public right not to have a highway obstructed). Similarly, constitutional liberties are enjoyed by all. The definitions of Luxmoore, L. J., may have been correct within the context of the particular section he was discussing, but it seems unsatisfactory that we have no technical term which connotes beyond a peradventure an absence of duty whether universal or particular.

As said before, liberties are in some contexts expressed by the word 'license'. Thus we speak of the plea of 'leave and license' in torts to property, and of a license as contrasted with a lease. Sometimes a license (that is to say, exemption from duty) may be given by an official acting in accordance with legal rules: examples are dog, radio, and operators' or driving licenses, which render legal acts that would otherwise be illegal. On the subject of licenses to use land, Vaughan, C. J., said in 1673: 'A dispensation or licence properly passeth no interest, nor alters or transfers property in anything, but only makes an action lawful, which without it had been unlawful.'[1] The latter part of this sentence expresses a legal liberty. But the term license is normally confined to a permission given by a human being in accordance with the law; it is not applied to permissions given directly by the law. Nor is it applied to all permissions by a human being; as has just been noted, a

[1] *Winter Garden Theatre, Ltd.* v. *Millennium Productions, Ltd.*, [1948] A.C. 173, 193; see also MILLER, op. cit. *supra* note 2, at 102–3. Although Vaughan C. J.'s dictum is still verbally maintained by the courts, one opinion holds that the law has developed in such a way that licenses for value are in reality interests.

lease is not a license, and neither is an easement. Finally, in political philosophy license means an immoral use of liberty.

Yet another word is 'freedom'. This is not much used by lawyers except in connection with the constitutional freedoms and the freedom of a municipality.

'Immunity' is sometimes used: thus the infant's immunity in contract is in reality a liberty not to pay what would otherwise be his debts. 'Authority' is another word, though in some contexts this means power. Other expressions are 'lawful', 'justified', 'justifiable', 'excuse', 'excusable', 'defense', 'exemption', 'protection', 'protected'; but these have their own troubles. Perhaps the most unreliable as terms of art are 'lawful' and its opposite, 'unlawful'. In *Lemy* v. *Watson*[1] it was held that a trade description was not lawfully applied before 1887 within the meaning of the English Merchandise Marks Act of that year, when it was misleading to the public, even though its use was not, before the act, a criminal offense. The decision may perhaps be explained by saying that the misleading application was a breach of contract. Sometimes other courts have gone further and distinguished between what is legal and what is lawful; legal is what is in conformity with the law; lawful connotes also a requirement of morality. Thus a conspiracy to do something immoral may be regarded as a conspiracy to do an unlawful act; or, at one time, a killing in the course of an immoral act was apparently regarded as a killing in the course of an unlawful act, and so as manslaughter. The usage is most unfortunate, particularly in criminal law; and there are signs that it is disappearing.[2] Finally, 'lawful' sometimes means the valid exercise of a legal power.[3]

Owing to the lack of legal expressions of clearly general import, a draftsman is forced to make use of a large variety of words if he wishes to express a wide conception; and he must then content himself with hoping that a particular contingency which he wishes to cover will not be held to be excluded from each of his particular words. For example, by the English Medical Act of 1860 'the granting of new charters to the said corporations respectively by and in the altered names and styles respectively, as provided in the Medical Act, shall not, in respect of such alteration of name or

---

[1] [1915] 3 K.B. 731.
[2] *The Queen* v. *Clarence*, 22 Q.B.D. 23, 36, 40 (1888); WILLIAMS, CRIMINAL LAW: THE GENERAL PART § 8 (1953).   [3] *In re* Coxon, [1904] § Ch. 252, 257.

style merely, alter or affect in any way the *rights, powers, authorities, qualifications, liberties, exemptions, immunities, duties, and obligations,* granted, conferred, or imposed to or upon, or continued and preserved to the said corporations respectively.'[1] If the wide meanings of 'powers' and 'liberties' now current in jurisprudential literature were accepted by the judges, there would have been no need to include in this list the words 'authorities', 'qualifications', and 'exemptions'; and 'obligations' could have been omitted as covered by the word 'duties'.

III. LEGAL LIBERTIES TO ACT AND NOT TO ACT

There was one point upon which Hohfeld was in error, or at least guilty of incomplete statement. It will be remembered that Hohfeld constructed a table in which privilege (or, as I am calling it, liberty) was made the opposite of duty and the correlative of no-right. The scheme may be exhibited as follows:

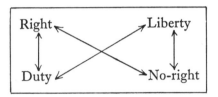

Here the vertical arrows couple the correlatives, so that a right in *A* against *B* implies a duty in *B* towards *A* and vice versa. The diagonal arrows couple what Hohfeld called opposites but which can better be called contradictories, because taken together they exhaust the relevant field (universe of discourse). For example, a no-right means the absence of a right. Either *A* has a right in a particular respect or he has no right (a no-right); there is no third possibility.

There is, however, an error in the table, namely in the unqualified word 'liberty'. Liberty is not, as such, the correlative of no-right, or the contradictory of duty. To make the table correct, one must write instead of 'liberty' the words 'liberty not'. For example, the correlative of your no-right that I should pay you $5 is my liberty *not* to pay you $5. The contradictory of my duty to pay you $5 is again my liberty *not* to pay you $5.

[1] 23 & 24 Vict., c. 66, § 3.

To explain this in more detail, it is necessary to consider the kinds of rights and duties. These may be either positive or negative, in the sense that a duty may oblige either to acts or to forbearances. My right against my debtor that he shall pay me the debt is a right of positive content; my right that he shall not assault me is a right of negative content.

The negative in the last example touches on the content of the right (that he shall not assault me), and is to be distinguished from a negative predicated of the right itself, i.e., a statement that a given right does not exist. The sentence: 'I have not a right that X shall pay me \$5' is an example of a denial of a right of positive content. The sentence: 'A child has not a right that his father shall not chastise him' is a denial of a right of negative content. Putting the last sentence another way, one could say: 'A father is not under a duty not to chastise his child.' This is a denial of a duty of negative content. It is a denial of any legal prohibition of chastisement. Observe that the two negatives perform different logical functions. The first denies the duty, while the second states that the duty denied is one of negative content, a duty to refrain from doing. This difference of function means that the negatives cannot be cancelled out. In the instance given, the sentence obviously does not mean the same as: 'A father is under a duty to chastise his child.' The latter affirms a duty of positive content, and, unlike the former, is an incorrect statement of the law.

Nor (one may add) does the former sentence mean: 'A father has a right (in the strict sense) to chastise his child.' This is because the child owes no duty to be chastised. He would not break a duty if he were not chastised.

The next step is the vital one in the argument. We will take the sentence: 'A father is not under a duty not to chastise his child', and by verbal magic change it into another sentence that in outward form appears quite different. This sentence is: 'A father has a liberty to chastise his child.' The two sentences have precisely the same meaning. Yet in the second two negatives have disappeared, namely, the negative serving to deny the duty and the negative expressing the fact that the duty denied is one of forbearance. In short, whereas the second sentence seems to assert something concerning the father, it is in meaning merely a denial—a denial of a legal duty of negative content.

It will be found that the same analysis holds for every other sentence asserting a liberty to do something. Such an assertion is in reality a *denial* of duty *not* to do the thing in question.

This is perhaps a unique phenomenon in our language. Several other words conceal a single negative behind an apparent positive, *e.g.*, 'black', 'cold', 'heathen', 'alien', 'layman'. 'Liberty' goes one better; it manages to conceal two negatives which are logically independent of each other. (The same is, of course, true of words of similar meaning like 'freedom' and 'privilege'.)

We may manufacture a compound noun 'no-duty', meaning an absence of duty. No-duty is the contradictory of duty. Using this expression, a liberty to do something becomes a no-duty not to do it. This gives a number of different ways of expressing the same thought, e.g.:

'A father has a liberty to chastise his child.'

'A father has not a duty not to chastise his child.'

'A father has no duty not to chastise his child.'

'A father has a no-duty not to chastise his child.'

The only need for the noun 'no-duty' is this, that lawyers commonly speak of a liberty (using various words to express the concept, not necessarily the word 'liberty'), and it is sometimes clearer to be able to translate this into the language of rights and duties. Therefore it is sometimes convenient to say that a liberty is a no-duty not to do something. One can always avoid using both the term liberty and the term no-duty by saying simply that there is not a duty not to do the act, i.e., by denying a duty to refrain from it.

The foregoing discussion was concerned with a liberty to do something. Now it is possible also to have a liberty not to do something. For example, I have a liberty not to pay my tailor any money, because it happens that at the moment I do not owe him any. This liberty not to pay means that I am not under a duty to pay, i.e., that I have a no-duty to pay. We thus reach the conclusion that a 'liberty not' means a no-duty, while a liberty means a 'no-duty not'.

What is the correlative of liberty not or no-duty? Since rights are correlative to duties, a denial of duty necessarily involves a denial of correlative right. Thus, the correlative of the negative concept no-duty (liberty not) is no-right, or the contradictory of a right. This is illustrated in the following sentences, all of which are equivalent in meaning to the corresponding ones previously given:

'My tailor has not a right that I shall pay him.'
'My tailor has no right that I shall pay him.'
'My tailor has a no-right that I shall pay him.'
'The child has not a right not to be chastised.'
'The child has no right not to be chastised.'
'The child has a no-right not to be chastised.'

Here, again, the noun 'no-right' is not necessary. It is simpler and more usual to say that a man has not a right than that he has a no-right. However, those who insist on finding a correlative for the expression 'liberty' (to do something) can be satisfied by being told that the correlative is a no-right in the other person that the thing shall not be done.

Just as the correlative of a no-duty (liberty not) is a no-right, so the contradictory of a no-duty is obviously a duty. This is where Hohfeld went wrong. He said that the correlative of a no-right is a privilege, and the contradictory (or, in his language, opposite) of a privilege is a duty. I have shown that to make these statements correct the word 'privilege' must be written as 'privilege not'.

If it is desired to take the concept of privilege or liberty as a starting point, this is equivalent to no-duty not, and its correlative is no-right . . . not, while its contradictory is duty not.

The discussion so far may be summed up by setting out two conversion tables, in amplification and correction of Hohfeld's, explaining what happens when a right or duty is repealed or denied. Reading downwards the concepts are correlative. Reading diagonally towards the right, the tables state what happens when a right or duty is repealed or denied. In other words, the concepts connected by diagonal arrows are legal contradictories; each is a denial of the truth of the other.

Rights of positive content	Their repeal or denial	Rights of negative content	Their repeal or denial

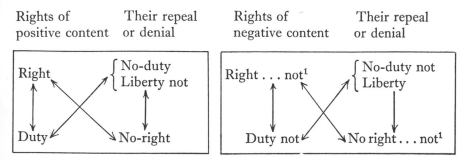

[1] The conduct to which a right obliges is the conduct of the person under the

Within each square the left-hand column may be taken to indicate an assertion of the present legal position, and the right-hand column to indicate what would happen if the law were altered or its existence denied. Or, the right-hand column within each square can be read as the assertion, and the left-hand column as its alteration or denial.

To give some further illustrations: I am under a duty to pay my taxes. If the tax statutes were repealed, I should have a liberty not (a no-duty) to pay taxes. Again, if *A* has a right that *B* shall not trespass on his land (right . . . not), *B* is under a duty not to trespass (duty-not); it is not true that *B* has a liberty to trespass (denial of liberty); it is not true that *A* has no right that *B* shall not trespass (denial of no-right . . . not).

The term no-right, which was invented by Hohfeld, has been derided by some writers, who observe that it is a purely negative expression. You might as well talk of a no-dog, it is said, as of a no-right; and again it has been remarked that a no-right may be an elephant. Oddly, these critics do not find anything laughable in the term 'liberty'; yet it is an even more negative expression than no-right, for a liberty is a no-duty not.[1] Whether no-right and no-duty prove to be sufficiently convenient terms to establish themselves in the language remains to be seen; it is not a final objection that they are of quaint appearance.

IV. LEGAL LIBERTY NEED NOT INVOLVE CHOICE

As remarked at the beginning, liberty in the sense in which that word is here used is not inconsistent with duty, for there may be a duty and a liberty of the same content. The real inconsistency is between duty and liberty not (i.e., no-duty). To repeat an example already given, the repeal of the tax laws could not give me a liberty to pay taxes, for I already have that liberty; it would give me a liberty not to pay.

[1] cf. WHATELY, LOGIC 137 (rev. ed. 1869): 'Many negative terms which are such *in sense only* have led to confusion of thought from their real character being imperfectly perceived. E.g. 'Liberty', which is a purely negative term, denoting merely 'absence of restraint', is sometimes confounded with 'Power'.

---

duty. There is never a right in the strict sense that the owner of the right shall do or not do something. A 'right . . . not' (right of negative content) is a right *that the other shall* not do something, and so with a 'no-right . . . not'. The dots in the table are intended to signify the missing words 'that the person under the (real or alleged) duty shall'.

This is a difference between the definition of legal liberty and that of philosophical liberty. A philosopher would say that if the law regulates every action of the citizen, prescribing in detail what it is his duty to do from morning to night, there is no liberty left. Liberty, for the philosopher, implies choice of conduct, and liberty merely to do one's duty (as, to pay taxes) is a poor kind of joke. The philosopher's use of the term is important and useful, but it is not the one generally needed by the lawyer. Once legal liberty is defined as the absence of a duty to act otherwise, it follows that there can be no liberty to perform a legal duty.

Those who remain unconvinced by this argument should reflect that any difficulty they feel is caused merely by our appropriation of the word 'liberty'. Replace this word by Hohfeld's 'privilege', and the difficulty would hardly arise. It is the word 'liberty' that, through its philosophical associations, raises in the mind the notion of choice. Now this, from the present point of view, is an irrelevant factor. The concept under investigation, whatever we may choose to call it, is the contradictory of duty and the correlative of no-right. Logically, the question of choice has nothing to do with this concept. If we decide to express the concept by the word 'liberty' (or, rather, 'liberty not'), this can only be on the distinct understanding that there may be liberty to perform a duty. From this point of view, it must be confessed, Hohfeld's 'privilege' is superior to 'liberty'; it does not import the irrelevant philosophy of choice.

This objection does not seem to be fatal to the use of the word 'liberty' in the table of jural relations, because in many legal contexts the word does not necessarily imply choice. For example: suppose that a convict's sentence has expired, and the governor of the prison says to him: 'You are at liberty to leave.' This means that the convict will not be prevented from leaving, and that he will not commit the crime of escape in leaving. It is a perfectly natural use of the language: none the less so because the convict is actually under a duty to quit the prison, his period of free board having come to an end. The statement 'You are at liberty to leave' does not imply the statement 'You are at liberty to stay.' It is true that in many contexts of ordinary life the speaker and hearer may understand from the word 'liberty' that a choice is intended. This is true even of legal documents: for example, the word 'liberty' in the United States Constitution implies an ambit of philosophical freedom.[1] But in legal discussions it is best to state precisely that there is a choice (i.e., that liberty and liberty not coexist), if that is meant and if it is important to express it, and to read the sentence, 'You are at liberty to leave', as meaning neither more nor less than it says.

As a further illustration of this, there is a doubt whether in present law a citizen is under duty to arrest one who commits a felony in his presence; but he certainly has a liberty and power to do so at common law. Even if there is a duty to arrest, it is meaningful to say that there is a liberty to arrest, for this means that arresting is not a tort to the person arrested.

In England, the Larceny Act of 1861 provides that a person to whom any property shall be offered to be sold, pawned, or delivered, if he has reasonable cause to suspect an offense under the act with respect to such property, 'is authorised, and, if in his power, required', to apprehend the party offering.[2] The word 'authorised' creates a liberty and power to arrest; the word 'required' creates a duty to arrest. There is no contradiction between the two concepts.

Where the law imposes a public duty, there is an immediate inference that a liberty exists to give effect to the duty, in accordance with the maxim that 'what the law requires it also justifies'. In other words, 'must' includes 'may', for otherwise the subject of the law would be placed in the embarrassing position of having to break one or the other of conflicting duties. Even an unenforceable duty may create a liberty. Thus the Act of Uniformity,[3] which is still technically in force in England, imposes a duty to attend divine service; but the only punishment named is 'the censures of the Church', which in effect makes the duty an unenforceable one from the legal point of view. Nevertheless the duty has some legal importance, for the duty of parishioners to attend their church is taken to create a 'right' in them to enter the church.[4] This 'right' is a liberty which cannot be revoked except for disorderly conduct;

[1] See Shattuck, *Meaning of the Term 'Liberty'*, 4 HARV. L. REV. 365 (1891).
[2] 24 & 25 Vict., c. 96, § 103. [3] 5 & 6 Edw. 6, c. 1, § 1 (1552).
[4] *Cole* v. *Police Constable* 443A, [1937] 1 K.B. 316, 330 (1936). Notice may be taken here that the word 'correlative' is sometimes confused with 'corollary'. A correlative, properly, is one of two things having a reciprocal relation such that one of them necessarily implies, or is complementary to, the other: e.g., husband–wife; parent–child; right–duty. A corollary is an immediate deduction from a given proposition, generally so obvious as not to require separate proof. When, in *Cole's* case, *idem* at 323, counsel argued that the 'right' of parishioners

and its meaning is that the parishioners do not commit trespass in entering the church, and have a right not to be prevented from entering the church except for due cause.

The only instance in Anglo-American law where a public 'must' does not include a public 'may' is in relation to trusts for indefinite public non-charitable purposes. The effect of some authorities seems to be that if the testator has said that his trustees 'may' devote property to such purposes, then they may; but if he says they must, then they may not. The latter rule has been the subject of criticism.[1] Of course it does not create conflicting duties, for the 'must' is void and the only duty is to apply the property for the benefit of those otherwise entitled.

In private law, owing to the concept of duties *in personam*, a 'must' (i.e., duty) in respect of one person need not necessarily involve a 'may' (liberty) in respect of another. In rare instances, the performance of a duty towards A is not a liberty towards B but is a breach of duty towards B. Suppose that X sells the same watch twice, the second purchaser not knowing of the first sale. Here X is under inconsistent legal duties—to deliver to the first purchaser, and to deliver to the second. Since he cannot perform both duties, he must be liable in damages to one purchaser. His performance of the one duty, being a breach of the other, is not the exercise of a liberty. To speak more precisely, his performance of his duty to one purchaser is a liberty towards that purchaser, but is not a liberty towards the other purchaser. Liberties, like duties, can exist *in personam*.

The lack of opposition between liberty and duty has had the peculiar consequence that in some cases a statute saying that someone may do something, or that it shall be lawful to do something, has been construed as creating not merely a liberty but a duty to do it.[2] *Prima facie*, however, these expressions create liberties

[1] E.g., Scott, *Trusts for Charitable and Benevolent Purposes*, 58 HARV. L. REV. 548, 563 (1945).

[2] *Yorkshire Copper Works Ltd.* v. *Registrar of Trade Marks*, [1954] 1 W.L.R. 554, 560 (H.L.); *Rex* v. *Worcestershire Justices*, 55 T.L.R. 657 (K.B. 1939); *De Keyser* v. *British Ry. Traffic & Elec. Co.*, [1936] 1 K.B. 224; *Julius* v. *Lord Bishop*, 5 APP. CAS. 214, 222-3 (1880); see 3 BURROWS, WORDS AND PHRASES 169, 342 (1944); MAXWELL, INTERPRETATION OF STATUTES 244 (10th ed. 1943); ODGERS, CONSTRUCTION OF DEEDS AND STATUTES 270, 281 (3d ed. 1952).

---

to attend church is correlative to their duty to do so, he should have said 'the corollary of'.

only.[1] It is submitted that only the clearest inference from other parts of the statute should be sufficient to give a mandatory meaning to words permissive in ordinary use.

It would be possible to escape from linguistic difficulties if we could invent a completely new technical term to occupy the place in the table of legal relations. The best and clearest term would be 'no-duty', so that instead of saying that X has a liberty to do something we should say that X has a no-duty not to do it. However, one can hardly hope to persuade the legal profession to use such an invented language. Thus it seems that the word 'liberty', notwithstanding the ambiguities to which it is subject, is the best existing term for denoting the jurisprudential concept.

V. LIBERTY AND RIGHT

Quite often a liberty is called a right, e.g., the right of self-defense, the right of combination, rights of way. The 'claim of right' in larceny is a claim of liberty. This use of the word 'right' is found even in statutes. It should, however, be avoided wherever strictness of language is required. 'Right' conjures up the idea of something that can be insisted on, whereas a liberty is purely a negative expression.[2] A right exists where there is a positive law on the subject; a liberty where there is no law against it. A right is correlative to a duty in another, while a liberty is not.

It might have been thought that the last proposition had been proved beyond doubt by the labors of the classical writers on jurisprudence; yet it is still persistently denied in some quarters. There are those who still assert that a liberty corresponds to duties, or at least is surrounded and supported by duties, or is given legal protection.[3] For example, the proposition that I have a liberty to walk along the street is not (it is said) a mere negative statement, because the liberty is correlative to the duty of everyone not to stop me from walking.

[1] cf. *In re* Baker, 44 CH. D. 262, 270 (C.A. 1890); *East Suffolk Rivers Catchment Bd. v. Kent*, [1941] A.C. 74 (1940); *Comment*, 14 CAN. B. REV. 160, 161 (1936).

[2] Of course, a right frequently co-exists with a liberty; e.g., my right against my debtor that he shall pay me co-exists with my liberty to receive payment. However, the exercise of a right against A may be a breach of duty to B. And it would not be illogical for the law to recognize a primary right as founding a sanctioning right even in some circumstances where the primary right would be illegal. See Williams, *The Legal Effect of Illegal Contracts*, 8 CAMB. L. J. 151 (1942).

[3] It is not common to come across these views in print. But see BUCKLAND, SOME REFLECTIONS ON JURISPRUDENCE 94–96 (1945).

The short answer to this is that the duty not to stop me from walking is merely the ordinary duty not to assault me, and this is correlative to my right not to be assaulted. The latter right is something different from my liberty to walk along the street, which is merely an expression of the fact that there is no law against my walking.[1]

Those who wish to find a 'right' (in the strict sense) to walk along the street sometimes say that it is correlative to the duty of others not to obstruct the highway so that I cannot pass along it. This obstruction would be a public nuisance, but the rule is that no member of the public can sue for damages sustained from a public nuisance unless particular damage is suffered, over and above that suffered by the rest of the public. Thus your duty not to obstruct my passage along the highway is, properly speaking, a duty owed to the state; the only duty you owe me in this respect is a duty not to cause me particular damage by obstructing the highway, which is correlative to my right not to receive particular damage. This is obviously different from my liberty to walk, which requires no reference to damage.

The argument that rights and liberties are the same is usually based on the proposition that every one has a right not to be interfered with in the exercise of his liberties. This, however, is a fallacy. There are in fact two different propositions involved, viz.:

'I have a liberty to do this'; and

'I have a right not to be interfered with in doing this.'

Even if in a particular context the second proposition is true as a matter of law, the two propositions mean different things. The first means that I do not commit a tort or other legal wrong by doing so-and-so. The second means that you commit a tort or other legal wrong by interfering with my doing so-and-so. These are different statements.

But the truth is that the second proposition does not invariably coincide with the first as a matter of law. It often does, because of the width of the law of tort, particularly in such torts as assault and false imprisonment. Yet circumstances arise in which there can be

---

[1] It can be said that you have no liberty to stop me walking. This means that you have no excuse if sued in tort for assault. It is an assertion that my general tort-right not to be assaulted applies to these particular facts. The sentence does not mean the same as the sentence, 'I have a liberty to walk down the street.'

K

a liberty to do something without a right not to be interfered with in doing it. These are the well-known instances of *damnum absque injuria.*

(1) It has already been shown that this is partly true of the public liberty of passage along the highway. (2) You and I are walking together when we see a gold watch lying in front of us. I have a liberty to run forward and pick it up. (Also a power by so doing to obtain a title good against all save the true owner.) But you may run faster than I and pick it up first; this will *de facto* be an interference with me in the exercise of my liberty, but will not be a tort or other legal wrong to me. My liberty is a bare liberty unsupported by a right in this particular respect. This was essentially the situation in *Mayor* v. *Pickles*:[1] the corporation of Bradford had a liberty to receive the percolating water but no right against other landowners to receive it. (3) After much inquiry I discovered a good cook who is willing to take employment with me. I have a liberty and power to employ her, but you commit no tort by offering better wages and so displacing me. (4) One who has a license to use land has a liberty, but according to the traditional position of the common law has no right against third parties not to be interfered with.[2] (5) I have a liberty to erect a house on the edge of my land (provided that I obtain any requisite governmental permission); but my neighbor has a liberty to dig a quarry on the edge of his land and so cause a subsidence of my house, thus rendering it impossible for me to build effectively. (The only exceptions are where I have an easement of support, or where the quarry would cause a subsidence of my land even if it were unweighted by buildings; in these two instances I should have a right of action.)

One of the clearest examples of a liberty unprotected by corresponding duties is the liberty of speech. It may be asserted that I possess this liberty; yet no one is under a duty to assist me in my speech, to listen to me, or (since I am neither a judge nor a parson) to preserve silence while I am speaking. The only relevant duty that can be discovered is the duty not to gag me; but this, of course, is

---

[1] [1895] A.C. 587.

[2] Some decisions, however, give a wider measure of protection, either by allowing an action for the tort of interference with contract—see *G. W. K. Ltd.* v. *Dunlop Rubber Co.*, 42 T. L. R. 376 (K.B. 1926), *appeal dismissed*, 42 T. L. R. 593 (C.A. 1926); PROSSER, TORTS § 106 (2d ed. 1955)—or by regarding the license as a 'clog or fetter' on the title of the licensor.

only part of the ordinary duty to refrain from assault. It has no specific connection with liberty of speech. A person who is not gagged may still fail to make others pay attention to him; he has no right to be heard. Were there such a right, every one who did not hear the speaker would break his duty. In truth the liberty of speech is, as Dicey showed, the residuum after subtracting all the particular duties to refrain from sedition, slander, etc.

From this discussion there emerges a principle of some importance in dealing with these fundamental legal concepts. This is that, in arguing from a concept to its correlative, the content of the concept must not be changed. It is not permissible to deduce from the proposition that A is under a duty not to gag B the proposition that B has a right to speak freely. Whenever there is the possibility of fallacy, the content of the right should be stated in the same language as the content of the correlative duty, and vice versa. If the verbal formula be changed, this may give rise to the suspicion that the content of the concept has been changed, and consequently that there is a flaw in the reasoning.

To test whether an alleged 'right' is a right in the strict sense, ask whether it has a legal duty correlative to it, and keep to the same formula when stating the duty. Thus it is fallacious to argue that the 'right' of a licensee to go upon land is correlative to a duty on the occupier not to set traps. Similarly the 'right of way' (as, by way of easement) is not a right, because there is no duty of way. A person entitled to a right of way has not a right to walk, because the other is under no duty that he shall walk. If the dominant owner decides to stay at home and not walk, this would be no tort to the servient owner. The 'right of way' is a liberty of way combined with the ordinary right not to be assaulted when exercising it and a right not to have the way obstructed.

There is another method of showing that 'right of way' is a misnomer. No one ever has a right to do something; he only has a right that some one else shall do (or refrain from doing) something. In other words, every right in the strict sense relates to the conduct of another, while a liberty and a power relate to the conduct of the holder of the liberty or power. A statement that a person has a right to do something generally means that he has a right in the strict sense not to be interfered with in doing it.

It may be thought that the phrase 'right of way' is not a favorable illustration of the argument, for it is, after all, a convenient and relatively harmless abbreviation of 'right not to be prevented from passing'. In so far as the first phrase means the second, it is a true right. A liberty of way under an easement is so closely coupled with a right that it is convenient to speak of the complex as a right of way. If a person were given a revocable license of way, that is to say a bare liberty of passing, we should hardly call it a right of way. This shows that 'right of way' is a contracted expression connoting a protected enjoyment, and involving a right proper.[1] While accepting the convenience of this language, it is still necessary to insist as a matter of analysis that the right and the liberty are distinct.

The use of the word 'right' in an extended sense to include liberties is inveterate and probably beyond recall; but there should at least be an awareness of the ambiguity. For right in the sense of liberty, Terry suggested the phrase 'permissive right'; for right as correlative to duty he suggested 'correspondent' or 'protected right'.

VI. SOME EXAMPLES OF FALLACIES

To give point to the argument, it is necessary to show how confusion of terms has in the past led to false reasoning.

The error has sometimes been made in conspiracy cases, and in those relating to restraint of trade. Thus Lord Parker said,

At common law every member of the community is entitled to carry on any trade or business he chooses and in such a manner as he thinks most desirable in his own interests, and inasmuch as every right connotes an obligation no one can lawfully interfere with another in the free exercise of his trade or business unless there exists some just cause for such interference.[2]

Here the first proposition is readily accepted, though in its ordinary meaning it refers only to a liberty; Lord Parker takes advantage of the ambiguity of the word 'entitled' to assume that it.

---

[1] Even a bare license cannot be revoked except upon reasonable notice, so that until the expiration of the reasonable notice the licensee is protected by a right not to be interfered with in derogation of the license. See *Minister of Health* v. *Bellotti*, [1944] K.B. 298 (C.A.).

[2] *Attorney General* v. *Adelaide S. S. Co.*, [1913] A.C. 781, 793 (P.C.); cf. *Sorrell* v. *Smith*, [1925] A.C. 700, 727–8; *Quinn* v. *Leathem*, [1901] A.C. 495, 534 (discussed in HOHFELD, FUNDAMENTAL LEGAL CONCEPTIONS 42 (1934); *Allen* v. *Flood*, [1898] A.C. 1, 14, 33 (1897) (from which it appears that this particular fallacy goes back to a book published by Erle).

is also a right in the strict sense, for he proceeds to find a correlative obligation, i.e., duty. Thus a tort of interfering with trade materializes out of the thin air of a logical fallacy. Other judges have pointed out the *non sequitur*.[1] Of course, the recognition of the tort may be socially desirable notwithstanding the illogicality of the argument used to establish it. Since judges do not readily admit to making law, a fallacy is often the only acceptable mode of establishing a new rule. But when the decision on the point of policy remains unavowed, one has no assurance that the relevant considerations have been weighed.

I have heard the reply made to this criticism that the liberty to trade necessarily involves a right not to be interfered with in trading, for otherwise what use is it? The answer to this is that the liberty to trade is of precisely the same 'use' as any other liberty; it states a protection from legal proceedings for breach of duty. This may be shown by taking a regulated profession. I have no liberty to practice as a medical practitioner, because I am not qualified. Dr. Smith has a liberty to practice, because he is on the medical register. His liberty to practice means that he commits no offense in practising. It does not in itself mean that he can sue others who in some way interfere with his practice. Whether he can sue others depends upon his rights, not upon his liberties.

The next clinical specimen is taken from an argument advanced by a great master of the common law. In an article in the *Law Quarterly Review*,[2] Pollock examined the legal effect where *A* purports orally to give *B* a chattel, but does not deliver it. For example, *A* says, 'I hereby give you this watch', but although *B* is waiting expectantly, nothing else happens. Pollock suggested that the words of present gift, though they do not pass the ownership of the chattel (for it is only delivery or a deed that can pass legal ownership by way of gift), nevertheless operate as a revocable license (and, indeed, a power) to take it. *B*, the imperfect donee, may therefore take the watch if he sees it lying about, and if he does so the delivery will become perfect and he will obtain ownership. But suppose that, before he can take it, it is stolen by a stranger. Can *B* sue the thief for conversion? Pollock suggested that he can, and the way in which he arrived at that conclusion was as

---

[1] Per Lord Dunedin in *Sorrell* v. *Smith* (cited above, p. 140 n. 2) at 727–8; *Allen* v. *Flood* (cited above, p. 140, n. 2) at 29, 151.

[2] Pollock, *Gifts of Chattels Without Delivery*, 6 L. Q. REV. 446 (1890).

follows: Anyone who has an immediate right to possession can bring trover, and *B* (in Pollock's view) has an immediate right to possession, because it would be lawful for him to take possession if he could.

Here again we have a covert transformation of terms. Pollock's proposition that an imperfect donee can sue a stranger in trover is not proved by the argument that precedes it. For the right to recover damages in trover is founded on possession or on an immediate right (in the strict sense) to receive possession of the chattel—not upon an immediate liberty to take possesion of the chattel. Conversion, like every other tort, is a legal wrong, a breach of duty towards the plaintiff. It is a violation of the plaintiff's right in the strict sense, not a violation of the plaintiff's liberty; in fact there is no such thing in analytical jurisprudence as a violation or breach of liberty. Pollock's argument is plausible only because of the ambiguity of the word 'right'. In fact the argument, or one very like it, was rejected by the English Court of Appeal in a recent case.[1]

The ambiguous use of the word 'right' caused the plaintiff in *Chaffers* v. *Goldsmid*,[2] to waste his money in fruitless litigation. It is frequently said by writers on the English constitution that there is a right in the subject to petition Parliament for the redress of grievances. What this means is that it is not a contempt of Parliament to do so; that there is a regular parliamentary procedure for receiving petitions; that petitions have absolute privilege in libel;[3] and perhaps that they have privilege in the law of sedition. The plaintiff, however, assumed not unnaturally that there was a right in the strict sense, and he accordingly sued his Member for damages for refusing to present a petition, and for a mandamus. The action failed. This case shows how important it is to have a precise legal terminology. If English law were codified, it would be undesirable to provide that a man has a right not to be assaulted and a right to petition Parliament, for the two rules have quite different effects and need different language for their proper expression.

The curious uncertainty of usage now prevailing is further illustrated by the following passage from a judgment of Evershed, M. R., in the English Court of Appeal, relating to a permission to use land.

[1] *Jarvis* v. *Williams*, [1955] 1 W.L.R. 71 (C.A. 1954).
[2] [1894] 1 Q.B. 186 (1893).
[3] *Lake* v. *King*, 1 Wms. Saund. 131, 85 Eng. Rep. 137 (K.B. 1667).

If the nature of the privilege given is a mere licence unsupported by consideration, it cannot strictly be stated that any 'right' to occupy had been conferred at all. No doubt, until it was revoked, the occupant, the licencee, could not be said to be a trespasser, but he could not claim and enforce in the courts any right to continue in occupation, still less exclusive occupation, of the property. But it might be that there could be a tenancy at will without consideration. In so far as there was a tenancy, that would appear to involve an exclusive right of occupation.[1]

Here the suggestion in the concluding sentence seems at first sight to contradict the earlier reasoning. The first part of the passage implies that a person has not a right to occupy if he cannot enforce in the courts a right to continue in occupation. Now a tenant at will (referred to in the concluding sentence) cannot enforce against his landlord any right to be allowed to continue in occupation; consequently he has not, against his landlord, a 'right of occupation'. However, the tenant at will has a right at common law against strangers not to be disturbed in his enjoyment of the land. On the other hand the gratuitous licensee, referred to in the earlier reasoning, was thought, when this judgment was pronounced, not to have a right against strangers. Hence it may be that the learned Master of the Rolls intended to refer to this distinction of right against strangers, but the judgment is not clear.[2]

VII. LIBERTY NOT AS AFFECTED BY THE CHARACTERISTICS OF DUTY

Since liberty not is a denial of duty, it takes its meaning from the duty that is denied.

(1) Some duties are to refrain from wilful wrongdoing, or negligence; others are strict. Liberties exhibit corresponding distinctions. Damage inflicted by negligent driving is a breach of duty; but damage inflicted by driving without negligence (inevitable accident) is done in pursuance of liberty.

(2) Some duties are imposed by the criminal law, others by the civil law. It might be convenient to speak correspondingly of criminal liberties and civil liberties; but the former expression is unusual, and the latter has the specialized meaning of constitutional liberties (including even constitutional criminal liberties).

---

[1] *Goldsack* v. *Shore*, [1950] 1 K.B. 708, 714 (C.A.).
[2] Possibly even this distinction has disappeared with the new protection given by the courts to the licensee; but the extent of this protection is disputed, and it is not certain that the decisions apply to a gratuitous licensee.

By the Canadian constitution, the provinces have legislative power in respect of 'property and civil rights in the Province'. In *Toronto Electricity Comm'rs* v. *Snider*,[1] the Privy Council held that a Dominion statute interfered with civil rights when it suspended liberty to lock-out or strike during a reference to a board. Now the statute did not make the lock-out or strike a tort or breach of contract but only made it a crime; hence it did not affect non-criminal liberties but only criminal liberties. Nevertheless it affected civil rights within the meaning of the constitution.

(3) Some duties are *in personam*; hence, as said before, it is possible for a 'liberty not' to exist against *A* but not against *B*.

VIII. THE NON-EMOTIVE CHARACTER OF LEGAL LIBERTY

The fact that conduct is a liberty does not necessarily imply any sort of approval of it by the law. *Non omne quod licet honestum est.*[2] It used to be thought that the aim of the criminal law was to suppress moral wrong-doing, but the growth of the deterrent theory of punishment and the realization that there are limits to effective legal action have modified this view. Thus the maxim of the enlightened legislator is: *Non omne quod inhonestum est prohiberi debet.* Yet even at the present day, proposals to restrict the law of abortion, incest, and sodomy on utilitarian grounds are sometimes met with the objection that 'the law cannot countenance that sort of thing'. The notion that the repeal of a prohibitory statute involves approving or condoning the conduct in question is extraordinarily persistent and is a serious obstacle to legislative change.

The strong emotive character of 'privilege' is one reason why it is unsuitable for use as a general synonym for liberty. Thus in one case Channell, J., expressed the opinion that it was inaccurate to speak of the privilege of a judge to be malicious, because such conduct would be wrong of him.[3]

The law may concede a liberty and yet strike at it indirectly, for example, by the law of public policy in contract. Lord Wright said that 'a legal liberty may form the basis of blackmail'[4]—not because the exercise of the liberty is legally or morally wrong, but because it

---

[1] [1925] A.C. 396, 403.   [2] PAUL, D. 50.17.144.
[3] *Bottomley* v. *Brougham*, [1908] 1 K.B. 584, 586.
[4] *Thorne* v. *Motor Trade Ass'n*, [1937] A.C. 797, 822.

is wrong to make certain forbearances a means of extorting money.

Different grades of liberty are also found in other contexts. In the law relating to by-laws (and, probably, other forms of delegated legislation) a distinction is drawn between what may be called a protected liberty and a bare liberty. A protected liberty exists when a statute expressly enacts that it shall be lawful to do so-and-so, or uses words that are construed as having the same effect; a bare liberty exists when the statute book merely refrains from forbidding the conduct in question. In the former case, a by-law forbidding the conduct is invalid for repugnancy; in the latter it is not.[1] A similar distinction prevails in the law of contract. The English rent acts are construed as conferring upon a landlord a protected liberty to charge his statutory tenant the standard rent, and a term in the previous contract that the rent shall be less than the standard rent is repugnant to this liberty, even though it is not repugnant to the liberty (also possessed by the landlord) of charging less than the standard rent if he likes.[2] Yet another variant of the protected liberty may be found in connection with self-defense. Some liberties are accompanied by a duty upon other persons to submit to the exercise of the liberty, while other liberties are not so accompanied. The liberty of a jailer to imprison the convict is a protected liberty in the sense that the convict is under a duty to submit and is not allowed to commit a battery in order to escape. In contrast, suppose that a lunatic, not knowing what he is doing, attacks a man; even if the lunatic is not liable in tort or crime, so that his attack is legally the exercise of a liberty, the person attacked has the usual liberty of self-defense.

---

[1] *Powell* v. *May*, [1946] K.B. 330; cf. *London M&S. Ry.* v. *Greaver*, [1937] 1 K.B. 367 (1936); *Gentel* v. *Sutters*, [1900] Ch. 10 (C.A.); *White* v. *Morley*, [1899] 2 Q.B. 34.

[2] *Dean* v. *Bruce*, [1952] 1 K.B. 11 (C.A. 1951).

Intention and Purpose in Law

ANTHONY KENNY[1]

There is a presumption in law that a man intends the natural consequences of his acts. This presumption has been discussed by English lawyers since 1961 in connection with a famous murder case. (*D.P.P.* v. *Smith* [1961] A.C. 290). The facts were as follows. Smith was driving a car containing stolen property when a policeman told him to draw into the kerb. Instead he accelerated and the constable clung to the side of the car. The car zig-zagged and collided with four oncoming cars; the policeman fell off in front of the fourth and was killed. Smith drove on for 200 yards, dumped the stolen property, and then returned. He was charged with murder and convicted by the jury. He appealed to the Court of Criminal Appeal which quashed the conviction and substituted one for manslaughter. The Crown took a further appeal to the House of Lords, which restored the conviction for murder.

It was never suggested that Smith intended to kill the policeman, but the prosecution contended that he intended to do him grievous bodily harm, as a result of which he died. It was a rule of common law (unaffected by the English Homicide Act of 1957) that a person who intentionally inflicted grievous bodily harm was guilty of murder if death resulted.

In his final direction to the jury, the trial judge, Donovan J., said

---

[1] Anthony Kenny, D.Phil. 1961 Oxon., is Fellow and Tutor in Philosophy at Balliol College, Oxford. The essay here is a revised version of *Intention and Purpose* 63 J. PHILOSOPHY 642 (1966), read in a symposium of the American Philosophical Association in December 1967. The author has written elsewhere on intention. See ACTION, EMOTION AND WILL (1963), and *Practical Inference*, 26 ANALYSIS 65 (1966). For assistance in preparing the earlier version of *Intention and Purpose*, the author is indebted to Messrs. R. Buxton, P. M. Hacker and J. Raz, and, for assistance with the revised version, to Professor H. L. A. Hart. (Footnote by editor.)

146

If you are satisfied that . . . he must as a reasonable man have contemplated that grievous bodily harm was likely to result to that officer . . . and that such harm did happen and the officer died in consequence, then the accused is guilty of capital murder.[1] . . . On the other hand, if you are not satisfied that he intended to inflict grievous bodily harm upon the officer—in other words if you think he could not as a reasonable man have contemplated that grievous bodily harm would result to the officer in consequence of his actions—well, then, the verdict would be guilty of manslaughter.

The Court of Criminal Appeal stated the presumption of intention thus:

As a man is usually able to foresee what are the natural consequences of his acts, so it is, as a rule, reasonable to infer that he did foresee them and intend them. But, while that is an inference which may be drawn, and on the facts in certain circumstances must inevitably be drawn, yet if on all the facts of the particular case it is not the correct inference, then it should not be drawn.

They said that it was for the jury to decide what Smith himself intended, and not what a reasonable man would intend.

The Lord Chancellor, giving judgement in the House of Lords, said:

The jury must . . . in such a case as the present make up their minds on the evidence whether the accused was unlawfully and voluntarily doing something to someone. . . . Once . . . the jury are satisfied as to that, it matters not what the accused in fact contemplated as the probable result or whether he ever contemplated at all, provided he was in law responsible and accountable for his actions. . . .

Criticism of the decision in Smith's case has mainly concerned what lawyers call 'the objective test'—the relevance of the question 'What would the reasonable man have foreseen?' At least three positions seem possible here. (1) To be guilty of murder, the accused need not himself foresee grievous bodily harm: it is enough that a reasonable man would have foreseen. (2) To be guilty of murder, one must foresee grievous bodily harm, but if a reasonable man would have foreseen grievous bodily harm, that proves that the accused himself foresaw it. (3) To be guilty of murder one must foresee grievous bodily harm; but if a reasonable

---

[1] The murder of a policeman acting in the execution of his duty was capital murder—i.e. punishable by death—according to the Homicide Act of 1957.

man would have foreseen grievous bodily harm then it is for the accused to prove that in a particular case he did not. (1) appears to be the plain sense of the Lord Chancellor's words. (2) appears to be the sense given to those words by Lord Denning, one of the judges in the House of Lords, in his lecture *Responsibility before the Law*. (3) appears to be regarded by most critics of the decision as the correct principle to apply. Certainly, most arguments in favour of the decision support only (3) and not (2) or (1): for instance, Lord Denning's argument that if we apply the subjective test, the accused will always be able to get off by lying. But (3) itself seems very ambiguous. Does a reasonable man ever get into a panic? If not, then what a reasonable man would have foreseen gives us little guidance as to what Smith, in a panic, foresaw. If so, then it seems that in order to arrive at a verdict in cases such as Smith's, the jury must know when it is, and when it is not, reasonable to get into a panic.

What I wish, however, to discuss is not the disputed principle 'If the reasonable man would have foreseen it, then Smith foresaw it', but rather a different principle: 'If Smith foresaw it, then Smith intended it'. This seems to have been accepted at all stages. The trial judge, indeed, treated 'you are not satisfied that he intended' as synonymous with 'you think he could not have contemplated', which seems to involve not only the equation of intention with foresight but also a confusion of 'he need not have foreseen' with 'he could not have foreseen'. Of course, the word 'contemplate' is not free from ambiguity; but even the Court of Criminal Appeal thought that where it was reasonable to infer that a man foresaw the consequences of his acts, then it was reasonable to infer that he intended them.

To somebody who is not a lawyer, it might seem that there was a further question relevant to Smith's intention: not only what he foresaw, but what he wanted. This, however, was ruled out. At the trial it was alleged that Smith said 'I only wanted to shake him off'. The trial judge said 'It may well be the truth—he did only want to shake him off; but if the reasonable man would realise that the effect of doing this might well be to cause serious harm to this officer, then, as I say, you would be entitled to impute such an intent to the accused.'

Leaving aside its application to Smith's case, the principle that a man intends all the consequences of his actions which he foresees appears to the layman far too sweeping. When the Protestant martyr Latimer refused to recant his beliefs he foresaw that he would be burnt as a heretic. Yet it would be absurd to say that he refused to recant in order to be burnt or with the intention of being burnt. In this case the consequences of his action were the result partly of other men's actions; but there is no need for human agency to intervene to prevent the foreseen consequences of an action from being intended. Feeling miserable, I may deliberately get drunk. In doing so, I foresee that I will have a hangover; but I do not get drunk in order to have a hangover, or with the intention of bringing on a hangover.

Should we say, then, that a man intends only those consequences of his action which he both foresees *and* wants? Consider a case invented by Glanville Williams.[1] Suppose that *D*, an eccentric and amoral surgeon, wishes to remove *P*'s heart completely from *P*'s body in order to experiment upon it. *D* does not desire *P*'s death (being perfectly content that *P* shall go on living if he can do so without his heart), but recognizes that in fact his death is inevitable from the operation to be performed. Williams says that such a case would clearly be murder, and murder because of an intent to kill. This certainly seems plausible. But Williams goes on to conclude from this that foresight *with certainty* is enough for intention, but not foresight which allows of doubt. But this needs serious qualification, as Williams himself makes clear. First, a degree of foresight of death much less than certainty may be all the foresight necessary for a murderous intent; secondly, a degree of certainty which would make a wanted result intentional would be insufficient to make an unwanted result intentional. I am guilty of murder if I push an enemy off a lifeboat to his death in a shark-infested sea; I do not commit suicide if I yield up my own place in the same lifeboat to another more deserving survivor.

To clarify these matters, we need to consider the whole concept of intentional action. Intentional actions appear to be a subclass of voluntary conscious actions. Not all actions of human beings are conscious: snoring, for instance, is commonly not conscious. Not all conscious human actions are voluntary: reflex actions such as blinking under stimulation are conscious but involuntary. Voluntary conscious actions, it seems, are conscious actions over which we have control. There are, of course, degrees of control;

[1] WILLIAMS, CRIMINAL LAW 35 (1953).

and so we might say that there are degrees of voluntariness. Breathing, for instance, is not completely voluntary, but admits of some degree of control. I can't choose whether to breathe or not, *simpliciter*; but I can hold my breath, and breathe in when the doctor tells me to. The nature of control, and therefore of voluntariness, is obscure. I leave this difficult topic unexamined. But henceforth, in discussing human actions, I shall have in mind voluntary actions. Some conscious voluntary actions are unintentional. They are those actions which one does not do on purpose, and which can be inhibited with an effort. Examples would be wincing in pain, fidgeting, sneezing, laughing, using an irritable tone of voice, mentally brooding over an injury. Intentional actions are distinguished from other conscious voluntary actions in virtue of the agent's state of mind with regard to the results and consequences of his actions.

I have in the past distinguished between *performances*, the bringing about of states of affairs in the world (e.g. killing a man, baking a cake, opening a door), and *activities* which go on for an indefinite time and have no particular terminus (e.g. running, laughing).[1] Substantially the same distinction has been made by von Wright as a distinction between *act* which is the effecting of a change, and *activity* which keeps a process going.[2] I adopt his terminology, and following him I shall make a distinction between the result and the consequence of an act. The result of an act is the end state of the change by which the act is defined. When the world changes in a certain way there may follow certain other changes, perhaps by natural necessity. In that case we may say that the second transformation is a consequence of the first and of the act which brought the first about. The relation between an act and its result is an intrinsic relation, and that between an act and its consequence is a causal relation. The consequence of one act may be the result of another and the activity involved in the two may be identical. For instance, the consequence of the act of opening the window may be that the room becomes cooler; but the room's becoming cooler is the result and not the consequence of the act of cooling the room; but it may be by one and the same activity— e.g. movements of my hand—that I both open the window and cool the room. Von Wright says: 'One and the same change or

---

[1] ACTION, EMOTION AND WILL 171–86 (1963).
[2] THE VARIETIES OF GOODNESS 115–17 (1963); NORM AND ACTION 39–42 (1963).

state of affairs can be both the result and a consequence of an action. What makes it the one or the other depends upon the agent's intention in acting, and upon other circumstances which we shall not discuss.' This could be misleading in two ways. In the first place, one and the same state of affairs cannot be the result and a consequence of one and the same act: it either is or is not the state of affairs by which the act is defined. Nor can one and the same state of affairs be both the result and the consequence of an activity: for an activity has no result in the sense defined by von Wright. In the second place, the distinction which von Wright draws between result and consequence applies to inanimate as well as to animate agents, and therefore can be made without any appeal to intention.

Let X be the movement of a body which brings about the state of affairs that p. Let p and q describe states of affairs in some close relation to each other such that q is the case because p is the case. Let A be the act of bringing it about that p, and B the act of bringing it about that q. An agent who brings it about that p in such a case will also bring it about that q. In doing A he will also do B. In order to apply von Wright's distinction between result and consequence we must restrict the pattern to cases where the connection between p's being the case and q's being the case is causal and not logical. Then we can say: that p is the result of A, and that q is a consequence of A, and that q the result of B. If there was a logical connection between the results then there would be a logical connection between act A and its consequence, which goes counter to von Wright's definitions. But in order to apply von Wright's distinctions to legal matters (e.g. provocation) it would be useful to extend his notion of consequence so that one state of affairs may be the consequence of another though it does not follow from it by natural necessity, but through the intervention of another human agent.

The pattern we have sketched is fundamental to the description of intentional action. But it applies also to non-human and human non-intentional action: for instance, a falling tile, by piercing the skull of a passer-by, may cause his death. Doing B by doing A is not necessarily intentionally doing either A or B.

The new factors which enter in with human action are the knowledge[1] and desires of the agent. For instance, if the agent

---

[1] I am using 'knowledge' to include cognitive states of mind which fall short

wants q (wants to do B), and does A in order to do B, then he knows that he is doing A and he knows that he is doing B by doing A and he wants to do B. He may or may not want to do A for its own sake, or as a means to some other end. If we consider these four factors—namely whether the agent knows that he is doing A, whether he wants to do A for any other reason aside from wanting to do B, whether he knows he is doing B and whether he wants to do B—there are, arithmetically speaking, sixteen possible combinations.

Of the sixteen arithmetical possibilities, four fortunately can be ruled out in advance since one cannot know that one is doing B by doing A unless one knows that one is doing A. There remain twelve cases:

1. An agent knows he is doing A, wants to do A, knows that he is doing B by doing A, and wants to do B. This is the case when somebody does A in order to do B but likes doing A in any case: for instance, philosophising to earn one's living.

2. The agent knows that he is doing A, knows that he is doing B by doing A, and wants to do B, but does not want to do A for any other reason than in order to do B. This is the commonest case of doing A in order to do B: for instance, using a knife to cut bread, paying a premium to insure against sickness.

3. The agent knows he is doing A and wants to do A and knows he is doing B by doing A but does not want to do B. This would be the case of a man getting out of bed knowing that he is waking the baby by doing so but not wanting to wake the baby.

4. The agent knows that he is doing A and knows that he is doing B by doing A, but neither wants to do A nor to do B. For instance, a husband may know that by being bad tempered he is driving his wife to leave him while regretting his temper and wanting the wife to stay.

5. The agent knows that he is doing A and wants to do A and wants to do B, but though by doing A he is doing B he does not know this. This would be the case of a man who by shooting at a stag kills, unknown to himself, the enemy whom he has long desired to kill.

6. The agent knows that he is doing A and wants to do B but

---

of strict knowledge. In what follows 'knows' should be used as 'knows or thinks it likely that'.

though in fact he is doing *B* by doing *A* he does not know this and does not want to do *A*. There were once some brewers, we are told, who brewed excellent beer in dirty vats. When they cleaned their vats the quality of the beer declined, until somebody surreptitiously introduced a dead rat into the vats, whereupon it improved. Initially they knew they were using dirty vats, they did not want to use dirty vats, they wanted to brew good beer and unknown to themselves they were brewing good beer by using dirty vats.

7. The agent does not know that he is doing *A* but wants to do *A*, he wants to do *B* but does not know that it is by doing *A* that he is doing *B*. For instance, an executive wishes to improve his chances of promotion by flattering the chairman of the board at a party. Unknown to himself the person he is now impressing is the chairman, to whom he has not been introduced.

8. The agent neither knows nor wants himself to be doing *A*, wants to do *B* but does not know that it is by doing *A* that he is doing *B*. A comedian wishes to amuse his audience. He does so, but only because, unknown to himself, he is wearing his shirt-tail outside his trousers.

9. The agent knows and wants himself to be doing *A*, but neither knows nor wants himself to be doing *B* by doing *A*. Hamlet knowingly and wantonly stabbed through the arras, but neither knew nor wanted himself to be killing Polonius thereby.

10. The agent knows he is doing *A* but does not want to do it. He neither knows nor wants himself to be doing *B* by doing *A*. A man may sneeze in a crowded tube train against his own wishes, and not knowing nor wanting himself to be giving others a cold by passing on germs to them.

11. The agent wants to do *A* but does not know that he is doing it; unknown to himself by doing *A* he is doing *B*, which he does not want to do. Let us suppose that the executive mentioned in No. 7, is, unknown to himself, talking to the chairman of the board whom he wants to talk to, but by doing this is boring and infuriating the chairman.

12. The agent neither knows nor wants to do *A*, nor does he want to do *B*, which unknown to himself he is doing by doing *A*. For instance, a surgeon in a field hospital killing a patient by using, unknown to himself, an unsterilized scalpel.

Intuitively, I think, the plain man would say that the agent does *A* intentionally only in cases 1, 2, 3, 5 and 9; and that he does *A*

L

in order to do *B* only in cases 1 and 2. In which cases does he do *B* intentionally or intend to do *B*? Again, I think, the plain man would say: only in cases 1 and 2. Bentham, who considered our cases 1, 2, 3 and 9, said that in a case such as 3 the performance of *B* was *obliquely intentional*,[1] and many lawyers agree with him in classifying such cases as intentional. This, it seems to me, is regrettable, for reasons I will give later.[2]

On the account which I have attributed to the plain man, an agent intends an action if he (a) knows he is doing it and (b) wants to do it either for its own sake or in order to further some other end.

When an agent wants it to be the case that *q* and not in order to make anything else the case, we may say that *q* is his ultimate end. If he brings it about that *q* by bringing it about that *p*, then we may say that *p* is a means to that end; if *A* is the act of bringing it about that *p*, then it is also natural to call *A* a means of bringing it about that *p*; and we can also call it a method of *B*-ing. That *p*, which is the result of *A*, we may say is a step towards the end (that *q*); and that *q*, which was the result of *B*, we may say is a consequence of *A*. An action may be both a means to an end, and an end in itself. This was so in case 1 above.[3]

Using this terminology, we can summarize the plain man's view thus. A man intends the ends he sets himself and the means he adopts to those ends. This doctrine can be expanded by the following theses.

(i) One intends the result of any act one does intentionally.

(ii) One foresees the result of any act one does knowingly.

(iii) One may do an act knowingly without intending its result, if one does it without wanting to.

(iv) If one does act intentionally, and its result is the consequence of the result of another act, then in doing that other act, one intends its consequence.

---

[1] PRINCIPLES OF MORALS AND LEGISLATION Ch. VIII.

[2] The plain man's intuitions do not rest only on the factors of knowledge and desire present: they are based partly also on some notion of the proximity of a consequence to the relevant act. By restricting consideration to cases where the consequence of one act is the result of another which the agent admittedly performs, I have tried to minimize this factor in the present discussion.

[3] An action may be an end in itself without its result being an end: if I jump over a fence for fun, being on the other side of the fence, though the result of the act of jumping over, is not an end in itself. An end which is not a means to any other end is an ultimate end; otherwise it is an intermediate end. Cf. TAYLOR, THE EXPLANATION OF BEHAVIOUR 28.

(v) If one does an act with a certain result in order to bring about a consequence of that result, then one also does the act of which the consequence in question is the result.

(vi) One may do an act whose result is the consequence of the result of another act, without doing that other act in order to perform the act first mentioned.

These theses leave open the following question: does one intend the foreseen consequences of one's ultimate end? Let us first suppose that these consequences are themselves wanted. It might be thought that this case could not arise: if the consequences are wanted must they not themselves be a further end beyond the ultimate end, which is absurd? This is not so unless the consequences are wanted enough to be brought about in any case independently of the end of which they are consequences. The case in point is where the agent reasons: 'I want q so I will bring it about that p; but if q then r will be the case also; but r is welcome so I will bring it about that p all the more willingly.' Even in such a case it would seem to me wrong to say that the consequences were intended, since they do not form part of the chain of practical reasoning which leads to the initial decision to bring it about that p. If this is so, then *a fortiori* consequences which are foreseen but which the agent is indifferent to or regrets are not intended. Of course, it may well be correct to hold the agent responsible for these consequences, but that only means that we can be held responsible for more than we intend.

Besides consequences we sometimes have to consider concomitant effects or side effects of people's actions. Let me explain the distinction. If A is bringing it about that p and B is bringing it about that q, and if q then r, then r is a consequence of both A and B. But in a case where we do not have if q then r, but if p then r, then r while a consequence of p is an effect which accompanies q and which we might call a concomitant of q. For instance, if I open the window to look out of it, and by opening the window cool the room, then the cooling of the room is a consequence of the opening of the window but a concomitant and not a consequence of my looking out of the window. We may explain the notion of a side effect as follows. If r is a concomitant of q and q is a means to s, then r will be a side effect of the action which is bringing about that s. For instance, noise is a side effect of fast travel in a motor car because it is a concomitant of the operation of the engine which is a means to the speed of travel. Concomitants, or side effects, of an end or an action may themselves be both foreseen and desired and adopted as ends: as in cases of killing two birds with one stone. Unless this is the case, however, it seems to me that they are no more intentional than consequences, with one exception to be made in the case of side effects. The exception depends on the distinction between necessary and chosen means. If there is only one means of achieving the agent's purpose then these are necessary means, but if the agent believes that there is more than one way of achieving his purpose then the means he adopts are chosen means. If he chooses a means which has a certain side effect knowing and wanting this side effect, then it seems that he intends this side effect, if that is his reason for choosing this means rather than another, even though he would never have performed the action at all were it not a means to his original purpose.

The account so far given does not do full justice to the layman's concept of intention. For instance, most plain men, as well as lawyers, would agree that the eccentric surgeon described by Glanville Williams intended the death of the patient whose heart he removed. This seems to be not simply because of the certainty of the death, but because of its immediacy. Yet on the account given the death would not be intentional. So we must make an exception to the present account for cases where—in the words of H. L. A. Hart—'a foreseen outcome is so immediately and invariably connected with the action done that the suggestion that the action might not have that outcome would by ordinary standards be regarded as absurd or such as only a mentally abnormal person would seriously entertain.[1] Because 'immediately' is a vague term, the layman's concept of intention does not have sharp edges. But the concept, it seems to me, is a coherent one, and most cases are clearly on one side or the other of the blurred line it draws.

This, however, does not mean that the concept has or should have any moral or legal significance. Why should the law, we may ask, interest itself in intention at all? The purpose of a law against φing is surely to prevent the state of affairs which is the result of φing. Why not then just forbid φing, without inquiring with what intention the φing was done, or indeed whether it was done intentionally at all?

There are reasons which may be brought out as follows. Let

[1] *Intention and Punishment* 4 OXFORD REVIEW 5 (1967).

us suppose that the law wishes to prohibit a certain action, and let us suppose this *actus reus* is described in a way which does not contain any reference to the state of mind of the agent: e.g. 'using a motor vehicle uninsured', 'doing an act likely to assist the enemy'. The law may wish this to be punishable (1) no matter whether the agent did know or could have known that he was committing the *actus reus*, (2) no matter whether he did know or suspect that he was doing so, but only if he could have known, (3) only if he knew or suspected that he was doing so, but no matter whether he wanted to commit it or not, (4) only if he did know and did want to commit it for some reason or other, (5) only if he did know, and only if he wanted to commit it for some specified reason, (6) only if he wanted to commit it for some specified reason and for no other further reason.

In the first case, the law will be one of strict liability and in order to secure a conviction, the prosecution will merely have to show that the action was performed by the accused. In the second case, they will have to show in addition that the accused could have known he was performing the action: if the knowledge could have been acquired by reasonable exercise of care, he will be said to have been acting negligently. In the third case they will have to show that he did at least suspect that he was performing the action, and if the suspicion was solid and the act unjustified, this will be a case of recklessness. In the fourth case, they will have to show that he not only knew, but also wanted, himself to be performing the action: i.e. that he was acting intentionally in the sense I have been explicating. In the fifth case they must prove not only that he was acting intentionally, but that he was acting with a specific intention (e.g. 'with intent to kill' or 'with intent to assist the Queen's enemies'). In the sixth case, they must prove that the end described in the specific intent was not a means to some further end (e.g. 'in order to bring peace to the world').

When we ask whether law should interest itself in intention (in the layman's sense) we are asking whether it should distinguish between the third case and the fourth. When we ask why it should interest itself in specific intents, we are asking why it should distinguish between the fourth case and the fifth. When we ask whether the law should distinguish between the fifth case and the sixth, we would commonly be said to be asking whether the law should interest itself in motives.

Now why distinguish (4) from (3)? Let us suppose that the *actus reus* is B and that it is prohibited in order to prevent its result that q. Now any case of this act's being performed recklessly must be a case where an agent performs another act A, foreseeing but not desiring that q as a consequence of A. For, if it were foreseen and desired that q, then the performance of B would be intentional and not reckless; whereas, if it were neither foreseen nor desired that q, then the performance of B would not be reckless but at worst negligent. So, in distinguishing between the intentional and the reckless performance of B, the law would in effect be distinguishing between the performance of some other act with foresight of q, and the performance of that act *in order to* bring about q.

In general, in English and American law, no such distinction is made, at least in cases where the foresight approaches certainty. In cases of homicide, in particular, despite varying statutory definitions of murder, the principle has been generally accepted which was enunciated by Lord Coleridge in the Clerkenwell Prison case of 1868 (*Desmond*): 'It is murder if a man did an act not with the purpose of taking life but with the knowledge or belief that life was likely to be sacrificed.'[1]

It might be argued however that the law *should* distinguish between doing A foreseeing that q, and doing A in order to bring about q. The argument might go as follows. The purpose of the law is to prevent q, and q is much more likely to occur if A is done in order to bring about q than if A is simply done while q is foreseen as more or less probable. Because, for instance, the latter activity, unlike the former, is compatible with taking precautions against the occurrence of q. Moreover, if A is performed and q does not in fact occur, then in the first case A is likely to be repeated until q does occur; not so in the second. If a bullet whistles past me and hits a cat on the wall behind, it is important for me to know whether the gunman was aiming at me and missed, or whether he was aiming at the cat reckless of the danger to me. If the former, I must take cover; if the latter, I may breathe a sigh of relief. In general, incompetent though we humans may be in giving effect to our desires, a state of affairs is more likely to come about, other things being equal, if we set out to bring it about than if we merely passively foresee it as a likely consequence of our other projects.

[1] Cox 146 THE TIMES April 28, 1868.

And so, if we are to punish no more than is necessary, there is good reason to distinguish case (4) from case (3) and in some cases to attach greater deterrent penalties to an act performed intentionally than to the same act performed recklessly.

I used to think these considerations decisive; but I now see that they are not. In the first place, this argument would not justify distinguishing between intention and foresight in a case in which a result is foreseen as certain. For if it is certain that q will follow the performance of A, then it is no more likely to follow from doing A with the intention of doing B than from doing A without any such intention. In the second place, as Professor Hart has pointed out to me, the law as it stands already provides an incentive to the man who foresees another's death as the likely outcome of an independent project to take precautions against the death's actually taking place. For if the precautions are successful then even if apprehended he can avoid the severer penalties for murder and risks only the penalty attached to the successful execution of his project. And if the law did distinguish between intention and foresight the incentive to take precautions would actually be lessened, since the agent would know that even if no successful precautions were taken, he still would not suffer the supreme penalty.

None the less there can be cases where it would be in the interests of society that there should be a greater deterrent penalty attached to intentional than to reckless homicide. Let us suppose that it is of great importance to Peter that Paul should not be in town on a particular day: perhaps Paul is a witness in a case against Peter, or is coming to claim an inheritance that will otherwise pass to Peter. On the one hand, Peter can kill Paul, giving a 100 per cent certainty that he will be absent on the crucial day. On the other hand, he can incarcerate Paul in a solitary spot, reducing the certainty of his absence, but also taking a serious risk that he may die before he is rescued. Let us suppose further that the chances of the crime being traced to Peter are equal in each case.

In such a situation, Peter has a greater motive for choosing the less violent course if the law distinguishes between intention and foresight than if it does not. Whether or not the distinction is made, of course, he takes a greater risk of suffering the supreme penalty by choosing the first method than by choosing the second, since the first involves a greater chance of Paul's death. But this increase of risk may be justified in his eyes by the increased chance which the first method provides of achieving his initial purpose. If this is so, and the penalties for intentional and reckless homicide are equal, the law offers him no further motive for choosing the second course. But if intentional homicide is punished more severely, he has such a further motive: for the penalties that he risks in the event that Paul dies and the crime is brought home, are less in the second case than in the first. Thus he has a sound reason for choosing the less anti-social course of action.

It may well be objected that such a case presupposes a greater interest in games-theory than can be demanded in the potential criminal; and that in any case the situations of this kind will be rarer than those which make it undesirable for the law to draw any distinction. This may be so. There are, however, other reasons which are sometimes brought forward in favour of the distinction, and these we should now consider.

One reason is that it is desirable, particularly if criminal law is to be administered by juries, that the word 'intention' should mean the same to lawyers as it does in ordinary language, and not be stretched to include foresight. Another is that there often appears to be a clear moral distinction between intention and foresight which it may be desirable that the law should reflect. For instance there seems to be a moral difference between appointing the best man to a job *knowing that* this will pain the rival candidate, and appointing him *in order to* pain the rival candidate. This type of difference, it seems, may occur also in matters of life and death. Consider the case of two nurses, each of whom is in possession of a poison and a pain-killing drug which are indistinguishable to the eye and have in some way been mixed up in the medicine cabinet so that she does not know which is which. Nurse *A* gives a pill to her patient, whose money she stands to inherit, hoping but not knowing that it is the poison. Nurse *B* gives a pill to her patient, who is in great agony, hoping but not knowing that it is the pain-killing drug. Neither nurse is blameless; but most people, I imagine, would feel that there was an important moral difference between the actions of the two, even if the patient dies.

As the law stands a moral distinction between the cases would probably be reflected in the difference between a verdict of murder and a verdict of manslaughter, since *A*'s desire for her patient's death would certainly constitute sufficient malice aforethought for murder; whereas it is doubtful whether the fifty-fifty risk taken by B would do so. However, if the risk was much more than fifty-fifty, both cases would probably count as murder, though we might well feel that there was still a moral difference between them.

We may ask, with regard to specific intents, the question we asked earlier concerning intent in general. Why ever have any laws of the form 'Never do A with the intent to B'? Why is it not sufficient either to prohibit A or to prohibit B?

It seems safe to presume that when the law forbids the doing of A with the intention to B, its aim is to prevent the taking place of q which is the result of B. If q is something which is held very important to prevent, such as death or the defeat of the state, then the law may consider it an insufficient precaution merely to forbid B. If someone wants to do B very much, and success in B will outweigh for him whatever penalty the law attaches to B, and failure to do B will bring no penalty, he may well consider an attempt to do B as a worthwhile gamble. Punishing attempts to do B is one way of making the gamble less worth while. On the other hand it may be too much to forbid the performance of A: for instance to forbid wounding under the same penalties as killing would be unfair, for this would punish also those who wound for socially desirable purposes, such as surgeons. So one might want to have instead a law against wounding with intent to kill. It would be possible for the law to forbid, as in some cases it does, simply the attempt to do A without specifying the acts in which the attempt must consist. But once again, punishing all acts done with a certain intention may involve punishing where there is no need. Sticking pins in a wax effigy of the commander-in-chief might be an act done 'with intent to assist the enemy'; but it would hardly be punishable under a statute which prohibited only 'acts likely to assist the enemy done with intent to assist the enemy'.

There remains to be considered the distinction between cases (5) and (6) above. So far as I know, no law has ever interested itself in the question whether a particular intention of an accused was his ultimate intention or not. However, 'purpose' is sometimes used to mean 'ultimate intention', and section 1 of the English Official Secrets Act, 1911, made it a felony 'if any person for any purpose prejudicial to the safety or interests of the state approaches any prohibited place'. In *Chandler* v. *D.P.P.* (1962 3 w.l.r. 694) the appellants, who were campaigners for nuclear disarmament, had been convicted of an offence under this section because they had tried to enter a prohibited airfield in order to prevent bomber aircraft from taking off. They claimed that their purpose in doing this was to lessen the likelihood of nuclear warfare, and that this, so far from being prejudicial to the state, was in its best interests. The appeal was dismissed by the House of Lords. The reasons given were not all consistent; but it was clear that if 'purpose' was taken to mean the same as 'ultimate aim', the statute would become completely vacuous. As Lords Reid and Devlin pointed out 'a spy could secure an acquittal by satisfying the jury that his purpose was to make money for himself, a purpose not in itself prejudicial to the state'.

It is time to return to the case from which we started. As a consequence of widespread dissatisfaction with the verdict in *D.P.P.* v. *Smith* the Law Commission was instructed in 1965 to examine the implications of the decision. It reported in 1967 in a paper entitled 'Imputed Criminal Intent' which recommended that a subjective and not an objective test should be applied in ascertaining the intent required in murder. The commission drafted the following clause: 'A court or jury, in determining whether a person has committed an offence (a) shall not be bound in law to infer that he intended or foresaw a result of his actions by reason only of its being a natural and probable consequence of those actions; but (b) shall decide whether he did intend or foresee that result by reference to all the evidence, drawing such inferences from the evidence as appear proper in the circumstances.' Moreover, they recommended that an intent to inflict grievous bodily harm should no longer be retained as an alternative to an intent to kill in the crime of murder; and they suggested a second draft clause which began 'Where a person kills another the killing shall not amount to murder unless done with an intent to kill. A person has an "intent to kill" if he means his actions to kill, or if he is willing for his actions, though meant for another purpose, to kill in accomplishing that purpose.' Many people found the expression 'willing for his actions to kill' to be obscure. It seems that if a man foresees death as the result of his actions, but does not therefore desist from his actions, he is willing for them to kill; and thus the intent to kill would be the same as foresight of death, a conclusion which the commissioners expressly wished to avoid.

The Criminal Justice Act of 1967 made the Commission's first draft clause into law. Significantly, it made no mention of the second clause. The definition of 'intent' must have been found unsatisfactory. The search for a definition suitable for legal use will have to continue.

PART TWO

Rational Justification

On Processes for Resolving Disputes

J. R. LUCAS[1]

I. HUMAN NATURE

Human beings, as we know them, are often selfish, but sometimes unselfish; their judgement is fallible, but sometimes in the course of argument different people come to hold the same view, which is, as far as we can see, reasonable and right; they are infinite in their complexity and aspirations, but finite in their capacities and achievements; they occupy the same public external world, but are each the centre of a private perspective, not necessarily shareable with others; they have values, which are neither necessarily the same for all, nor actually different for each; they can help one another, and need to, but can hurt one another, and often do.

These propositions about human nature are not self-evident, though I believe them to be true. They have been, and still are, often denied, at least implicitly, but I shall not in this book attempt to show that they are true. I shall assume their truth and show what then will follow if human beings are living together in communities, and what different things would follow if human nature were different. Many of the varying political ideals that have been put forward from time to time have drawn their strength from some other idea of human nature, perhaps partial, perhaps wrong, but such as to warrant the different form of society that is being argued for.

We can see how political institutions depend upon the nature of the men constituting political communities by considering one by

[1] J. R. Lucas, B.A. 1948, B.A. 1951, Oxon., is Fellow and Tutor in Philosophy, Merton College, Oxford. His work reprinted here consists of the first sixteen pages of THE PRINCIPLES OF POLITICS (O.U.P. 1966). Other writings of relevance to legal philosophy include: *The Lesbian Rule* 30 PHILOSOPHY 195 (1955); *On Not Worshipping Facts* 8 PHILOSOPHICAL Q. 144 (1958); *The Philosophy of the Reasonable Man* 13 PHILOSOPHICAL Q. 97 (1963); *Against Equality* 40 PHILOSOPHY 296 (1965). (Footnote by editor.)

one the propositions I have put forward about human nature, and how things would differ if each in turn were false, while the others remained true. There would be no conflict, no law, no State, if men did not live in the same public external world in which they could interact with one another: nor if they had no values in common, and could neither hurt one another nor be in need of another's help. No coercive machinery would be needed, either, if no men were ever 'bloody-minded'—that is, if men, though having different desires and interests and different ideas of what was right, were all prepared to abide by decisions duly made by the proper authorities in the proper way. Again, if men's judgement were not fallible, and we all knew what in general ought to be done even though we were often not willing to do it, we should not need the present apparatus of legislatures and law courts to establish laws and determine their application. Or again, if human affairs were not so complicated, or if we were all omniscient, it would be feasible, as Locke believed, to draw up a precise constitutional determination of areas of potential conflict where governmental adjudication was needed, and areas which should be guaranteed free from governmental interference.

These primitive polities, ἀναγκαιόταται πολιτεῖαι, reveal the rationale of different facets of our own more complicated political institutions. We shall think them out further in the next section as foils to illustrate, by contrast, the social organisation required by human beings as they actually are, capable of interacting in the same world, having some values the same; sometimes selfish, fallible in their judgements, and imperfectly informed.

These five characteristics of human nature fall into two groups. First the two general conditions, which are necessary if there is to be any possibility of communal co-existence at all:

A(i)   Some Interaction.

A(ii) Some Shared Values.

Second, three conditions of *imperfection*, or, to use a more neutral word, limitation:

B(i)   Incomplete Unselfishness.

B(ii) Fallible Judgement.

B(iii) Imperfect Information.[1]

---

[1] cf. the characterisation of human nature given by H. L. A. HART in THE CON-CEPT OF LAW 189–95 (1961), which can be summarised again under five heads, namely:

The first two conditions are prerequisites of there being any community at all. If we were disembodied spirits not inhabiting any common world and incapable of impinging on one another—incapable even of communicating with one another—, then we could not co-exist in any common life. Equally, if we co-existed, but had no values in common, then, although we might impinge, we could not communicate or co-operate at all. But although it is necessary that we should be able sometimes to interact and have some values in common, it is not necessary that we should always be interacting, and have all values the same. Indeed, it is barely possible that we should, if we are to remain separate individuals. Each man, if he is to be different from other men, must have some sphere of consciousness and thought, of experience and aspiration, that is his own, and is not shared with everybody else: and each man, if he is to be a man, and conscious of himself as an agent, and not merely a puppet, must have some angle on life that is peculiarly his, some realm of choices that is under his own control, and therefore likely to be different from those that others might have chosen. I would not be a man at all, if, besides my publicly observable behaviour, I could not think to myself, feel feelings, contemplate ideas, and make plans for my future actions before carrying them out. To have a mind of my own is to be able to wish, privately, as well as to act, publicly. Nor could I call even my soul my own unless I could choose for myself, and not be bound always to endorse some common set of values. Although it is a good and joyful thing to dwell together in unity, we cannot—logically cannot, if we are to be *we*, in the first person plural—be entirely of one mind or share all our experiences or live all our lives together. We are individuals, different, unique. And therefore we can have no absolute community with other people, but must always remain to some extent strangers and aliens, as all the others are.

    (i)   Human Vulnerability.
   (ii)   Approximate Equality.
  (iii) Limited Altruism.
  (iv) Limited Resources.
   (v) Limited Understanding.

Hart's condition (iii) corresponds to B(i) above; his condition (v) to B(ii) and B(iii) together. His condition (i) states the most important part of what is covered by A(i) and A(ii) together. His condition (iv) is important for a lawyer or an economist developing the concept of property, but does not hold in his sense of all communities—for example, intellectual or religious ones. His condition (ii) is better expressed by saying that human powers are *comparable*.

M

Human beings are able to interact and do have some shared values. It is a contingent but highly important fact that all, or nearly all, men can feel physical pain, and that physical pain can be caused to one man by another, and will be felt by that one man alone, and not by the other who is causing it, nor by anybody else. Pain is not only regarded as bad: it is an irruption into one's private personal experience which demands one's attention, and in extreme cases absorbs it so much that one cannot attend to or think about anything else. It is also a contingent and highly important fact about men that one man can kill another, and that death is generally regarded as something bad and to be avoided. Also that men need food, drink, and many other material goods, which other men may hinder them from obtaining, but which they can no less help them to secure. Also that human beings at some stages in their life need, and often enjoy, the companionship of other human beings.

These contingent facts about human beings mean that there are a number of shared values, of evils to be avoided and goods to be pursued, common to all, or almost all, mankind; and therefore that there can be a set of pains and penalties and of rewards and inducements that will be effective in conforming human behaviour to required patterns. But although these contingent conditions are highly important in shaping human life as it actually is, it is possible to erect a system of coercion and enforcement on a much more slender and less contingent basis than these. Whenever we have autonomous agents interacting with one another or acting in a common world, each with some set of values, not all of them concerned exclusively with his private experience, then each agent will be liable to be caused distress through the actions of another agent. To have a set of values—that is, to care for something—is, for any being not totally omnipotent, to be *vulnerable*. And therefore anyone who ever wants to *do* anything in a public external world, as well as anyone who ever wants the co-operation of anybody else, or who even values the good opinion of anybody else, is vulnerable. Even tortoises[1] are vulnerable in this way, and could be subject to a form of coercion. Although a recalcitrant tortoise could not be killed or made to suffer pain by other tortoises, it could be prevented from doing anything. Anything it did, a group of other tortoises could undo: or they might stand in a circle round it, and

---

[1] cf. HART, THE CONCEPT OF LAW 190 (1961).

in effect imprison it. This is not a contingent fact about tortoise life, but a necessary consequence of there being a common, public, external world in which individuals can do things. If one individual can do something, another may be able either to prevent him doing it or to undo it: and unless one is incomparably stronger than all the others, a sufficient number of them will be able to prevent or frustrate all his actions: for an action that cannot be prevented or frustrated by no matter how many other individuals is *eo ipso* not an action in a public world at all, but must, by definition, be confined to some private sphere of activity. Nobody can stop a tortoise from speculating: but if that is all that a tortoise wants to do, so that he will not regard it as an evil to be prevented from doing anything else except speculate, then he will not want to do anything to which any other tortoise might object, so that there will be no need of any penalty or punishment to prevent or deter him from doing anything that other tortoises might not want him to do.

Imprisonment is the paradigm punishment. A man who is imprisoned is thereby debarred from doing anything, whatever it is, that he may want to do in the public, external world. So that if there is anything that he wants to do in the public, external world, imprisonment will be regarded by him as an evil and something to be avoided, and if there is nothing in the public external world that he wants to do, if he has achieved an attitude of utter ἀταραξία, complete indifference, towards external things, then he is harmless, and it does not matter that he cannot be influenced or deterred. For all other men, the loss of liberty is an evil on a different logical level from the infliction of pain: it is an evil we are vulnerable to simply because we are rational agents. It is for this reason we are peculiarly sensitive on the score of the liberty of the subject, and it is for this reason that while we have been able to dispense with the rack and the thumbscrew, and perhaps the gallows, gaols will continue to be necessary, and adequate, as means of coercion, so long as there are men recalcitrant enough to need to be coerced.

II. OTHER NATURES AND IDEAL COMMUNITIES

If human nature were different, human society would be different also. The first two conditions—A(i), that human beings inhabit the same public, external world, in which they can interact with one another, and A(ii), that they have values which are neither necessarily the same for all, nor actually different for each—cannot be other than they are if communal life is to be possible at all. The three principles of imperfection, however, could be different, and if they were, communal life would be very different also. Many political ideals have drawn their strength from some variant view of human nature.

The three principles of imperfection have the same logical form. Each says that human beings are *sometimes, but not always*, unselfish, right, well informed. They deny that we are never unselfish in our decisions, right in our judgements, well informed in our opinions, as well as that we always are. In the terminology of the schoolmen, they are of the form I as well as O, and rule out the corresponding E propositions as well as the A ones.

The principles can thus be denied in two ways. They can be denied pessimistically, by denying to man even the limited excellences they ascribe to him. Or they can be denied optimistically, by denying that man's excellences are limited at all or are in any way less than perfect.

Of the pessimistic alternatives, one need not detain us. Nobody denies B(iii), Imperfect Information, in a pessimistic vein, and maintains that men never know anything. It is a pessimistic denial of B(i), denying that men are ever the least bit unselfish, that underlies the political philosophy of Hobbes. Hobbes misconceived human nature as being entirely selfish, and therefore altogether precluded the possibility of moral government freely supported by reasonable men, and made government out to be necessarily a tyranny, only tolerable in that the selfishness of tyrants was likely to be less obnoxious than the law of the jungle. More recently, thinkers have despaired more of man's reason than of his unselfishness, and have denied B(ii), that men have any judgement, albeit only fallible, rather than B(i), that men are ever the least bit unselfish: people may be willing to compromise, and not pursue their own interests without regard to other people's interests, but, they say, we cannot conceive of a discussion or an argument leading to a solution which can be held to be fundamentally reasonable and right. On such a view, all principles of Natural Law or Natural Justice are mistaken; there is no room for the Reasonable Man of the English common law; political philosophy can discuss forms and procedures, but not questions of substance and principle.

Most political thinkers have erred, however, in thinking too much rather than too little of human capacities, and have denied the *O* part, rather than the *I* part, of some of the principles of imperfection, assuming that men were perfectly unselfish, perfectly rational, or perfectly informed.

Let us first consider the assumption of perfect information—the denial of B(iii): it is often felt that obedience, far from being a virtue, is a vice. To act in obedience to another's wishes is to act heteronomously, and only autonomous actions are really moral, are the authentic actions of a self-respecting man. And so we yearn for a society in which nobody is ever told to do anything, but each person knows for himself what he ought to do. The Stoics had such an ideal. If each man were to recognise his station and its duties and perform the task that fell to him, then indeed all men could live together in a universal commonwealth. The kingdom of autonomous agents continues to fascinate us to this day. We feel that to each of us there is a job assigned and waiting to be done, and that we should all be allowed to get on with our respective tasks without interference from outside.

Only when we reflect on our being but imperfectly informed, do we accept the need for some outside organisation of our activities, and are reconciled to some degree of heteronomy. I am not able to will many maxims to be universal laws because I do not know enough about the rest of mankind, where they are, what they need, or what they are doing, to be able to legislate for them. Even in deciding my own course of action I am often ignorant of how other people are situated and what they expect of me. Often therefore I must obey orders, carry out instructions, or take things on trust, because I have not the time or the opportunity to make an independent assessment of my own. More than this, often it is a condition of the success of an enterprise that independent assessments shall not be acted upon: in an army or a business it is more important that bad orders shall be carried out than that subordinates should remedy the mistakes of their superiors. In less extreme cases the Stoic and Kantian ideal of the independent individual's determining for himself by exercise of pure practical reason his station in the universe and the path along which duty calls him is still misleading, because the universe is not so determinate as to fix either my particular moral position in it, or the particular actions I ought to undertake. Rather, the universe affords many indifferent positions and paths of duty, and it is only in virtue of my own or other people's, often arbitrary, decisions that a particular moral situation arises, or a particular course of action is marked out as obligatory. Arbitrary decisions are rationally opaque, and other men's reasons, even where they exist, are often unknown to me. Therefore, knowing that I do not know everything, and believing that morality is largely other-regarding, I must be prepared, if I wish to be moral, to let my actions be determined by other men's wills, and to some extent and in this sense to act heteronomously, and to allow that obedience must, on occasion, be a virtue.

If we assume not perfect information, but complete unselfishness, we have the conditions for what I might call an 'Areopagite' community, of the type envisaged by Milton and Mill. They assume the conditions of Some Interaction and Some Shared Values A(i) and A(ii), Fallible Judgement B(ii), and Imperfect Information B(iii). Areopagites are fallible and not perfectly informed, but they are possessed by a deep love of truth, and are anxious only to discover the truth, and not to establish the rightness of their own views because they are their own. An absence of intellectual *amour propre* characterises the Areopagite frame of mind, and it is only in the absence of this species of selfishness that Milton's and Mill's argument for freedom of discussion holds good. Provided everyone puts forward opinions only because he thinks them to be true and not because they are the ones he happens to hold, and provided he will abandon them if they are shown to be false, and would prefer to be cured of his own errors rather than have to point out those of other people, unfettered debate and discussion is possible. And if each Areopagite is liable to some errors of judgement or information, then the more debate and discussion there is, the more errors will be exposed, and the more the truth will be established.

If we allow that men are sometimes selfish and sometimes misinformed, but deny that their judgement may ever be at fault, our view of society will be that which lies behind the thought of Mr. Frank Buchman. People are selfish, but if only people could get over their selfishness, then, granted they were correctly apprised of the facts, they could live lives of Absolute Honesty, Absolute Integrity, Absolute Justice, and the like. There is no allowance for the fact that men can in good faith still disagree, or that men with the best intentions can still be utterly wrong; and, correspondingly, there follows the conclusion that where people disagree, it must be due to bad faith. There is a suggestion of this view of human nature, characterised by Some Interaction and Some Shared Values A(i) and A(ii), Incomplete Unselfishness B(i) and Imperfect Information B(iii), but not Fallible Judgement B(ii), in President Eisenhower's belief that if only all men of Good Will could get together, a satisfactory solution of all problems must emerge.

If we drop two of the conditions B(i), B(ii), B(iii) at the same time, we develop even more idealised visions of communal existence. Thus if we assume Some Interaction and Some Shared Values A(i) and A(ii) and Fallible Judgement B(ii), but not Incomplete Unselfishness B(i) nor Imperfect Information B(iii), we have the form of life assumed in the higher ranks of the Civil Service. Civil Servants are unselfish and devoted to the public interest: they are well informed, and believe themselves to be perfectly informed—they believe that everything that can be said can be said on paper, and that all papers are to be found in the files of their own department. But they recognise that their judgements may be wrong, and that therefore an exchange of views between departments or mutual discussion and criticism within a department is the proper way to conduct the administration of State.

If to the Stoic assumption of perfect information we add that of perfect rationality, while still allowing that men are often selfish, we approximate towards the position of Kant or, in our own time, Professor R. M. Hare.[1] Both writers acknowledge that men are often guided by self-love or self-interest, but both play down the significance of ignorance and fallibility: they believe not only in Autonomy but in Universalisability, and believe that on this basis a complete system of morality can be erected. Kant assumes without question that there is always only *one* maxim which the man possessed of Good Will can at the same time will to be a universal law of nature: and although Mr. Hare allows that 'Fanatics', as he terms those who disinterestedly differ from normal moral standards, do exist, it is, he believes, an important and fortunate fact that they are few in number.[2]

The nearest we can get to a community of individuals characterized by Imperfect Information B(iii), but not Incomplete

[1] R. M. HARE, THE LANGUAGE OF MORALS (1952); FREEDOM AND REASON (1963).
[2] R. M. HARE, FREEDOM AND REASON 172 (1963).

Unselfishness B(i) nor Fallible Judgement B(ii), is the Visible Church as sometimes idealised. The body of Christian people are, ideally, completely unselfish. Unlike the Areopagites, they have little feeling for their own fallibility—partly perhaps because they avoid contentious topics of debate,[1] partly because they often construe Our Lord's promise that the Holy Spirit will guide them into all truth[2] as meaning also that the Holy Spirit will guide them into nothing but the truth. Christians differ from Stoics in their strong sense of non-self-sufficiency, their sense of being only children who do not know enough to be completely independent autonomous agents, and in their consequently heteronomous ethics. And we may represent this, with some considerable strain, as the acceptance of B(iii), the principle of Imperfect Information.

We end with the completely ideal society, characterised by Some Interaction and Some Shared Values A(i) and A(ii) only, without any principles of imperfection. We may reach it in three ways. It is clear that if the Visible Church on earth is what is characterised by Some Interaction and Some Shared Values A(i) and A(ii), together with Imperfect Information B(iii), then what is characterised by Some Interaction and Some Shared Values alone, without Imperfect Information, will be the Church above, in which we have perfect information, and know even as we are known.[3] If Kantian man is perfected from his self-love, his Good Will becomes a Holy Will, and the Kingdom of Holy Ends-in-themselves clearly constitutes a heavenly city for that philosopher. The passage from the higher Civil Service to Heaven is more difficult, but we can follow it out if we look back to the origins of the Civil Service beyond Jowett to Plato's *Republic*, where διαλεκτική, the method of discussion in which the Guardians engage in their pursuit of truth and the common good, is transmuted, in the metaphysical books of the Republic, from a tentative method of winnowing out truth from error by the give-and-take of argument, to a mystical and infallible intuition of the Forms as they really are; and as the philosopher comes to apprehend the Form of the Good, he is, as it were, transported into the world of the Forms, the Platonist's Heaven.

III. COMMUNITIES AND DISPUTES

A community is a body of individuals who have a common method of deciding questions that may arise among or between them. It is

---

[1] ROMANS xiv. 1.   [2] JOHN xvi. 13.   [3] I CORINTHIANS xiii. 12.

by virtue of their having in common a way of deciding questions, a way of achieving a common mind about important matters, that a number of individuals who necessarily are not *necessarily* going to agree about everything, are united into a single body. Two may walk together so long as they happen to agree; but for them to be more than casual companions who happen to have fallen into each other's company, they must acknowledge some principle for determining where they are to go and what they are to do, other than the contingent concomitance of their separate wills. Even a married couple counts as a community in this sense because they must have some way of settling disputes—e.g. that in the last resort the husband shall decide, as laid down in the 1662 Prayer Book, or that in the last resort the wife shall decide, as in America— so that they may stick together and not drift apart or break up like couples engaged in some passing love affair.

For human beings disagree. They inhabit the same world and have different points of view. There will be disagreements not only about ideas, but about actions; in particular, members of a community will disagree about what shall be done by, or in the name of, their community. These disagreements we shall call disputes. A dispute is about how a community shall act—though often the 'action' in question is that the community shall let one, or the other, party get his own way. Often disputes can be resolved by rational discussion and argument, but since men are less than perfectly rational and their judgement is fallible, their disputes will not always be resolved by argument alone, but will be unresolved disputes; if human beings are also both bloody-minded and able to hurt one another, they will be tempted to settle their unresolved disputes by force, each party trying to bring about the state of affairs that he desires by every means within his power, hurting anyone who attempts to stop him, and avoiding being hurt himself, so far as he can. It is a characteristic of civilised life that unresolved disputes do not become conflicts of force, but are settled some other way. Philosophers have often imagined what life would be like if unresolved disputes were settled by force, and have given vivid descriptions of how unpleasant it would be. I go further, and make it part of the *definition* of a community that disputes between its members are never settled by force, but by some method common to all its members. It is in virtue of this that we can talk of a community's being a single entity. The members of a community are not always of one mind, necessarily not always of one mind. What is common to them is not their views on all questions, but a way, a *method*, of settling, or at least of *deciding*, those *disputes* that cannot be resolved by argument alone. A community, therefore, is defined as a body of individuals who have a common method of deciding disputes. There are, of course, other, more amorphous groups which lack a common method for settling disputes, but they are for that reason less definite entities than communities.

Hobbes' contention that every Commonwealth must have a Sovereign can be understood, and seen to be by and large true, if we take it as meaning that every community must have a supreme method of settling disputes. For if, as with the married couples, there is only one rule, it is supreme; and if there is more than one rule, there must be some further rule, a 'meta-rule' to adjudicate between the two rules in cases of conflict and to decide which one is applicable; for example, the Anglo-American couple who agreed that the husband should decide all important, the wife all unimportant, issues, and that the wife should decide which issues were important and which not.

In a sense, therefore, and subject to certain qualifications, there must be only one method of settling disputes within a given community, if it is to be an alternative to recourse to force. This is not to say that all disputes must be settled in exactly the same way, but that all the methods must form a single coherent system. In Great Britain we have in one sense many methods of settling disputes— the Queen's Bench, the Courts of Equity, the Appeal Court, the High Court of Parliament; but in another sense we have only one, namely that in no dispute that is likely to arise are there two methods available, likely to give different results, both equally applicable, neither superior to the other, and with no method of deciding which method is to be preferred. Usually it is obvious from the nature of a dispute which method is the correct one to apply; the Queen's Bench Division does not prove wills or grant divorces. Sometimes, when more than one method is available, some definite person, say the plaintiff, has the right to choose which one shall apply in his case. On other occasions, where two jurisdictions appear to compete, one jurisdiction is authorised to decide whether itself or the other is the appropriate one for the case; or one court is superior to the other, and can always overrule its decision, as in this country the High Court of Parliament can override any judicial decision. In this sense, then, a society can have only one method of settling its disputes. For suppose there were more than one. Then there would be a possibility of their giving different results. It would be in the interests of the one party that one method should be the method adopted and of the other that the other should. There would thus be a dispute about methods of settling the original dispute. And with *this* dispute there would be no *method* for deciding it. So that if there really are two distinct methods, which are not woven together, by a method for deciding between them, into a single system, then there will be no method of always obtaining settlement of disputes; and if a dispute that was irresoluble by other means arose, the community would fall apart.

IV. DECISION PROCEDURES

It is because human nature is as we have described it, and, in particular, because of the fallibility of human judgement, that we need to have, and can have, the methods of settling disputes that we actually do have. If men were all much more reasonable than they are, there might be differences of opinion among them, but these would be easily resolved by discussion and argument, and they would all agree in the end on how a question ought to be decided. There might still be difficulty in carrying out the decision, but there would be none in knowing that it was the right decision. In fact, however, even when fully informed of the relevant features of a case, we often disagree about the right solution, and this disagreement often remains unresolved by argument. It is of crucial importance, however, that although we often do have irresoluble disagreements it is not the case that we always disagree. Even on moral questions we sometimes reach agreement, and there are other types of question on which agreement is almost invariable. We nearly always agree about the number of people in a given room at a given time, about the date, about questions of personal identity. And this fact, that we can recognise procedures more easily than right results, enables us to agree on methods of settling disputes even if we cannot agree on a solution directly. As in other branches of philosophy, we can set up a 'decision procedure' on whose validity we agree and about whose application there can be little doubt; and by means of such a decision procedure we can settle indirectly issues on which we could not reach agreement direct.[1] Two friends, each of whom thinks it is the other's turn to buy the drinks, may agree to toss for it. This is an effective method for settling the dispute, because they both know without any serious doubt what constitutes tossing for it, the way in which one sets about doing it, and how the fall of the coin is to be interpreted. In a similar vein they may agree on a more serious matter to refer the dispute to a third friend to arbitrate: and again this is an effective method, because they can have no serious doubt whether the person they address is that third friend or not, nor how the words he utters are to be taken. Thus it is often possible to have almost complete agreement about a method, a procedure, or a form, for settling disputes, when we are unable to reach any sort of agreement about the rights and wrongs of the dispute itself, the content of the dispute, the substantial issue at stake. Therefore, if we attach, as we do, paramount importance to being able to settle disputes, we shall need to establish *methods* of settling disputes, about which methods themselves there can be very little dispute.

In order that there should be no dispute about methods, it is necessary that the established method shall have or shall be given some identifying marks so that every party to a dispute shall be able to recognise it as *the* method to which he should have recourse. The mediaeval monarchs wore their crowns and modern states put their policemen into uniform. An American story illustrates the logical importance of uniform.[2] A leading bandit in New York State was arrested; 'Will you go quietly?' asked the officer who arrested him, 'or must I handcuff you?' 'What's the charge?' 'Income-tax.' 'I'll come along', and he entered the waiting police-car without resistance, and was driven to the police station, which was full of policemen. Only as his executioner drew his gun, did the bandit realise that these were not policemen at all, but members of the rival gang, dressed for the occasion. The policeman's uniform, like the crown of the mediaeval monarch, or the *fasces* of the Roman magistrate, commands immediate respect, so that people obey without actually having to be coerced. It is obviously better that physical violence should not have to be employed, if only for

[1] The term 'decision procedure' is used in mathematical logic in a technical sense, different from that in this essay.

[2] Also actual incidents in Britain: see THE TIMES 11 December 1965, p. 8, col. 5, and 11 May 1966, p. 12, col. 2. For the citizen's views of the problem, see letter in THE TIMES 2 February 1966, p. 13, col. 5.

reasons of economy, to save wear and tear on the police force: on reflection, we can go further than this and see that it is logically necessary for people to be able to recognise 'Authority' and give way before it, if they are to be members of a community at all, and not outlaws. If a man involved in a dispute with his neighbour was unable to call a policeman, unable to find a magistrate to summon his neighbour to appear, unable to invoke the protection of a king, because there was no means of telling policemen, magistrates or kings apart from other folk, then there would be no way of settling the dispute. If there was a state in which bandits regularly dressed up as policemen, people would not obey putative policemen for fear they might be bandits, unless compelled to at pistol point. A policeman could not stop a car by holding up his hand, but must always shoot its tyres. People would obey only when coerced, and might then be obeying the police or bandits for all they knew: one lot of people dressed as policemen meeting another lot of people dressed as policemen would shoot it out: and every encounter and dispute would end in a resort to violence.

For these reasons, the officers of the law need to be clearly recognisable as such, and legal systems characteristically secure this by making it an offence for any persons or procedures to appear to be authorised when they are not. Hobbes makes the same point, that there is 'requisite, not only a declaration of the law, but also sufficient signs of the author and authority. The author, or legislator is supposed in every commonwealth to be evident because he is the sovereign, who having been constituted by the *consent*[1] of everyone, is supposed by everyone to be sufficiently known.'[2] The 'consent' here mentioned is that when, at the institution of a commonwealth 'a multitude of men do agree, and covenant, every one, with every one, that' whatever body the majority of them shall choose, 'every one, he that voted against as well as he that voted for, shall *authorise*[3] all the actions and judgements of the body'.[4] Hobbes' account here has often been criticised, as being broken-backed—because on his view agreements are not binding unless and until there is somebody in a position to enforce them—and as being redundant—because once a sovereign is established, any contract there might be would be between individual subject and sovereign, and not between subject and subjects. These

---

[1] My italics.   [2] LEVIATHAN 178 (Oakeshott ed. 1946).
[3] Hobbes' italics.   [4] LEVIATHAN 113 (Oakeshott ed. 1946).

criticisms are cogent. Nevertheless it is at this point that Hobbes comes nearest to realising that sovereignty is a matter of agreement as well as of coercion, and that for a sovereign to be a sovereign he must be able not only to coerce the recalcitrant, but to be recognised as sovereign, that is, for it to be agreed by his subjects, however unwillingly, that he is their sovereign. This is true not only of a Hobbesian sovereign, but of any method of settling disputes. The method must be one about which there is agreement, at least to the extent of its being agreed that it is the relevant method, that is, of its being recognised as *the* method. Various methods of settling disputes have been adopted in their time. The ancient world looked for omens and auspices, the Middle Ages had trial by ordeal and trial by combat, often recourse has been had to some random process, but the pre-eminent method has always been the decision either of one person or of more than one person after the arguments on each side of the case have been put. . . .

Morals and the Criminal Law

GRAHAM HUGHES[1]

General jurisprudential discussion does not often become the concern of a wide audience. Outside a small specialist circle even the cultivated public is for the most part unaware of the exchange of mighty blows that so consumes the academics. But occasionally a controversy is, or is thought to be, of such central importance or of such practical implication that it breaks out of the cloister and becomes a subject of general notice. This has happened recently in England over the question of the relationship between the criminal law and general morality.

The discussion was set off by a lecture delivered by Lord Devlin (Sir Patrick Devlin as he then was) as the 1959 Maccabaean Lecture in Jurisprudence of the British Academy, under the title, 'The Enforcement of Morals'.[2] A partial explanation of the interest aroused by this lecture is no doubt to be found in the person of its author. British judges do not often speak publicly on basic jurisprudential topics, and when a judge of Lord Devlin's eminence does so his pronouncements are rightly given close attention. Again, Lord Devlin had taken as his text certain important statements of policy advanced in the Report of the Wolfenden

---

[1] Graham Hughes, B.A. 1948, M.A. 1951, Cantab., LL.B. 1950 Wales, LL.M. 1962 New York Univ., is Professor of Law at New York University. This paper is a revised version of *Morals and the Criminal Law* 71 YALE L. J. 662 (1962). Other relevant writings by Mr. Hughes include: *Criminal Omissions* 67 YALE L. J. 590 (1958); *The Existence of a Legal System* 35 N.Y.U. L. REV. 1001 (1960); *Professor Hart's Concept of Law* 25 MOD. L. REV. 319 (1962); *Jurisprudence*, 1964 ANN. SURVEY AM. L. 685; *Jurisprudence*, 1965 ANN. SURVEY AM. L. 639; *Jurisprudence*, 1966 ANN. SURVEY AM. L. 711. (Footnote by editor.)

[2] THE ENFORCEMENT OF MORALS by Sir Patrick Arthur Devlin. London: Oxford University Press, 1959, hereinafter cited as DEVLIN. Lord Devlin's lecture is now reprinted in a collection of essays, DEVLIN, THE ENFORCEMENT OF MORALS (London: Oxford University Press, 1965). The citations in this article are to the pagination of the original publication.

Committee on Homosexual Offences and Prostitution[1] and this Report had itself been a matter of lively public discussion. But the feature of Lord Devlin's lecture that aroused most interest and generated most heat was that his central thesis appeared to be an attack on a view of the nature and function of the criminal law which had been accepted for so long by an important section of public opinion that it might fairly be called the orthodoxy on this point. The position under attack is the utilitarian or Benthamite view of morality and law.

I

In Bentham's view, man is placed 'under the empire of *pleasure* and of *pain*'.[2] Under his principle of utility all human action is to be scrutinized against the criterion of its tendency to produce pleasure or pain and judged by the final balance in the pleasure–pain ledger, by the felicific calculus. Pleasure and pain are not here to be understood in the grossest physical sense, for they include emotional enrichments and deprivation. (Bentham includes in his list such pleasures as friendship, good reputation, benevolence, and knowledge and their corresponding pains.)[3] Man must be taken in his actual constitution and subjected to an essentially social, communal judgment: 'That which is conformable to the utility, or the interest of a community, is what tends to augment the total sum of the happiness of the individuals that compose it.'[4] By the judgment of the legislator it is bad for X to do that which brings him 5 units of pleasure if it is likely in sum to bring 6 units of pain to others. For Bentham, there is no other admissible test of the rightness or wrongness of action and, in the first instance, the test must be the same whether we speak in moral or legislative terms.

If [the partisan of the principle of utility] finds in the common list of offences some indifferent action, some innocent pleasure, he will not hesitate to transport this pretended offence into the class of lawful actions; he will pity the pretended criminals, and will reserve his indignation for their persecutors.[5]

But the criteria for the advisability of criminal legislation are not at all stages the same as the criteria for the simple moral judgment

---

[1] COMMITTEE ON HOMOSEXUAL OFFENCES AND PROSTITUTION, REPORT, Cmd. No. 247 (1957) (Wolfenden Report).

[2] BENTHAM, THEORY OF LEGISLATION 2 (Hildreth ed. 1876).

[3] ibid. pp. 20–27.   [4] ibid. p. 2.   [5] ibid. pp. 3–4.

of condemnation. Even though an act may be condemned as immoral by the operation of the principle of utility, there may be other outbalancing reasons why it should not be condemned by the criminal law. The chief of these, in Bentham's exposition, would be that the punishment would be inefficacious as a deterrent, that is, where it would not prevent the disapproved conduct; secondly, that the punishment would be unprofitable, that is, where the mischief produced by the criminal prohibition would be greater than the mischief produced by letting the disapproved act go unpunished; and, thirdly, that the punishment would be needless, that is, where the mischief may be prevented without the punishment.[1] In all these cases, Bentham would have the acts go unpunished, even though they were morally reprehensible under the principle of utility.

Moreover, Bentham recognized that when legislators calculate the harmfulness of conduct they must pay attention to the attitude of the public at large towards such conduct, however irrational such attitude may seem to be. His position here is put in a powerful passage, which deserves quotation for its particular relevance to this topic:

> But when I say that *antipathies and sympathies are no reason*, I mean those of the legislator; for the antipathies and sympathies of the people may be reasons, and very powerful ones. However odd or pernicious a religion, a law, a custom may be, it is of no consequence, so long as the people are attached to it. The strength of their prejudice is the measure of the indulgence which should be granted to it. . . . The legislator ought to yield to the violence of a current which carries away everything that obstructs.
>
> But ought the legislator to be a slave to the fancies of those whom he governs? No. Between an imprudent opposition and a servile compliance, there is a middle path, honourable and safe. It is, to combat these fancies with the only arms that can conquer them,—example and instruction. He must enlighten the people, he must address himself to the public reason; he must give time for error to be unmasked.
>
> It is to be observed, however, that too much deference for prejudices, is a more common fault than the contrary excess.[2]

As a system of moral philosophy the principle of utility has come under telling attack. It has been pointed out that the notions of

---

[1] BENTHAM, PRINCIPLES OF MORALS AND LEGISLATION 281–8 (Harrison ed. 1948). [2] BENTHAM, THEORY OF LEGISLATION 76–77.

N

pleasure and pain are subjective, so that what X may experience as pleasure Y may experience as pain. In this way there may be a clash of interests, and Bentham provides no guide for the individual who is faced with such a clash. Indeed, according to the notion of the empire of pleasure and pain, man must ineluctably act in a way that brings pleasure to him. He can have no reason for acting in any other way whatever harm his acts may bring to others. If a good action is one that brings more pleasure than pain, it is then difficult to see in what sense the individual can be said to act wrongly except in the sense of a social judgment of what is pleasure and pain for the greatest number. Again, it has been said that pleasure and pain are not susceptible to nice calculation. The moral arithmetic here must be very sketchy and must often be no more than an intuition or guess. But, as his defenders have insisted, Bentham was not in fact so much interested in constructing a moral philosophy as in erecting a method of approach for the legislator. His primary interest was in law-making and law reform. Viewed in this light, many of the weaknesses of the principle of utility disappear. Thus, in practice we are not so much concerned with the individual's view of what is for him pleasure or pain as with a social view of what is pleasure or pain for the greatest number. It is in the sphere of public decisions with respect to the greatest happiness of the greatest number that the principle of utility is designed to operate, rather than in the individual's guiding of his personal life. And when the technique is confined to the making of public decisions, the clash between individual and public interest is no longer strictly relevant. The objection of the roughness of the calculation also loses much of its force when made in this context. For, though in personal life there may be agonizing choices between two courses of action where the pleasure–pain account is nicely balanced, the ledger in public decisions, such as those reflected in criminal legislation, will be read in millions of units and all that will be required is reasonable conviction of a substantial benefit. As Dicey put it, one does not need to weigh butcher's meat in diamond scales.[1]

This Benthamite approach does not of course reduce criminal legislation to a process of strict calculation. In the first place, there may be genuine dispute about the actual consequences of conduct

[1] DICEY, LAW AND PUBLIC OPINION IN ENGLAND DURING THE NINETEENTH CENTURY 141 (2d ed. 1914).

that it is sought to prohibit or no longer to prohibit, or about the consequences of the prohibition or its removal. So, one may argue about the precise deterrent effect of capital punishment, or about the possible spread of homosexuality if the criminal prohibition were removed. The resolution of such arguments clearly depends very much on the available information about social practices and the impact of laws. Again, even if in agreement about the actual consequences of conduct or of criminal prohibition or, more often, while still in disagreement about them, one may also dispute whether certain consequences should be regarded as harmful. That is to say that even in the public sphere there may be disagreements about pleasures and pains. This disagreement may take two forms. It may be a simple denial by one side that an admitted consequence is harmful at all. So, one may agree that to remove the criminal prohibition from homosexual conduct will lead to an increase in such conduct but may simply not regard this as harmful. Secondly, the disagreement may be less abrupt and more quantitative, i.e., one may agree that a spread of homosexuality is harmful but may regard it as much less harmful than does the other side and, on the other hand, may regard the effect of law enforcement in this field as much more harmful than does the other side. Disagreements of the first kind (a total clash over the harmful character of an admitted consequence) are probably rare, and the more typical conflict is between two views of the degree of harm involved, usually complicated by a disagreement over the actual consequences to be expected. Thus, the Benthamite approach neither eliminates clashes over values nor does it provide any simple resolution of such conflicts; it is not a legislative computer. This cannot be better demonstrated than by the dramatic twentieth-century shift away from Bentham's own emphasis on individual liberty in his context of *laissez-faire* economics.

But what is, or ought to be, enduring is the Benthamite method of public debate about public decision-making. Bentham's values may not always be our values but his method of discussion ought to be our method. In the first place, he insisted upon obtaining the best possible information for decision-making, demanding careful investigation of actual social behavior and institutions, delicate projection of contemplated legislation in terms of its probable effects, and public scrutiny and discussion of such information. In so doing, Bentham became the great forerunner of modern sociological and realist schools of jurisprudence. The other fundamental aspect of his method of discussion was an insistence upon an explicit statement of value positions and their defense, as far as this may be possible, in rational debate. Legislation and decision-making, he felt, must be examined in the arena of reasoned discussion in the light of information about their probable consequences and the values which they profess to serve. This is the method of modern democracy; it is the method of the common law courts in England at their best; it is the method of the United States Supreme Court. It involves the recognition that though rational argument cannot solve disputes about conflicts of values, such argument can solve a host of problems on which there is no real dispute about values and that, even when such a dispute exists, the insistence on reasonable public discussion is of the greatest importance in aiding judgment and influencing opinion. This is a tradition which we readily accept and in which we are now immersed, but it is no more than two centuries old and Bentham was its prophet and nurse.

If Lord Devlin's lecture involved no more than a disagreement with what is probably the majority of current intelligent opinion on the evaluation of the present state of the law in the field of sexual offenses and certain other fields, its appearance would not have been so profoundly important. What does make Lord Devlin's thesis so disquieting is that it constitutes an attack on the whole Benthamite position of rational debate about public decision-making. It is here that Lord Devlin's views become dangerous and here that they must be resolutely opposed.

Lord Devlin begins by recognizing that the present law of sexual offenses in Britain is haphazard and not always closely linked with popular moral notions. The question he wishes to consider is whether there are any principles which can regulate the embodiment of the moral law in the criminal law. The inquiry must be a general one and cannot be confined to the field of sexual morals. The question is:

What is the connexion between crime and sin and to what extent, if at all, should the criminal law of England concern itself with the enforcement of morals and punish sin or immorality as such?[1]

There is, already, in these opening passages an identification of

[1] DEVLIN 4.

the concepts of immorality and sin which is disturbing to the secular-minded reader. Lord Devlin is to be excused somewhat here for he was concerned with the report of the Wolfenden Committee which had set a bad example by equating immorality and sin. The vital passages in the Report of the Committee are those which put forward:

Our own formulation of the function of the criminal law so far as it concerns the subjects of this enquiry. In this field, its function, as we see it, is to preserve public order and decency, to protect the citizen from what is offensive or injurious, and to provide sufficient safeguards against exploitation and corruption of others, particularly those who are specially vulnerable because they are young, weak in body or mind, inexperienced, or in a state of special physical, official or economic dependence.

It is not, in our view, the function of the law to intervene in the private lives of citizens, or to seek to enforce any particular pattern of behaviour, further than is necessary to carry out the purposes we have outlined.[1]

The Committee recommended:

That homosexual behaviour between consenting adults in private should no longer be a criminal offence [following on the argument] which we believe to be decisive, namely, the importance which society and the law ought to give to individual freedom of choice and action in matters of private morality. Unless a deliberate attempt is to be made by society, acting through the agency of the law, to equate the sphere of crime with that of sin, there must remain a realm of private morality and immorality which is, in brief and crude terms, not the law's business. To say this is not to condone or encourage private immorality.[2]

In Lord Devlin's view this amounts to setting up a concept of private immorality which is to be prohibited criminally only if it infringes certain further criteria, and it is with this view that he proceeds to take issue.

Lord Devlin believes that 'a complete separation of crime from sin . . . would not be good for the moral law and might be disastrous for the criminal'.[3] The opposite point of view to this, he suggests, is that which holds that 'A state which refuses to enforce Christian beliefs has lost the right to enforce Christian morals.'[4] But, he goes on, 'If this view is sound, it means that the criminal law

---

[1] WOLFENDEN REPORT 13.   [2] ibid. pp. 61 and 62.
[3] DEVLIN 6.   [4] ibid. p. 7.

cannot justify any of its provisions by reference to the moral law. It cannot say, for example, that murder and theft are prohibited because they are immoral or sinful.'[1]

Much is involved in these statements. How far the administration of the law and the control of crime depend on a sense of sin, if by that is meant a religiously oriented sense, is arguable, but it is no doubt true that a strong and widely held acceptance of religious teaching is on the whole a valuable supporter of law enforcement agencies, unless the law itself offends against religious tenets. If for a sense of sin we substitute the notion of a sense of infringing morality without the religious connotation, then it is difficult to see how such a sense could ever be completely separated from the state of the law. To contemplate such a possibility is to ignore the interdependence of law and morality while seeming to defend it. The pressure exerted by generally held views of what is right and wrong upon legislatures when legislating, the support that the law in its administration receives from such widely held feelings, and, in turn, the support that general feelings of right and wrong receive from law enforcement are inevitable facts of the system of social control. The exact nature of the interdependence may be debated, the comparative importance of the law as compared with general feelings of morality may be the subject of controversy, but the existence of some interdependence is unquestionable. But this still leaves open the question of whether it is wise and proper to prohibit criminally any particular species of conduct. It is probable, for example, that the 'sense of sin' to which Lord Devlin refers, is most often felt by most people with respect to aspects of their behavior into which the criminal law does not enter at all. It is, for the most part, with respect to cowardice, cruelty to others, or parsimony that the sense of sin is felt. With all this the criminal law has very little to do. There are indeed situations in which a sense of wrongdoing might be keenly felt by the individual, where the criminal law might well interfere, but where, in common law jurisdictions, it has chosen not to do so. An example of this would be the absence of a legal duty to aid others in peril.

The greatest confusion is introduced, however, by Lord Devlin's casual shifts from general references to morality to specific references to 'sin', 'Christian morals' and the 'moral law'. (The

[1] DEVLIN 7.

'moral law' is an ambiguous term which seems to attempt to get the best of both worlds by being free of overt theological implications but at the same time obliquely implying authoritative attributes by the use of the word 'law'.) It is difficult here to give precision to significant ideas which are peculiar to Christian morality. Lord Devlin's examples of murder and theft seem particularly ill chosen. One has not heard that it was or is legal to murder and steal in Classical Greece or Rome, in modern Muslim countries or in Soviet Russia. The criminal prohibitions of murder and theft are of course extremely easy to defend on utilitarian grounds. This is not to deny the importance of the sense of horror that most men have at the contemplation of killing. The derivation of that sense, and how much it owes to immemorial law enforcement may be left to the psychologists and anthropologists for there is no need to inquire into it nor into any religious beliefs in order to justify the present state of the law. Indeed, if one addresses oneself seriously to the question of what issues in the contemporary criminal law appear to be vitally connected with specifically Christian beliefs, or the beliefs of specific Christian sects, it is only in very controversial fields such as the prohibition of contraceptive practices, abortion, sterilization and euthanasia that examples occur. Here the arguments rage, and to refer one to Christian morals is to beg the questions and not to answer them.

Lord Devlin himself indeed proceeds to bring his generalities on Christian morals and the moral law to a practical concentration on certain aspects of sexual morality. 'It is true', we are told, 'that for many centuries the criminal law was much concerned with keeping the peace and little, if at all, with sexual morals. But it would be wrong to infer from that that it had no moral content. . . .'[1] It is difficult to see why anyone should dream of making such an inference unless he took the peculiar view that morality was restricted to questions of sexual behavior. Yet at times Lord Devlin himself seems to approach this view for he tells us, very oddly, on the same page that, 'Rules which impose a speed limit or prevent an obstruction on the highway have nothing to do with morals.' It is, to say the least, possible to argue that it is much more immoral deliberately to choose to exceed a speed limit and so put one's fellows in great danger than to take a minority view of the proper object of sexual activity.

[1] DEVLIN 7.

In another general attack on the position which he characterizes as a separation of law and morality, Lord Devlin lists a
number of existing criminal law principles whose justification he
cannot find in any utilitarian principle of 'the preservation of order
and decency' and which therefore must be justified, he argues, in
terms of some moral law which cannot be pinned down in concrete terms.[1] The examples put forward are the general denial of
the consent of the victim as a defense in criminal law and in particular the rejection of consent as a defense in cases of euthanasia,
suicide, attempted suicide, abortion, incest and duelling.

On the point of consent generally it would seem that Lord
Devlin is a little too emphatic about the present state of the law.
The authorities on the scope of consent as a defense are meagre but
they seem to be in conflict with Lord Devlin's proposition that,
'It is not a defence to any form of assault that the victim thought his
punishment well deserved and submitted to it.'[2] The position in
fact appears to be that in the general crime of assault at common
law the consent of the victim will be a defense provided that no
serious bodily harm was caused. But in homicide and cases where
serious bodily harm is caused consent is not admitted as a defense
and it is true that in a utilitarian context this position is debatable.

We do start here with a firm moral position, amply ratified by
utilitarian tests, that the infliction of harm on an individual without his consent is to be condemned and is eminently proper for
criminal sanction. Whether the consent of the victim should
cause a reversal of this judgment depends on somewhat conflicting
views about paternalism in society and also on practical doubts
about the possibility of obtaining satisfactory evidence of full and
free consent. Whether a collective judgment about what is commonly accounted a harm should yield to an individual's personal
appraisal of what is harm for him, an appraisal which may be
perverse by collective standards, is admittedly a problem with
which any version of utilitarianism must wrestle. As an explanation
of the present state of the law it is clearly true that the emphatic
condemnation of the infliction of serious harm, even with the
consent of the victim, by Christian religious doctrine is a major

---

[1] DEVLIN 8–9.
[2] ibid. p. 8. See Hughes, *Consent in Sexual Offences* 25 MOD. L. REV. 672
(1962); Hughes *Two Views on Consent in the Criminal Law* 26 MOD. L. REV.
233 (1963).

factor. And in this sense the condemnation certainly springs from a moral position. The only point perhaps that needs to be made in answer to Lord Devlin is that it is a moral position which is not closed to debate and one where the issues are seen to be difficult and complicated once one demands a better warrant than the declaration of a religious belief. As a result of secular examination of Christian doctrine in this area controversy is now keen and some shifts in the law have already taken place. Thus, since Lord Devlin wrote, both suicide and attempted suicide have ceased to be criminal offenses in Britain.[1] There is a body of opinion in favor of legalizing euthanasia; the crime of abortion is increasingly subject to modification in a number of jurisdictions. Similarly it is not easy to find utilitarian reasons why incest should be a crime, unless perhaps for eugenic reasons or in circumstances where it would amount to some other existing crime.[2] Indeed, at present the great majority of prosecutions for incest are in cases where the act at the same time amounts to some other sexual offense. As for duelling, it is easy to find utilitarian reasons for its prohibition. Such combats have an obvious tendency to lead to bodily harm or death and so all the arguments cited above with respect to the relevance of consent here apply.

The examples offered by Lord Devlin thus fall for the most part into that area of the criminal law which is presently the subject of keen debate. That debate has arisen precisely because it is felt by many people that there are no good utilitarian reasons for the perpetuation of criminal sanctions for some of these acts. To cite their presence in the criminal law as a rebuttal of the utilitarian position is thus not a tenable argument. In some instances, it shows no more than that the criminal law is in an antiquated and unreasonable state. At best, as with arguments for preserving criminal prohibitions on abortion and incest, this position can be presented as a moral position by an appeal to religious belief. But, though this may characterize the position as a moral one, it is not in itself a sufficient warrant for translating it into a criminal prohibition. The task of the investigator and legislator must be one of constant inquiry into the accuracy of the reflection of existing values in the criminal law and a constant appraisal of those values themselves,

---

[1] Suicide Act, 1961, 9 & 10 Eliz. 2, c. 60.
[2] See Hughes, *The Crime of Incest* 55 JOURNAL OF CRIMINAL LAW, CRIMINOLOGY AND POLICE SCIENCE 322 (1964).

in so far as they are open to rational appraisal. It is dangerously easy to point to an existing criminal prohibition as evidence of a community value, when in fact the law may lag well behind mores. It is even more dangerous to be dissuaded from examination of the alleged community value merely because it is expressed in an ancient criminal prohibition.

III

Lord Devlin proceeds in his inquiry by framing three questions which he suggests are helpful to the discussion. The first and second are as follows:

1. Has society the right to pass judgment at all on matters of morals? Ought there, in other words, to be a public morality, or are morals always a matter for private judgment?
2. If society has the right to pass judgment, has it also the right to use the weapon of the law to enforce it?[1]

The use of the word 'right' here is odd. As a matter of fact social attitudes of approval or disapproval grow up with regard to modes of conduct. To say that they are matters of morals is to say that they are modes of conduct about which such attitudes exist. What then can be meant by asking if there is a 'right' here? It would appear from the general trend of Lord Devlin's argument that he is referring here by 'matters of morals' to matters of sexual behavior, but, even so, it seems unhelpful to talk in terms of rights. Lord Devlin is not adverting here to the advisability of passing laws on such points because this is the subject matter of his third interrogatory. He clearly treats the first and second questions as something anterior, and it is in this sense that it is difficult to see what can be meant. Indeed, in turning to his answer to this self examination we find that the reply only amounts to a declaration that there is such a thing as public morality, i.e., widely held attitudes of approval or disapproval towards certain modes of conduct. But surely no one ever doubted this. His discussion is more enlightening when he turns to the subject matter of his third question:

3. If so [i.e., if society has the right to pass laws on matters of morals] ought it to use that weapon in all cases or only in some: and if only in some, on what principles should it distinguish?[2]

[1] DEVLIN 9.   [2] ibid.

Lord Devlin's three questions thus resolve themselves into only one legitimate question, which might be phrased as follows: 'In what circumstances should a legislature criminally prohibit a course of conduct which is disapproved by widely held public opinion? [If the difference is felt to be one of substance, the word "immoral" may be substituted for "disapproved by widely held public opinion".]'

This is certainly itself a moral question and in that sense it is quite meaningful to debate whether it is right for a legislature to pass a law. If that is all that is to be understood by speaking of the legislature's having a right the reference is acceptable.

Before society may intervene, Lord Devlin suggests, there must be a 'collective judgment' of disapproval against the conduct in question. But it is not at all clear what he means by 'collective judgment' for he admits that 'Some people sincerely believe that homosexuality is neither immoral nor unnatural', but suggests that there is a collective judgment against it.[1] Even though one clearly cannot offer a criterion of any precision for measuring the diffusion and strength of public feeling that ought to influence a legislature in debating the advisability of a criminal prohibition, it is, nevertheless, a matter that deserves as close an inquiry as may be possible. A great many laws are kept on the books by assertions of public revulsion which might not stand up on examination. Three factors deserve consideration: (1) the proportion of the community who disapprove of the practice, (2) the strength of their disapproval (will they riot or attack those who practise it if it is legalized?) and (3) the qualitative nature of the majority and minority groups (a strong majority of cultivated opinion may be significant even if it is but a minority of public opinion as a whole). The importance of these inquiries is too easily obscured by the simple demand for a 'collective judgment', though it is true that Lord Devlin does return later to the question of the strength of the disapproval.

Lord Devlin also tells us that the collective judgment is only justified if 'society is affected' by the practice. In terms of the 'right to pass judgment' this does not mean very much, but in terms of the advisability of legislation it means a great deal and appears to be a strange surrender of Lord Devlin's major argument that the utilitarian test is unsatisfactory. And it is followed by a

[1] ibid. p. 10.

strange linking of the collective judgment with certain subsidiary prohibitions of an obviously utilitarian aspect.

If society is not prepared to say that homosexuality is morally wrong, there would be no basis for a law protecting youth from "corruption" or punishing a man for living on the "immoral" earnings of a homosexual prostitute. . . .[1]

But this seems greatly misconceived. The drinking of alcohol is not generally regarded as immoral in itself, yet there are laws prohibiting minors from drinking on licensed premises. Heterosexual activity is not *per se* immoral, yet there are laws prohibiting assaults on young girls (even with their consent) and laws making it criminal to live on the earnings of a female prostitute. To prohibit acts of a similar nature in a homosexual context need not involve a general judgment about homosexual acts between consenting adults.

The same analytical lapse marks Lord Devlin's reference to monogamy, which he regards as an institution that is 'built-in' to our society. 'The institution of marriage would be gravely threatened if individual judgments were permitted about the morality of adultery. . . .'[2] This view appears to be shared by Dean Rostow in his comment on Lord Devlin's lecture. After referring to the prosecutions of Mormons in the United States, he writes:

Should we not then conclude that monogamy is so fundamental a theme in the existing common morality of the United States that the condemnation of polygamy as a crime is justified, even though in the end the repugnance to it rests on 'feeling' and not on 'reason'?[3]

But the relationship between the institution of monogamy and the criminal law is or may be much more complex than these comments indicate. To what extent are individual judgments about adultery not permitted? In England adultery is not a crime, though it is of course a ground for divorce. Bigamy is a crime but as such has come under a good deal of attack. It has been suggested that it be removed from the statute-book in its present general form and reincorporated as a sexual offense where it involves fraud on a female and, on the other hand, reduced to a summary offense

---

[1] DEVLIN 10.   [2] ibid. p. 11.
[3] Rostow, *The Enforcement of Morals* 1960 CAMBRIDGE L. J. 174, 190.

against the registration laws where it involves two parties one of whom knows the other to be already married.[1] One must agree with Lord Devlin and Dean Rostow that it is difficult to conceive of any Western system abandoning monogamy as an institution. Indeed, even in non-Western and non-Christian countries the trend is towards monogamy, presumably because it is an efficient, useful and easily organizable mode and because it expresses recognition of the equality of the sexes. But there is always the question of how much debate and how much change we can contemplate in our society. Monogamy exists at the moment side by side with a heavy divorce rate and, presumably, side by side with a great deal of adultery. Monogamy is thus only protected by the criminal law to a limited extent, and what is ensured and protected is not the indissoluble sexual union of one man and one woman but rather a form of registration entailing certain legal consequences which again can be dissolved in certain eventualities. It is thus quite possible to conclude that the criminal prohibition of bigamy is or ought to be aimed at suppressing two evils: (1) the procurement of sexual relations by fraud, and (2) the confusion of a public system of registration on which a host of rights, duties, powers and privileges depends. Any other conclusion indeed is difficult to accept unless one takes the frankly religious position of regarding bigamy as a defiling of a sacrament. Making bigamy a crime is thus just as defensible on utilitarian grounds as is making a crime of rape or voting twice.

Later in his lecture, Lord Devlin gives it as his view that 'Adultery of the sort that breaks up marriage seems to me to be just as harmful to the social fabric as homosexuality or bigamy.'[2] Adultery is not a crime in England, he thinks, because 'a law which made it a crime would be too difficult to enforce; it is too generally regarded as a human weakness not suitably punished by imprisonment'.[3] That adultery is a human weakness is not a very convincing reason for not punishing it. So is cheating on one's income tax returns. The sensible reason for not punishing adultery is surely the recognition that happy marriages are not made by the criminal law. It may be difficult to measure the social value secured by some criminal sexual prohibitions, but it can scarcely be doubted

---

[1] Williams, *Language and the Law* 61 L. Q. REV. 71, 76–78 (1945); Williams, *Bigamy and the Third Marriage* 13 MOD. L. REV. 417, 424–7 (1950).
[2] DEVLIN 22.   [3] ibid.

that no good at all would ensue in Britain from declaring adultery
to be a criminal offense.

IV

Lord Devlin attacked the approach of the Wolfenden Committee as
being 'wrong in principle' in endeavoring to specify those circumstances in which it may be proper for the criminal law to intervene.
The Wolfenden Committee with regard to sexual offenses had
characterized these circumstances among others as including the
'exploitation and corruption of others'. Lord Devlin suggests that
this is so wide a characterization that it 'can be supported only if it
is accepted that the law is concerned with immorality as such'.[1] It
may well be that the exploitation and corruption of others is so
wide a formulation as not to be of much practical help in a given
case. Indeed it may be a mistake to attempt to confine the proper
conditions for legal intervention within any single comprehensive
formula. But the task should rather be of intensive investigation
of social consequences in each particular case. The danger of Lord
Devlin's approach is that an Establishment evaluation of collective
judgments in society should replace the social research that is
necessary. The alarming tendency of Lord Devlin's thesis becomes
more apparent when he turns to the question of how the collective
judgment of society is to be ascertained. 'It is', he tells us, 'that of
the reasonable man. He is not to be confused with the rational man.
He is not expected to reason about anything and his judgment may
be largely a matter of feeling.'[2] 'Immorality then, for the purpose
of the law, is what every right-minded person is presumed to
consider to be immoral.'[3]

Here is an overt rejection of rationality startling in its frankness.
The yardstick is to be the feeling of right-minded people, though
we are not told who are to be considered 'right minded'. Without
qualification, this remarkable statement has a frightening evocation
of the notorious Nazi law of 1935 that empowered the judges to
punish acts that deserved punishment 'according to the healthy
instincts of the people'. Much of the sting is, however, removed by
the qualifications that Lord Devlin proceeds to offer. We are told
that 'there must be toleration of the maximum individual freedom
that is consistent with the integrity of society'[4] and that 'nothing
should be punished by the law that does not lie beyond the limits

[1] DEVLIN 13.   [2] ibid. p. 15.   [3] ibid. p. 16.   [4] ibid. p. 17.

of tolerance'.[1] The first is a very large admission and the second almost tautologous. We are told further that 'majority dislike' is not enough; there must be a 'real feeling of reprobation'. So, with respect to homosexual behavior, 'I do not think one can ignore disgust if it is deeply felt and not manufactured. Its presence is a good indication that the bounds of toleration are being reached.'[2] It is this feeling of disgust that is taken, in Lord Devlin's view, to justify the criminal prohibition of cruelty to animals.

The prohibition of cruelty to animals had earlier been considered by Bentham as an exercise in the theory of utility. His answer had been forthright:

It may come one day to be recognized that the number of legs, the villosity of the skin, or the termination of the *os sacrum* are reasons equally insufficient for abandoning a sensitive being to the same fate [i.e., the caprice of a tormentor]. What else is it that should trace the insuperable line? Is it the faculty of reason, or, perhaps, the faculty of discourse? But a full-grown horse or dog is beyond comparison a more rational, as well as a more conversable animal, than an infant of a day, or a week, even a month old. But suppose the case were otherwise, what would it avail? The question is not, Can they *reason*? nor, Can they *talk*? but, Can they *suffer*?[3]

Is this not much more satisfactory than to rest content with the mere observation of the reasonable man's wave of disgust? The Benthamite method compels us to do our best to express our disgust in the language of values. The value here advanced is that the infliction of suffering on any sensate creature is to be deplored and prohibited, unless there are very compelling reasons that outbalance this value (as in the case of vivisection). If we pursue this rigorous method into the example of homosexual behavior, it can be seen that the reaction of disgust which it is alleged is felt by the majority of right-thinking men is much less easy to state in the form of a defensible value judgment. Here the disgust is perhaps more akin to the disgust which some people may feel about gluttony or snoring or wearing gaudy ties. One cannot help suspecting that the morality of an established caste is being too uninquiringly proffered here as the morality of the right-thinking majority. For is it not a strange society that is disgusted at private,

---

[1] ibid.   [2] ibid.

[3] BENTHAM, PRINCIPLES OF MORALS AND LEGISLATION 412 n. 1 (Harrison ed. 1948).

consensual, homosexual behavior, but can look with equanimity upon fox and stag hunting? Such an Establishment morality sustained a severe shock recently in Britain when the men and women in a jury box could not be persuaded to condemn *Lady Chatterley's Lover* as an obscene book.[1] It is not beyond the bounds of possibility that proper inquiry might reveal that, while the ordinary man contemplates homosexual behavior with aversion and distaste, the knowledge of its practise by others does not disgust him so deeply as Lord Devlin suspects. The disgust of the ordinary man is a dangerous guide for legislation, but judicial reliance upon notions of what disgusts the ordinary man is even more dangerous. Popular prejudice, wrote Bentham,

> serves oftener as a pretext than as a motive. It is a convenient cover for the weakness of statesmen. The ignorance of the people is the favourite argument of pusillanimity and indolence; while the real motives are prejudices from which the legislators themselves have not been able to get free. The name of the people is falsely used to justify their leaders.[2]

Lord Devlin pursues this matter of the criminal prohibition of homosexuality by saying:

> We should ask ourselves in the first instance whether, looking at it calmly and dispassionately, we regard it as a vice so abominable that its mere presence is an offence. If that is the genuine feeling of the society in which we live, I do not see how society can be denied the right to eradicate it.[3]

It is not easy to see how a judgment that uses terms such as 'abominable vice' can be made 'calmly and dispassionately'. But, passing over this, we find again in the quoted passage the unhelpful reference to a society's 'rights' to pass laws. There is no suggestion of an inquiry into the harm such homosexual behavior does to society, into the effectiveness of criminal prohibition as a check, or into the evils which may attend criminal prohibition. The only yardstick is the depth of disgust. As was seen earlier in the quotation from Bentham, the utilitarian method does not deny the

---

[1] *The Queen* v. *Penguin Books Ltd.*, [1961] CRIM. L. REV. (Eng.) 176; *The Trial of Lady Chatterley* (Rolph ed. 1961); Clark, *The Law and Lady Chatterley*, [1961] CRIM. L. REV. (Eng.) (pts. 1–2) 156, 224.

[2] BENTHAM, THEORY OF LEGISLATION 78 (Hildreth ed. 1876).

[3] DEVLIN 18.

relevance of the majority's passionate disapproval of a mode of conduct when contemplating its criminal prohibition. But the utilitarian method leads one to evaluate that disgust in terms of stated values, and, if it is found to be irrational, to bow to it only with the greatest reluctance while continuing with strenuous attempts to eradicate it through education. What is contemplated in Britain as a consequence of the removal of the criminal prohibition on acts of homosexuality done in private between consenting adults? Would there be riots in the streets? Would homosexuals be stoned? If so, why does this not happen in the great majority of European countries where such conduct is not criminally prohibited? Can it be that the British are disgusted so much more easily than the French or Italians?

To the qualification that the feeling of disgust must pass beyond the limits of tolerance, Lord Devlin adds others, *viz.*, that the law should be 'slow to act' in making criminal prohibitions on matters of morals and that 'as far as possible privacy should be respected'.[1] This is a welcome admission that the individual's freedom of choice is a value to be set against the reprobation of the right-thinking man. The law, too, Lord Devlin tells us, ought to be concerned with the minimum and not the maximum of moral behavior.[2] These reservations, however, although they appear to temper the severity of Lord Devlin's approach, are not finally reassuring, for we are offered no guide as to their comparative importance when set beside the reprobation of the 'right-minded person'.

Towards the end of his lecture Lord Devlin gathers up his arguments and illustrations into a central thesis. Society, he argues, depends for its stability upon the existence of a common morality. This is as essential to its continuance as the freedom from external aggression or from internal rebellion. It is, therefore, not possible to mark out, as the Wolfenden Committee sought to do, a sphere of private morality or private sin which can never be the law's business. Thus he notes:

The error of jurisprudence in the Wolfenden Report is caused by the search for some single principle to explain the division between crime and sin. The Report finds it in the principle that the criminal law exists for the protection of individuals. . . . But the true principle is that the law exists for the protection of society. It does not discharge its function

[1] ibid. p. 19.   [2] ibid. p. 20.

O

by protecting the individual from injury, annoyance, corruption, and exploitation; the law must protect also the institutions and the community of ideas, political and moral, without which people cannot live together. Society cannot ignore the morality of the individual any more than it can his loyalty; it flourishes on both and without either it dies.[1]

Earlier he had observed:

I think, therefore, that it is not possible to set theoretical limits to the power of the State to legislate against immorality.[2]
The suppression of vice is as much the law's business as the suppression of subversive activities; it is no more possible to define a sphere of private morality than it is to define one of private subversive activity.[3]

We may agree tentatively with Lord Devlin that any attempt to plot an area of human activity that can never be the business of the criminal law will be difficult and dangerous. Certainly privacy cannot be the sole criterion, though activities which are carried on privately are always less susceptible to law enforcement and attempts at law enforcement in such areas always lead to attendant dangers of blackmail. Lord Devlin himself gives the example of a large proportion of society choosing to get drunk every night in the privacy of their homes, his inference being that if this were to happen it would be appropriate for the criminal law to intervene. On the other hand, it is arguable that if society came to such a pass the criminal law could do little to rescue it. But, granting the point that it is possible to conceive of private, immoral practices becoming so widespread that they are as much a danger to society as armed rebellion, the inquiry cannot stop at that point.

In the first place condemnation of behavior as 'immoral' is not sufficient to establish it as a danger to society. Lord Devlin suggests that the criminal law exists for the protection of society rather than, or as well as, for the protection of individuals. But as Bentham said, 'An act cannot be detrimental to a state, but by being detrimental to some one or more of the individuals that compose it',[4] even though those individuals may not be identifiable. The 'immorality' with which the criminal law is concerned thus becomes that species of conduct which is likely to harm specific individuals or an indefinite number of unidentifiable individuals, which is capable of sufficiently precise definition to be the subject

---

[1] DEVLIN 23.   [2] ibid. p. 14.   [3] ibid. p. 15.
[4] BENTHAM, PRINCIPLES OF MORALS AND LEGISLATION 313.

of law enforcement, and which is by its nature susceptible to law enforcement—always provided that the attempt to suppress it by law enforcement will not do more harm than good. Within this context there may be wide divergences by minority groups from conventional mores which do not necessitate the intervention of the criminal law. It is after all to be hoped that one of the chief values of our 'common morality' is tolerance and that this is a value always to be weighed carefully when considering penal legislation. To contend that a minority sexual practice and subversive activity are equal attacks upon the 'common morality' and equally deserving of criminal prohibition is to neglect that painstaking inquiry into the consequences of behavior and the efficacy of prohibition which should always precede criminal enactments. What ideas are so built into our 'community of ideas' that to abandon them would mean destruction? What institutions and practices are so fundamental that their modification would mean disintegration? There is room for much disagreement here, and if history teaches us anything it is that 'fundamental institutions' and 'built-in ideas' often may decay and be modified without any consequent catastrophe for the society in question. 'A rebel', Lord Devlin tells us, 'may be rational in thinking that he is right but he is irrational if he thinks that society can leave him free to rebel.'[1]

As it stands, this is a dangerous statement. If it is confined to armed rebellion and treasonable activities it is innocuous. If it has a wider meaning, as it seems to have in the context, it is alarmingly totalitarian. Our society rightly allows many lesser modes of rebellion, if by these are meant deviations from the common morality. The Benthamite argument will always be that such deviations should go untouched unless and until they satisfy the utilitarian tests for the passage of criminal prohibition.

The weakness of Lord Devlin's position here is perhaps demonstrated by a curious passage at the end of his lecture where he discusses the crime of abortion. '[A] great many people nowadays', he complains, 'do not understand that abortion is wrong.'[2] (The use of the word 'understand' here would seem to indicate some revelation granted to the author and which many people have unfortunately not enjoyed.) Lord Devlin then goes on to admit that the law prohibiting abortion functions very imperfectly and in practice is invoked only when something has gone wrong and the

[1] DEVLIN 25.   [2] ibid. p. 24.

woman has died, or where a professional abortionist is involved.
The result is that abortion is in fact illegal because it is dangerous,
is dangerous because it is performed by the unskilled, and is
performed by the unskilled because it is illegal. It is therefore an
excellent example of more harm than good resulting from a
criminal prohibition. While admitting this aspect of the matter,
Lord Devlin's comment is that this shows 'what happens to the
law in matters of morality about which the community as a whole is
not deeply imbued with a sense of sin . . .'.[1] But since he has
admitted that many people do not think abortion is wrong, it is
evident that by morality here he does not mean commonly shared
attitudes of approval and disapproval but rather the morality of
a church group.

This is expressed most frankly in the concluding paragraph of
Lord Devlin's lecture, which deserves to be quoted in full.

A man who concedes that morality is necessary to society must
support the use of those instruments without which morality cannot be
maintained. The two instruments are those of teaching, which is
doctrine, and of enforcement, which is the law. If morals could be
taught simply on the basis that they are necessary to society, there
would be no social need for religion; it could be left as a purely personal affair. But morality cannot be taught in that way. Loyalty is not
taught in that way either. No society has yet solved the problem of how
to teach morality without religion. So the law must base itself on
Christian morals and to the limit of its ability enforce them, not simply
because they are the morals of most of us, nor simply because they are
the morals which are taught by the established Church—on these
points the law recognizes the right to dissent—but for the compelling
reason that without the help of Christian teaching the law will fail.[2]

This passage is unconvincing mainly because it is never made
clear what is meant by 'morality'. To say that 'morality is necessary
to society' seems to imply that morality is an additive which might
be removed so as to secure the collapse of society. If morality is
taken to mean widely shared attitudes of approval and disapproval
towards modes of conduct, then morality is coexistent with and
coterminous with society and to speak of morality and society as
separate entities is meaningless. The question at issue is whether
particular attitudes of disapproval toward *particular* modes of
conduct ought to be supported by the prohibitions of the criminal

[1] DEVLIN 25.   [2] ibid.

law. On this point a paraphrase of Lord Devlin's argument could perhaps fairly be put as follows: There are some particular attitudes of disapproval which are necessary for the maintenance of society. The most effective way of maintaining these attitudes is through religion. The law must therefore support the churches by adding to their influence the weight of criminal prohibition, where that can be effective. This is something of a mutual bargain. The law must enforce Christian morals because without the help of Christian teaching generally the legal system as a whole would be in danger.

This position can be attacked on various points. It provides no test at all for deciding what disapproved conduct is so dangerous to society that it deserves criminal prohibition. It makes the very large assumption that society cannot remain stable without religion, an assumption that seems to be effectively contradicted by the experience of many contemporary societies. And it makes the quite unjustified leap, even on its own premise, that the law must enforce Christian morals simply because the Christian church is generally speaking an effective upholder of the legal system. This is a point of view that in England the Anglican church has itself abandoned, having spoken out plainly in recent years in favor of the abolition of the criminal prohibitions on homosexual behavior between consenting adults and on suicide.[1]

v

It may be well in conclusion to summarize briefly the relationship between the criminal law and general moral feelings that is here advocated and to indicate finally how Lord Devlin's position endangers this view.

Fortunately for humanity there is for the most part very wide agreement in any given society about what values deserve to be protected and consequently about what constitutes bad conduct that deserves to be discouraged. There is such general agreement about the evil quality of killing, physical violence, theft and damage to property that there is no need constantly to be enunciating our scheme of values on these points. The hard core of the criminal law has thus been pretty constant in all societies at all

---

[1] Church of England Moral Welfare Council, SEXUAL OFFENDERS AND SOCIAL PUNISHMENT (1956); Report of a Committee appointed by the Archbishop of Canterbury, OUGHT SUICIDE TO BE A CRIME? (1959).

times in recorded history. With the movement of opinion there is a contraction of some areas of the criminal law and an expansion of others. So the definitions of murder and manslaughter have become narrower over the centuries while, on the other hand, the last two centuries have seen a much expanded list of offenses of fraud and dishonesty. It will be commonplace to say that these changes reflect social, economic and intellectual developments that modify the set of public values. What the Benthamite position demands is that we should not unreflectingly accept any part of our criminal law simply because it is there and has been there for a long time, and that we should not hastily enact any fresh prohibition without long and painful debate. The examination of existing law and the debate about proposed laws should be conducted by making as explicit a statement as is possible of the values that the law is designed to protect, by a careful investigation of the harm done to those values by the conduct prohibited or which it is sought to prohibit, and by a careful consideration of the probable efficacy of legal prohibition. In this debate the prevalence of feelings of disgust or revulsion in the community towards given conduct is one factor to be considered and no more than that. It can never replace careful investigation of the social consequences of conduct and criminal prohibition, and if that careful investigation returns a verdict contrary to that of the disgusted majority, then that majority feeling must be ignored, unless to ignore it would lead to disturbance of a kind more harmful than the prohibition in question. The legislator cannot be wiser than he is, but he does not have to be as stupid as the stomach of the man in the street.

This method of proceeding, that Bentham advocates, is rational only in the sense that rational argument is possible after an explicit statement of values, assuming that there is agreement about these values. The element of irrationality that inheres in any value judgment inheres in this method also and the method is advanced therefore not because it is wholly rational but because it is as rational as you can get and frankly confesses its irrational aspects.

The quarrel with Lord Devlin is thus not that he substitutes an irrational method for a wholly rational one. By suggesting that the utilitarian method purports to be a wholly rational one and by appearing to plead for a necessary element of irrationality, Lord Devlin is in fact winning a hollow victory. The objection is that

Lord Devlin is denigrating the element of rationality that is possible and is, indeed, elevating irrationality to a dangerous peak. He does this by concentrating, as the central point in his thesis, on the feelings of reprobation of the man in the street and by correspondingly denying the efficacy of the utilitarian examination of conduct which generates such feelings in the man in the street. Dean Rostow, in commenting on Lord Devlin's lecture, suggests that Lord Devlin has so qualified and modified this central point that his final position is much the same as that of those who seem to disagree with him and that the difference is at the most a shift of emphasis.[1] But it is surely a shift of emphasis that assumes vital proportions, such an enormous difference of degree that it becomes a difference of kind. For the quarrel with Lord Devlin is ultimately a quarrel about values. It is the value that he gives to the revulsions of the reasonable man that is challenged, on the ground that the acceptance of his evaluation would threaten other and more important values in our society. In opposition to Lord Devlin's quietist acceptance of majority feeling we may finally set a memorable passage from Bentham:

I suppose myself a stranger to all the common appelations of vice and virtue. I am called upon to consider human actions only with relation to their good or bad effects. I open two accounts; I pass to the account of pure profit all the pleasures, I pass to the account of loss all the pains. I faithfully weigh the interests of all parties. The man whom prejudice brands as vicious, and he whom it extols as virtuous, are, for the moment, equal in my eyes. I wish to judge prejudice itself; to weigh all actions in a new balance, in order to form a catalogue of those which ought to be permitted, and of those which ought to be forbidden.[2]

This is commended as a better text for the legislator than Lord Devlin's lecture.

[1] Rostow, *The Enforcement of Morals* 1960 CAMB. L. J. 174, 197.
[2] BENTHAM, THEORY OF LEGISLATION 55.

Principled Decision-Making and the Supreme Court

M. P. GOLDING[1]

Times change and with them the fashions, even fashions in legal thinking. In the not too distant past, some of the most respected voices among our legal theorists called for a less 'legalistic' law and minimized the role of 'logic' and 'reason' in the judicial process. It is not clear how representative of the legal community the proponents of such views were; they seemed to have regarded themselves as voices crying in the wilderness. Nor is it always clear, to me at least, what it was that was being attacked and what it was that was being advanced. Yet it is not uncommon for these views to be taken as the typical American contribution to jurisprudence. Although no American can fail to be influenced in some measure by these conceptions, it is interesting to notice that some of our most distinguished writers have called for a return to reason in law, especially in high places, i.e., the Supreme Court.

Perhaps this is the 'inevitable reaction, long overdue'.[2] Even Judge Arnold, whose hard-boiled realism and rapier-like style have suffered no decline, seems to accept 'reason' as an 'ideal'. He has, nevertheless, severe reservations that 'reason would replace the conflicting views now present on the Court if the Court had more

[1] M. P. Golding, B.A. 1949 U.C.L.A., Ph.D. 1959, Columbia Univ., is Associate Professor of Philosophy at Columbia University. The essay here is reprinted from 63 COLUM. L. REV. 35 (1963). Mr. Golding's other writings on legal philosophy include: *Kelsen and the Concept of 'Legal System'* 47 ARCHIV FÜR RECHTS-UND SOZIALPHILOSOPHIE 355 (1961); *Principled Decision-Making* 73 ETHICS 247 (1963); NATURE OF LAW (ed. 1966); *History of the Philosophy of Law* in ENCYCLOPEDIA OF PHILOSOPHY 254–64 (Edwards ed. 1967). (Footnote by editor.)

[2] Henkin, *Some Reflections on Current Constitutional Controversy* 109 U. PA. L. REV. 637, 654 (1961).

time for the "maturing of collective thought".[1] Whether the Court is overworked is a question that probably can best be answered by the demigods who inhabit our Mount Olympus, and whether diminishing its workload will result in opinions grounded more in reason and principle is certainly problematical. Few would deny that such a result is desirable; however, it is no easy task to formulate the nature of such opinions or the criteria whereby we could determine whether such a result had been achieved.

A notable undertaking along these lines is the Holmes Lecture of Professor Herbert Wechsler.[2] This lecture has already occasioned a minor literature, in part focusing on matters of interest to constitutional lawyers and in part focusing on matters of a more theoretical nature.[3] Although its main thrust may be of a more practical scope, no one can deny that Professor Wechsler's lecture raises important issues of jurisprudence and legal philosophy.[4] In what follows I shall attempt to deal with some of these issues. Notwithstanding their broad scope, I shall in general confine

---

[1] Arnold, *Professor Hart's Theology* 73 HARV. L. REV. 1298, 1312 (1960). See also Griswold, *The Supreme Court, 1959 Term—Foreword: Of Time and Attitudes—Professor Hart and Judge Arnold* 74 HARV. L. REV. 81 (1960); Hart, *The Supreme Court, 1958 Term—Foreword: The Time Chart of the Justices* 73 HARV. L. REV. 84 (1959).

[2] Wechsler, *Toward Neutral Principles of Constitutional Law* 73 HARV. L. REV. 1 (1959), reprinted, with some introductory remarks, in WECHSLER, PRINCIPLES, POLITICS, AND FUNDAMENTAL LAW 3–48 (1961) [hereafter cited as WECHSLER, page references to the book].

[3] Miller & Howell, *The Myth of Neutrality in Constitutional Adjudication* 27 U. CHI. L. REV. 661 (1960); Mueller & Schwartz, *The Principle of Neutral Principles* 7 U.C.L.A. L. REV. 571 (1960).

[4] I do not think that the full significance of Professor Wechsler's ideas has been exhausted by the critical articles I have seen. The article by Mueller & Schwartz, cited above n. 3 and hereafter cited as Mueller & Schwartz, is a helpful one. I cannot feel the same about the article by Miller & Howell there cited. My paper was completed before the publication of Dean Rostow's Cohen Lecture in which Professor Wechsler is subjected to severe criticism. See Rostow, *American Legal Realism and the Sense of the Profession* 34 ROCKY MT. L. REV. 123 (1962). I think that my paper goes some way toward clarifying some if not all of the issues that he raises. Admittedly, the nature of principled judicial decision is a complex topic; many of its facets are hardly touched here. Regarding Dean Rostow's article, I shall make only a few remarks. First, I do not think that the model of principled decision that I outline—and which I think is the nub of Professor Wechsler's view—is at all identical with 'mechanical jurisprudence'. Secondly, even Dean Rostow implies, but does not make explicit, various standards that ought to control the *procedures* of his 'result-oriented' jurisprudence. It would seem that the explication of those standards would follow the lines that I present here. Thirdly, it is 'results' that we expect from the courts; not mere results, however, but *just* results. We cannot understand this except in terms of 'principle'.

myself to the Supreme Court, partly because Professor Wechsler
so restricts himself, but mainly because it occupies a special
position in our legal system—a position which, I shall try to show,
makes it particularly susceptible to the demands he makes of it.

I. NEUTRALITY AND PRINCIPLED DECISION-MAKING

If I do not misinterpret Professor Wechsler's lecture, my approach
to these issues differs somewhat from his. Nevertheless, I believe
that without overstretching Professor Wechsler's language what I
have to say can be fairly found in it; therefore I shall follow the
main lines of his exposition. The differences between our
approaches to these great issues of legal philosophy—if there
really are any differences—arise from my difficulty in comprehend-
ing the meaning of the expression 'general and neutral principles
of law'. In one place, Professor Wechsler speaks of 'generality' and
'neutrality' as 'surely the main qualities of law'.[1] Surely Professor
Wechsler is not here endorsing Austin's exclusion of particular
commands from the realm of law.[2] Although it may be that
generality and neutrality are in *some* sense inherent in the very

[1] WECHSLER 23.

[2] See AUSTIN, THE PROVINCE OF JURISPRUDENCE DETERMINED AND USES OF THE
STUDY OF JURISPRUDENCE 24 (Hart ed. 1954):

'A law is a command which obliges a person or persons. But, as contra-
distinguished or opposed to an occasional or particular command, a law is a
command which obliges a person or persons, and obliges *generally* to acts or
forebearances of a *class*.'

'In language more popular but less distinct and precise, a law is a command
which obliges a person or persons to a *course* of conduct.'

Austin gives the following example (ibid. p. 120):

'If Parliament prohibited simply the exportation of corn, either for a given
period or indefinitely, it would establish a law or rule: a *kind* or *sort* of acts
being determined by the command, and acts of that kind or sort being *generally*
forbidden. But an order issued by Parliament to meet an impending scarcity, and
stopping the exportation of corn *then shipped and in port*, would not be a law or
rule, though issued by the sovereign legislature.'

Compare Kelsen's remarks:

'But there is no doubt that law does not consist of general norms only. Law
includes individual norms, i.e., norms which determine the behavior of one
individual in one non-recurring situation and which therefore are valid only for
one particular case and may be obeyed or applied only once. Such norms are
"law" because they are parts of the legal order as a whole in exactly the same
sense as those general norms on the basis of which they have been created.'

KELSEN, GENERAL THEORY OF LAW AND THE STATE 38 (1946); see Golding,
KELSEN AND THE CONCEPT OF 'LEGAL SYSTEM' 57 ARCHIV FÜR RECHTS-UND
SOZIALPHILOSOPHIE 355 (1961).

concept of law, whereby we distinguish a legal order from a lawless tyranny, not each and every rule of law need be 'general' and 'neutral'. It is, in fact, impossible to tell by inspection of a given legal rule or principle,[1] in isolation from the context of its application, whether it is 'neutral' or 'general' in any significant sense. Trivially, almost every legal rule is 'general' and there are also levels of generality.[2] Scores of legal rules, purposely designed to favor one party or group over another, are 'un-neutral' with respect to social advantage. Since mere inspection does not reveal whether a rule or principle is 'general' or 'neutral' in the sense required by Professor Wechsler's argument, the key to neutrality and generality must be found elsewhere.[3]

This key is to be found in the *process* or *procedure* of judicial decision-making. The question that uncovers these qualities is: what are the distinguishing characteristics of principled decision-making?[4] I shall attempt to answer this question in outline and, in so doing, indicate how generality and neutrality are built into the very concept of 'principled decision' as embodying his notion of neutral principles of law. That he has in mind also the process or procedure of judicial decision-making may be seen from his contrast between 'courts of law' and a 'naked power organ'.[5]

A. The analogue in moral philosophy

The above question has its analogue in the history of moral philosophy. To be sure, there are differences between moral and legal reasoning; however, the similarities, especially in regard to

---

[1] 'Rules' and 'principles' are often distinguished, but I shall not over complicate my exposition by doing so here.

[2] Mueller & Schwartz p. 577, quite correctly drives home the question, 'how general is general?'

[3] Professor Wechsler quite rightly rejects 'impartial', 'disinterested', and 'impersonal' as substitutes for his adjective 'neutral'. WECHSLER xiii. What is of crucial interest to the community is not what the judge *feels* about the parties or the case before him, although this is not uninfluential, but rather how he administers the law. There are standards of judicial impartiality.

[4] The specific question which Professor Wechsler poses is: 'what, if any, are the standards to be followed in interpretation [?] Are there, indeed, any criteria that both the Supreme Court and those who undertake to praise or condemn its judgments are morally and intellectually obligated to support?' ibid. pp. 15–16. The *kind* of answer which he gives is interesting. He does not say what these standards or criteria are, but rather tells us something *about* them, namely, they must be 'general' and 'neutral'. The approach, then, is 'formalistic', although he assumes a background of democratic values. [5] ibid. p. 27.

Professor Wechsler's treatment of judicial neutrality, are sufficient to justify a brief discussion here. One can not disregard the
fact that Professor Wechsler elaborates his ideal of the judicial
process within the scope of the broad ethical conceptions of
political theory.

In no analysis of moral notions does principle play a greater role
than in Immanuel Kant's. He rejected the view that the rightness
or wrongness of an act is determinable by a straightforward
reference to its consequences. The 'moral value' of an act, says
Kant, 'does not depend on the reality of the object of the action but
merely on the principle of volition by which the action is done
without any regard to the objects of the faculty of desire'.[1] Rather,
two of the necessary constituents of a morally right action are:
(1) that it be done on principle; and (2) in conformity with a principle.[2] Not every putative principle, however, is a genuine moral
principle. It is the function of the various formulations of the
Categorical Imperative to serve as a test of putative principles.

It would be out of place to give here an extended account of
Kant's ethical theory, a theory not without its serious difficulties.
For my present concerns we need consider only a few points. In
developing his conception of a genuine moral principle Kant
appeals to a very simple consideration. Every moral decision makes
a universal claim: if an act is right for me, it must be right for
every similarly situated person. For me arbitrarily to make an
exception of myself is clearly the very negation of principle.[3] So
also, to distinguish some individual, or class of individuals,
arbitrarily and thus claim that it is right for me to treat him, or
them, differently from the way I treat others, is the very *negation*
of principle. To act in such ways is not to act on principle or in
conformity with a principle, and to decide to act in such ways is
not to make a principled decision. What Kant is doing in developing his notion of a genuine moral principle is to build into it—or
rather show how there are built into it—the notions of generality
and neutrality in one of their modes.

[1] KANT, *Foundations of the Metaphysics of Morals*, in CRITIQUE OF PRACTICAL
REASON 61 (Beck ed. 1949).

[2] Kant also requires that it be done for the sake of principle, i.e., out of a sense
of duty. But this is not relevant here.

[3] How this statement is related to the idea expressed in the previous sentence
need not concern us here. See generally Edgley, *Impartiality and Consistency* 37
PHILOSOPHY 158 (1962); Monro, *Impartiality and Consistency* 36 ibid. p. 161 (1961).

The obvious question elicited by Kant's view is: what are reasonable grounds for difference of treatment? This question raises a tremendously difficult problem for Kant. Most people would say that in determining whether I am permitted to make an exception of myself or some other individual in a given case it is legitimate to appeal to the consequences that my action would have; but this way is barred to Kant. Nevertheless, Kant's notion is not without its practical importance, for it throws a 'definite *onus probandi* on the man who applies to another a treatment of which he would complain if applied to himself . . .'.[1] It is important, also, to recognize the scope of Kant's notion: it is not restricted to differences made in respect of *persons*. Rather, it applies equally to *circumstances* or situations. Thus, moral action, or principled moral decision-making, must not only be 'impartial' with respect to persons, but also must be 'impartial' with respect to similar circumstances. No putative principle of action can be a genuine moral principle if it allows me to act differently in similar circumstances, unless a significant distinction between the circumstances can be shown to exist. Here again, the *onus probandi* falls on the person who would make such a distinction. As a consequence, consistency, in one of its modes, is built into the concept of principled moral decision-making.

It is evident that, for Kant, one's mere likes and dislikes cannot be the ground of moral action or principled moral decision-making. But insofar as Kant pretends to be analyzing our common moral notions, I think that he goes wrong in believing that our likes and dislikes, or as we should say now, our values, are irrelevant to moral action and principled decision-making.[2] Nevertheless, he is correct in his rejection of *mere* likes and dislikes as the basis of morality.

The same rejection is found in Bentham, whose utilitarian moral philosophy is quite different from Kant's. The principle of sympathy and antipathy, namely, 'that principle which approves of

---

[1] SIDGWICK, THE METHOD OF ETHICS 380 (6th ed. 1907); cf. WECHSLER 155 (remarks on the issues of the Nuremberg Trial).

[2] There certainly are occasions when it would be silly to say that one ought not to take one's likes and dislikes into account. As has often been pointed out, it would generally be foolish for a man to ignore his likes and dislikes in deciding whether to marry a certain woman. Kant might hold, however, that such a decision is morally neither right nor wrong; but it is not difficult to think of situations in which a couple might have an obligation to marry, according to Kant.

certain actions . . . merely because a man finds himself disposed to approve or disapprove of them' is

a principle in name [rather] than in reality: it is not a positive principle of itself, so much as a term employed to signify the negation of all principle. What one expects to find in a principle is something that points out some external consideration, as a means of warranting and guiding the internal sentiments of approbation and disapprobation: this expectation is but ill fulfilled by a proposition, which does neither more nor less than hold up each of those sentiments as a ground and standard for itself.[1]

Thus, Bentham, whose universalistic ethical hedonism assigns to likes and dislikes a central role in moral judgment, is at one with Kant in rejecting the method of *ad hoc* evaluation.

In operating the hedonic calculus, Bentham tells us that we must 'take an account of the *number* of persons whose interests appear to be concerned . . .'.[2] In so doing, each person is to be considered impartially. 'Each is to count for one, and no one for more than one.' Bentham nowhere justifies this impartiality. Clearly, it is not deducible from the Principle of Utility (the greatest happiness principle). Rather, he assumes it, because without it the Principle of Utility would not be a principle at all. Part of the meaning of principled decision-making is that persons or similar circumstances are to be treated in the same manner, unless a relevant distinction is shown to exist.

B. *The characteristics of principled decision-making*

In what follows I shall develop more fully the nature of principled decision, but it may be useful to summarize a few of its salient features at this juncture. A decision or judgment is principled only when it is guided by some 'external consideration', i.e., a guiding principle that contributes to the deliberation on the case. Such a principle is a *reason* (or part of the reasons) for the decision. It cannot be a reason for the decision unless it determines, at least to some extent, the outcome of the process of deliberation. This means that a principle cannot be so flexible as to allow for free-wheeling discretion. Furthermore, in applying a principle, the

---

[1] BENTHAM, AN INTRODUCTION TO THE PRINCIPLES OF MORALS AND LEGISLATION 15–16 (1823 ed.).
[2] ibid. p. 31.

instant case must be treated as an instance of a more inclusive class of cases, i.e., the case at hand is treated in a certain manner because it is held to be proper to treat cases of its type in that manner. In this way every principled judgment makes, or rests upon, a universal, or general, claim. When the given case is treated differently from the way in which it is held to be proper to treat cases of its type the decision-maker is required to distinguish it from these cases. Here, too, such distinctions must be drawn in a principled way: it is not sufficient to justify the different treatment of persons or circumstances simply on the ground that one is dealing with one person or circumstance rather than another. That is to say, in principled decision-making one is permitted to make exceptions of this sort only insofar as they fall within a class of cases considered appropriate for the different treatment.

Although the nature of distinction-making in principled decision-making is a complex topic deserving separate, detailed treatment, brief discussion about it is in order here. First, it is obvious that in many cases people disagree on whether there exists significant enough differences between apparently similar persons or circumstances to permit their being treated in disparate ways. But this fact in no way affects the account of principled decision I am presenting. This account does not assume or require that people agree in their judgments. It is quite consistent with it that two parties should be opposed in their judgments and yet both be principled. Second, when such distinctions are made, the criteria for determining which differences are significant or relevant must be drawn in a principled way.[1] Not just *any* distinction—which can always be found—will do.

Briefly put, the requirements for principled decision are: (1) that a reason for the disposition of the case be given; and (2) that the case be so decided because it is held to be proper to decide cases of its type in this way. It is in the meeting of the requirements for principled decision that the qualities of neutrality and generality are achieved. Naturally, I have presented them only in their barest outline. To do more would be to broach the most intricate problems in the analysis of moral reasoning. I have also formulated these requirements in a most general and broad way, so as to be acceptable to a wide variety of moral theories. It is

[1] See Mueller & Schwartz pp. 578–80.

worth mentioning that these requirements are part of a minimal analysis of the concept of 'distributive justice'.

It is important to recognize the fact that the above requirements constitute necessary conditions of a principled decision. I do not doubt that more is required in order to explicate the notion of a *justified* decision. It is especially important to recognize that I have been discussing the way one ought to go about justifying a judgment, and not the psychological process of reaching a judgment.[1] One's decision is principled if one supports it by reasons or reasoning of this kind. Of course, in situations in which people are expected to make principled decisions it is expected that the psychological process will accord with the above procedures. (It is what we expect of a principled man.) And it seems to me that this does happen at least sometimes. On the other hand, even when a decision is a so-called 'guts reaction' it might be a mistake to underrate the role of these procedures, for they may have been 'internalized'.

From the above delineation of principled decision-making it follows that the typical kind of argument that will be employed in both deliberation and criticism is that of *reductio ad absurdum*. One's judgment is 'tested not only by the instant application but by others that the principles imply'.[2] When a principle is advanced in support of a decision and this principle would necessarily permit some given case to be treated in a manner different from the way in which by hypothesis it must be treated, one is forced either to distinguish the cases or, failing this, to reject the principle. Rationality, of which principled decision is an element, requires pragmatic consistency of this sort.[3] Obviously, one's decisions lose their moral force when we indulge in inconsistency. Professor Wechsler quite correctly characterizes the criteria of principled decision as ones which we are 'morally and intellectually obligated to support'.[4]

In contrast with principled decision-making is the method of *ad hoc* evaluation. Professor Wechsler gives numerous examples from our constitutional politics, past and present, of the *ad hoc* type of evaluation. Whether, and in what circumstances, this

---

[1] See generally WASSERSTROM, THE JUDICIAL DECISION 26–38 (1961).

[2] WECHSLER 21.

[3] Another way of attacking the reasoning behind a judgment is to call into question the alleged facts that it supposes; but I am not concerned with this here. [4] WECHSLER 16.

method is to be deplored is beyond the scope of this paper. The analysis of principled political decision-making is, of course, a complex topic. The factor of *compromise*, which plays such an important part, would seem to add another dimension to the treatment that has been given so far. I recognize that compromise may also be an element in judicial decision in a number of ways, but this would require separate consideration beyond the scope of this article.

II. PRINCIPLED JUDICIAL DECISION-MAKING

Previously, I alluded to the fact that principled judicial decision-making is both similar to and different from principled moral decision-making. The truth of the matter as I see it is that with two provisos principled judicial decision is formally congruent with principled moral decision. The two provisos are, first, that a legal system is able to stipulate in a large measure the principles that must be employed in deliberation and, second, a legal system may stipulate what grounds are and what grounds are not legitimate grounds for the different treatment of persons or circumstances. So, for example, a legal system may stipulate that mere racial difference is (or is not) an acceptable ground for the different treatment of individuals in certain types of cases.

Within the scope of these limitations it still remains possible to speak of principled judicial decision-making. Our legal system has no privileged status. Not only are systems possible that differ from ours in content, but so also can principled decisions occur within the framework of such systems. For in such systems courts can function as 'courts of law' and may embody in their procedures 'the main constituent of the judicial process . . .'.[1] Thus, when a legal system does make racial (or other) differences relevant, it is still possible for principled judicial decision to exist, so long as the requirements for principled decision are met within the terms of the law that the system lays down. Principled legal judgment is not so much a matter of content as it is of form. Neutrality and generality are to be found not in the content of the law but in its application or administration. Principled judicial decision-making is possible in a tyranny. This is worth stressing, if only because Professor Wechsler's ideas move within a liberal democratic context. But I should also suppose that if we range states along a

[1] ibid. p. 21.

P

scale—'ideal' democracy at one end and 'ideal' tyranny at the other—there is a point of no return, a point at which the form and content of the tyranny become inseparable, making it impossible to speak of principled judicial judgment.[1]

A legal system, then, may broadly fix the starting-points of deliberation and the criteria of relevant distinctions. It is the lesson of American jurisprudence that this fixity has its limits and that a degree of discretion is inevitable. But we still demand that, so far as possible, courts be principled in their exercises of this discretion. This applies with greatest force to the Supreme Court when it has constitutional questions before it. Lower courts often have no choice once the higher courts have spoken. (One need only think of the different results in cases after *Brown* v. *Board of Educ.* had the Court affirmed the separate-but-equal doctrine in regard to public education.) But the Supreme Court, when ruling on constitutional issues, has no higher guide than the Constitution itself. Of course, there are times when 'the relative compulsion of the language of the Constitution, of history and precedent' do combine to make the answer clear; but frequently they do not. Professor Wechsler maintains, and I agree, that the due process clauses ought to be read as 'a compendious affirmation of the basic values of a free society . . .'.[2] Furthermore, it is possible to overstate the specificity of other provisions of the Bill of Rights addressed to more specific problems. They, too, must be read as 'an affirmation of the special values they embody rather than as statements of a finite rule of law . . .'.[3] Constitutional interpretation by the Supreme Court, then, most closely approximates moral decision-making, and when it is principled it will rest 'on reasons with respect to all the issues in the case, reasons that in their generality and neutrality transcend any immediate result that is involved'[4] in the way outlined above.

I should now like to consider in detail some further points in connection with Professor Wechsler's exposition. But before I turn to Professor Wechsler's allusion to some opinions of Holmes as

[1] It seems, again, that by contrast democratic states are the most moral, for not only must they adhere to the requirements of principled decision-making in the courts but also in the legislature. I shall not develop this point here, however, but simply point out that even in such case it is plain that there may be 'partial' or 'un-neutral' laws.   [2] WECHSLER 24, 26.

[3] ibid. It is obvious that Professor Wechsler is no 'strict constructionist'.

[4] ibid. p. 27.

possible exemplars of principled judicial decision and examine some aspects of Professor Wechsler's appraisals of review, I think it important to make clear why the question that forms the subject of his paper is the same for the critics as it is for the Court.

The reason is quite simple. The ground rules for the *intelligent* discussion of any issue—and, as Professor Wechsler correctly indicates, what he says is true not only of a critique of the Court, but 'applies whenever a determination is in question, a determination that it is essential to make either way'[1]—are exactly the same as the general requirements for principled decision-making. Consider for a moment what distinguishes *constructive* criticism from useless criticism, what distinguishes a discussion that is worthy of one's participation from a discussion that is not, and the truth of this will be apparent. No criticism is worth listening to unless it is constructive to some degree. The contrast with this is criticism of the mere 'I like it' or 'I don't like it' variety. Autobiographical remarks such as these are of interest only when it is important to know what someone's preferences are. But they mark the end of discussion, not its beginning; they function as 'conversation stoppers'. Discussion ends when we come to the bedrock of differences in preference, but it cannot begin there.[2] Constructive criticism and useful discussion can proceed only when reasons for a judgment are advanced that not only include but go beyond the case at hand.[3] If these reasons, or principles, are not ruled out *ab initio* as unacceptable (e.g., in law when contrary principles are stipulated), then debate typically continues in the *reductio ad absurdum* manner. Would the critic treat such and such similar cases in the same way as he treats the instant case? If not, how does he distinguish them? Failing this, must he not reject the reason or principle on which his judgment rests? Just as a factual proposition is shown to be false if it implies a false statement, so also is a practical principle shown to be unacceptable if it leads to pragmatic inconsistencies, or when it would require treating some given case

---

[1] ibid. p. 16.

[2] See BENTHAM (cited above p. 214 n. 1), p. 6. Of course, even when this point is reached, the argument may continue over the *facts* of the issue. See p. 216 n. 2, above.

[3] I think that Professor Wechsler goes too far when he says that an attack upon a judgment of the Court involves the assertion that the reasons which prevailed with the tribunal are *irrelevant*. WECHSLER 16. The reasons may have been relevant but inconclusive.

in a way in which *ex hypothesi* it may not be treated. Nothing that I have said in this paragraph is incompatible with the view that all our judgments rest ultimately on our preferences, and that differences in judgment rest on fundamental and perhaps ineradicable differences in preference.[1]

The utilization of the above type of *reductio* argument is well illustrated by Mr. Justice Holmes's dissent (his first as a member of the Court) in *Northern Sec. Co.* v. *United States*,[2] to which Professor Wechsler refers.[3] The question in this case was whether, under the Sherman Act, 'it is unlawful, at any stage of the process, if several men unite to form a corporation for the purpose of buying more than half the stock of each of two competing interstate railroad companies [Northern Pacific and Great Northern], if they form the corporation, and the corporation buys the stock.'[4] A majority of the Court, emphasizing the power of Congress to regulate interstate commerce, held that such activity is unlawful, given the effect that such an arrangement is bound to have upon competition between the railroads. Holmes, in his brilliant way, proceeded to give the Court a lesson in statutory construction, in how 'to read English intelligently'.[5] His language sparkles with 'neutrality'. In this case, involving J. Pierpoint Morgan and James J. Hill, Holmes wrote that 'we must read the words before us [the Sherman Act] as if the question were whether two small exporting grocers should go to jail'.[6] He rejected the argument of counsel for the Government as leading to the unacceptable conclusion that there is 'no part of the conduct of life with which, on similar principles, Congress might not interfere. . . . Commerce depends upon population, but Congress could not, on that ground, undertake to regulate marriage and divorce.'[7] The Government's principle must be rejected, for it would lead to treating a case in a way in which it may not be *ex hypothesi*. Driving home this point, he continues:

---

[1] It is often incorrectly thought that aesthetic evaluation, which seems most intimately and immediately bound up with our likes and dislikes, is an exception to the kind of principled decision which ought to apply to the courts and their critics. But that this is not so may be seen from the distinction we draw between good and bad art critics. The evaluations of the bad critic are always *ad hoc*, a mere expression of likes and dislikes. The evaluations of the good critic are constructive. He gives reasons for his judgment and in so doing shows how the work of art may be improved, even though he might not have the talent to do it better himself.   [2] 193 U.S. 197, 400 (1904).   [3] WECHSLER 33.
[4] 193 U.S. at 401.   [5] ibid.   [6] ibid. p. 402.   [7] ibid. pp. 403 and 402.

This act is construed by the government to affect the purchasers of shares in two railroad companies because of the effect it may have, or, if you like, is certain to have, upon the competition of these roads. If such a remote result of the exercise of an ordinary incident of property and personal freedom is enough to make that exercise unlawful, there is hardly any transaction concerning commerce between the States that may not be made a crime by the finding of a jury or a court.[1]

Again, an unacceptable conclusion. Furthermore, Holmes writes: 'If I am [wrong], then a partnership between two stage drivers who had been competitors in driving across a state line, or two merchants once engaged in rival commerce among the states, whether made after or before the act, if now continued, is a crime.'[2] This also is too hard for Holmes to swallow, and when a principle leads to constitutionally impermissible conclusions it must be rejected. We see Holmes in this dissent playing the part of the critic, rejecting the argument of the Government and the judgment of the majority because in part they fail to adhere to the requirements for principled decision. It should be mentioned that it is one thing for the critic to show that some given decision is not principled and another to show that it is wrong. The superficial reader of Professor Wechsler's article is liable to get the impression that there is no difference between the two.

Perhaps one of the most difficult theoretical points in Professor Wechsler's paper concerns the place of values in principled judicial decision-making. I am not sure that I have understood his position on this or, if I follow it, that I agree with what he has to say. Before attacking this issue head-on, it is useful to consider an example provided by Holmes's dissent in the *Abrams* case,[3] to which, together with his dissent in *Gitlow*,[4] Professor Wechsler invidiously compares[5] the main opinion in *Sweezy* v. *New Hampshire*.[6]

It seems that for Holmes the crucial point in *Abrams* was that of intent. It is, he says,

too plain to be denied that [the leaflet urges] . . . curtailment of production of things necessary to the prosecution of the war. . . . But to make the conduct criminal, that statute requires that it should be 'with intent

[1] ibid. p. 403.   [2] ibid. p. 410.
[3] *Abrams* v. *United States*, 250 U.S. 616, 624 (1919).
[4] *Gitlow* v. *New York*, 268 U.S. 652, 672 (1925).
[5] WECHSLER 35–36.   [6] 354 U.S. 234 (1957).

by such curtailment to cripple or hinder the United States in the prosecution of the war.' It seems to me that no such intent is proved.[1]

Passing on to the question of the freedom of speech, Holmes argues that

it is only the present danger of immediate evil or an intent to bring it about that warrants Congress in setting a limit to the expression of opinion where private rights are not concerned . . . [B]y the same reasoning that would justify punishing persuasion to murder, the United States constitutionally may punish speech that produces or is intended to produce a clear and imminent danger that it will bring about forthwith certain substantive evils that the United States constitutionally may seek to prevent.[2]

Professor Wechsler, apparently conceding that Holmes's position is framed in terms of 'neutral and general principles', queries in a footnote: 'Is it possible, however, that persuasion to murder is only punishable constitutionally if the design is that the murder be committed "forthwith"?'[3] This is instructive, aside from the common law point being made, for it shows that even what Professor Wechsler takes to be a 'neutral principle' may be objectionable. It is important to keep in mind that Holmes regarded *Abrams* as dealing with the expression of political opinion, and, although stating that 'persecution for the expression of opinions seems to me perfectly logical',[4] he believed that our Constitution opts for a particular value. This is the 'theory of our Constitution', which is 'an experiment, as all life is an experiment'.[5] This 'theory' is that 'the ultimate good desired is better reached by free trade in ideas— that the best test of truth is the power of the thought to get itself accepted in the competition of the market. . . .'[6] This is the root of the 'clear and present danger' restriction.[7] Holmes, therefore, asserts that 'while that experiment is part of our system I think that we should be eternally vigilant against attempts to check the expression of opinions that we loathe and believe to be fraught with death, unless they so imminently threaten . . .'.[8] To this should be

---

[1] 250 U.S. p. 626.   [2] ibid. pp. 628 and 627.   [3] WECHSLER 35–36 n. 83.
[4] 250 U.S. p. 630.   [5] ibid.   [6] ibid.
[7] See HAND, THE BILL OF RIGHTS 58–59 (1958):

'The only ground for this exception which I have ever heard is that during the interval between the provocation and its realization correctives may arise, and that it is better to accept the risk that they may not be sufficient than to suppress what, however guilty in itself, may prove innocuous.'

Did Homer nod in *Abrams*?   [8] 250 U.S. at 630.

added Holmes's dissenting remark in *Gitlow*: 'If, in the long run, the beliefs expressed in proletarian dictatorship are destined to be accepted by the dominant forces of the community, the only meaning of free speech is that they should be given their chance and have their way.'[1]

The *Abrams* dissent illustrates at least one way in which values enter into constitutional interpretation. It is important not to press too far his analogy between expression of opinion and persuasion to murder. Aside from the matter of intent, the essential problem *Abrams* poses is that of putting two values in the balance for the purpose of deciding the case. On the one side we have national security, which it is the legitimate function of government to protect, and on the other the 'theory of our Constitution'. It is not a question of Holmes's 'choosing' these values. (I think that the use of the phrase 'choosing a value' in legal writing is unfortunate.) The Constitution, so to speak, has chosen them, in Holmes's understanding. And he further takes it that the Constitution chooses to risk the 'experiment' which the 'theory of our Constitution' involves. He sees that risk as going as far as a 'clear and present danger' to national security. It is not, as Judge Learned Hand implies, that these opinions 'may prove innocuous'. They may, in fact, be 'destined to be accepted by the dominant forces of the community'. It is, moreover, 'perfectly logical' to suppress them. But this is not the 'theory of our Constitution'; one can not maintain this 'theory' *with all its attendant risks* and at the same time permit the suppression of opinion in the name of national security. Of course, there is a limit—that of 'clear and present danger'. To breach this limit, however, is to subvert the 'theory', the value of freedom of expression, which the Constitution has chosen.

I am not here concerned with whether Holmes's reading of the 'theory of our Constitution' is correct: I am sure that many constitutional lawyers would find it disputable. I am concerned, rather, with what it illustrates, namely, that constitutional interpretation does not occur within a vacuum of values. By this I do not simply mean that judges bring with them a personal set of values or that the determination of constitutional or other questions frequently reflects a 'choice of values'; my meaning is, rather, that affirmations of various values are written into the

[1] 268 U.S. at 673.

Constitution, 'values that must be given weight in legislation and administration at the risk of courting trouble in the courts'.[1] The Court, then, cannot avoid taking these values into account in constitutional adjudication. To do otherwise would be to fail to adhere to the requirements for principled decision-making. These values supply *substantive* criteria of principled judgment. We are entitled to reject any principle of decision that, if acted upon, would lead to the frustrating of accepted values. But this is workable only when values are not in competition.

Is it possible to speak of principled judicial decision-making when more than one value is at stake, when it is impossible for a plurality of values to be fulfilled in equal measure? Certainly one would like to emphasize together with Professor Wechsler 'the role of reason and of principle in the judicial, as distinguished from the legislative or executive, appraisal of conflicting values . . .'.[2] But what is that role? Certainly one would like to agree with him that the virtue or demerit in a judgment turns 'entirely on the reasons that support it and their adequacy to maintain any choice of values it decrees . . .'.[3] But what is the test of adequacy? I cannot see much in the way of an answer to these questions in Professor Wechsler's lecture.

The above questions raise the most complicated problems in the analysis of legal reasoning. I fail to grasp Professor Wechsler's position if it consists in the statement that one ought to, or even can, supply 'neutral principles' for 'choosing' between competing values. I can, of course, choose between two competing values by reference to a third value which is more comprehensive or supreme, that is, when there is already an ordering of values. Assuming such an ordering, it seems to make sense to speak of 'reasoned choice between competing values'. Although I doubt it, perhaps this is precisely what Professor Wechsler is implying in his comment on the 'preferred position' controversy when he says that it has virtue 'insofar as it recognizes that some ordering of social values is essential; that all cannot be given equal weight, if the Bill of Rights is to be maintained'.[4] But it is difficult to see how the ordering itself is to be made on 'neutral principles'.

Perhaps, however, even lacking such an ordering of values, all is not lost for principled decision-making. Another brief glance at Holmes's dissent in *Abrams* will illustrate what I have in mind.

[1] WECHSLER 26.   [2] ibid. p. 23.   [3] ibid. p. 27.   [4] ibid. p. 35.

Two values were involved in the deciding of this case—national security and freedom of expression—neither of which could be ignored. What Holmes did was to make his best judgment as to the point beyond which one cannot go if the value of national security is to be maintained, as he believed it must, when it competes with the value of free expression, which on his understanding of the Constitution ordinarily has precedence. That point is 'clear and imminent danger', which now functions as a standard or criterion to be applied in situations when these two values are in competition. This standard, though clearly and eminently vague, will now function for him as a principle of decision in this and other cases of its type. We may apply to this principle the type of critical evaluation that I have heretofore adumbrated.

Thus, when, in deciding a case, a tribunal is faced with two competing values and there is no good reason to be advanced for preferring one value over another, so that the preference given to one value is entirely arbitrary, if you please, we may still require that the tribunal formulate a standard or criterion that shall function as a principle of decision in this and other cases of its type. This principle is general in the sense that it covers but also transcends the instant case. It is not, of course, inherently 'neutral' in any sense, except that there may be neutrality in its application i.e., it may be applied in a principled way. Would the decision-maker apply this principle in such-and-such similar cases? If not, how does he distinguish the cases? Failing this, must he not reject the principle? What I have just said obtains not only in cases in which there are two competing values, but also, more broadly, in cases in which there are two (or more) countervailing considerations, e.g., two conflicting principles, which must both be taken into account such that the presence of one of them does not in all cases rule out the applicability of the other. Granted that both such countervailing considerations have weight, the decision-maker is required to draw a line fixing their limits.

It seems to me that the aspect of principled decision I have just described is not so remote from what Professor Wechsler demands of the Court in his appraisal of judicial review. To this extent his position seems perfectly intelligible, although I confess my inability to understand him if he requires that the 'choice of values' itself be made on 'general and neutral principles'. I am also uncertain that I understand how Professor Wechsler can demand that courts decide 'on grounds of adequate neutrality and generality' and at the same time maintain that courts should decide 'only the case they have before them'.[1] There is, of course, an obvious sense in which a court *does* decide *only* the case that is before it. But if a tribunal is to be principled, what it must do in essence is to anticipate the kinds of criticism that might be made of its decision. It must attempt to explain away at least the more apparent inconsistencies. In doing this the tribunal, in effect, 'decides' cases which are not before it. I think that we will see that this is precisely what Professor Wechsler is demanding in some of his appraisals of judicial review. Before turning to some phases of these appraisals, I should like to raise a question that I think is of importance for the subsequent discussion. I have argued that, in a case the resolution of which depends upon taking into account countervailing considerations, principled judgment requires that the decision-maker formulate a general criterion that shall serve as a principle of decision in cases of its type. Will this procedure always be wise? Are there not areas of the law, such as those involving problems of procedural due process, in which it may plausibly be argued that it is better to have each case come up for decision in its own right than to have the Court lay down in advance general principles of judgment? I shall come to this in a moment.

There is hardly any need to show in detail how Professor Wechsler's comments on some older cases illustrate the requirements of principled decision thus far presented. Were not, he asks, the principles which the Court affirmed 'strikingly deficient in neutrality, sustaining, for example, national authority when it impinged adversely upon labor, as in the application of the Sherman Act, but not when it was sought to be employed in labor's aid'?[2] The deficiency in neutrality here must be that the Court failed to articulate a significant ground for such disparity of treatment. So also must we understand his remark that some decisions are now read 'with eyes that disbelieve' in part because 'the Court could not articulate an adequate analysis of the restrictions it imposed on Congress in favor of the states. . . '.[3] Professor Wechsler further speculates 'whether there are any neutral principles that might have been employed to mark the limits of the

---

[1] WECHSLER 21.   [2] ibid. p. 32.   [3] ibid.

commerce power of the Congress in terms more circumscribed than the virtual abandonment of limits in the principle that has prevailed'.[1] I think it obvious that any such principles could be no more or less 'neutral' than Holmes's criterion of 'clear and present danger'. The commerce power of Congress poses problems of federalism and cases involving the reach of the commerce power necessarily bring into play countervailing considerations. The neutrality of such limiting principles would not inhere *in* the principles, just as it does not inhere in the limiting principle of 'clear and present danger', but rather, if at all, in the manner of applying them, i.e., in principled application.

III. PRINCIPLED DECISION-MAKING AND CIVIL RIGHTS

We come finally to those cases that pose for Professor Wechsler the hardest test of his belief in principled adjudication, namely, those involving the white primary, racially restrictive covenants, and segregation in the public schools. The decisions in these cases, he believes, 'have the best chance of making an enduring contribution to the quality of our society of any that I know in recent years'.[2] Yet he questions how far they rest on 'neutral principles' and are, thus, entitled to approval in the only terms which he acknowledges to be relevant to a judicial decision.

The problems in the first two categories of cases arise under the prohibitions of the fourteenth or fifteenth amendments which have been held to reach not only explicit deprivation by statute but also action of the courts and of subordinate officials purporting to exert authority deriving from public office.[3] Although I do not find all of his ingenious solutions compelling, Professor Pollak has admirably discussed[4] the issues involved in such detail that it would be unprofitable to retrace this ground here. I propose, therefore, to limit myself to one point, and then conclude with a defense of the desegregation decision, arguing that it does exhibit characteristics of principled judgment, although the Court's opinion in *Brown* v. *Board of Educ.*[5] is not entirely satisfying.

The main issue presented by the primary and covenant cases

---

[1] ibid. p. 33.   [2] ibid. p. 37.
[3] ibid. pp. 37–38, citing, *inter alia, ex parte Virginia*, 100 U.S. 339, 347 (1880).
[4] Pollak, *Racial Discrimination and Judicial Integrity: A Reply to Professor Wechsler*, 108 U. PA. L. REV. 1 (1959).   [5] 347 U.S. 483 (1954).

concerns the notion of 'state action'. One supposes that the paradigm of 'state action' in these areas would be a statute that explicitly discriminates on racial grounds. But as soon as we move away from this everything becomes less clear. May the Democratic Party of Texas, which is a 'private' organization, exclude Negroes from its primaries? If a 'private' party is free to enter into a restrictive covenant, may a state be charged with infringing the fourteenth amendment if its courts give effect to such an agreement? Professor Wechsler asks: 'What is the principle involved? Is the state forbidden to effectuate a will that draws a racial line, a will that can accomplish any disposition only through the aid of law, or is it a sufficient answer there that the discrimination was the testator's and not the state's?'[1] If I understand Professor Wechsler's complaint, it is that the Court has failed to lay down, in the cases dealing with these issues,[2] a criterion of 'state action', or of 'unconstitutional state action', or of 'discriminatory state action'.[3] In these cases one is forced to take account of the countervailing considerations of 'state' and 'private' action. If a 'private' party is by hypothesis free to discriminate, except when prohibited by law, at what point does such discrimination become invalid when it is enabled, permitted, or enforced by an organ of a state? As Professor Wechsler asks, what is the principle involved?

I suggested above that there might be areas of the law, such as procedural due process, in which it is inadvisable to lay down criteria or standards of the type under consideration here. There is an almost immeasurable variety of cases which could conceivably involve the notions of 'state' and 'private' action. In *Smith* v. *Allwright* the Court maintained that the discrimination practiced by a party entrusted by Texas law with the determination of the qualifications of participants in the primary was 'endorsed', 'adopted', and 'enforced' by the state. This conclusion was reached only after close attention to the *role* played by such primaries in the electoral process, rather than by an application of a general criterion.[4] Perhaps this, too, is an area in which it is best to

---

[1] WECHSLER 40.

[2] Principally, *Smith* v. *Allwright*, 321 U.S. 649 (1944), and *Shelley* v. *Kraemer*, 334 U.S. 1 (1948).

[3] See the suggestive article of Horowitz, *The Misleading Search for 'State Action' Under the Fourteenth Amendment*, 30 SO. CAL. L. REV. 208 (1957).

[4] *Smith* v. *Allwright*, 321 U.S. 649 (1944); cf. *Terry* v. *Adams*, 345 U.S. 461 (1953). Professor Wechsler inquires whether the decisions in *Smith* and *Terry*

proceed on a case-by-case basis, and the Court, in refusing to lay down a criterion, has chosen wisely.

But if it is proper for the Court to approach the problems of 'state' and 'private' action in this way, it is, nevertheless, not unfair to ask the Court to give some explanation for the apparent inconsistencies among the cases it has decided. If it is true that not every instance of judicial cognition of private discrimination is state action prohibited by the fourteenth amendment, can we distinguish those classes of cases in which it obtains from those in which it does not?[1] The requirements of principled decision impose such a task on the Court. In other words, the question whether the Court should refrain from laying down a criterion in cases of the sort I have mentioned really goes to the knotty issue of the *scope* of the criterion that the Court ought to give: how broadly, or how narrowly, should the principle be framed? This question is of great practical significance, for principles enunciated by higher courts inevitably affect decisions of lower courts. Moreover, an articulated principle stands as a commitment by the higher court itself with respect to future cases in which the fact situation may be slightly different. On the one hand, principles seem to have a way of fixating themselves in the mind of the decision-maker and impel him, in the next case, to go farther than he may really want. On the other hand, a narrowly formulated principle might supply no guidance to a lower court. Of course, no one supposes that principled decision is an easy task. (Perhaps it is to just these issues that Professor Wechsler's remark that courts should decide 'only the case they have before them'[2] is addressed.) The complexity of this problem is increased when we consider its relation to the doctrine of precedent; but I am not prepared to deal with these matters at this time.

The question of school desegregation hardly seems susceptible of judicial neutrality. It stirs even in Professor Wechsler the

---

[1] See Pollak (cited above p. 227 n. 4) pp. 12–16.   [2] WECHSLER 21.

---

mean that religious parties are proscribed, and whether such a proscription would not infringe rights protected by the first amendment. WECHSLER 40. My answer is that the first topic of consideration would be the role of such a party in the electoral process. If it plays the role of the Democratic Party or Jaybirds in Texas or the Democratic Party in a Louisiana locality, there is good reason for proscribing it. Are not the rights of members of other religious groups infringed in such a situation?

'deepest conflict' in testing his thesis.[1] Fortunately, the decision in *Brown* does not hinge on the slippery notions of 'state' and 'private' action, although they may become relevant in cases arising from devices adopted by states seeking to avoid the consequences of that decision. In order to determine whether and in what respects this case departs from the model of principled decision-making, which I take to be what is most comprehensible in Professor Wechsler's conception of 'neutral principles', it will be useful to have before us the heart of the Court's opinion:

We must consider public education in the light of its full development and its present place in American life throughout the Nation. Only in this way can it be determined if segregation in public schools deprives these plaintiffs of the equal protection of the laws. . . . Such an opportunity [education], where the state has undertaken to provide it, is a right which must be made available to all on equal terms.

We come then to the question presented: Does segregation of children in public schools solely on the basis of race, even though the physical facilities and other "tangible" factors may be equal, deprive the children of the minority group of equal educational opportunities? We believe that it does. . . . To separate them from others of similar age and qualification solely because of their race generates a feeling of inferiority as to their status in the community that may affect their hearts and minds in a way unlikely ever to be undone. . . .

We conclude that in the field of public education the doctrine of "separate but equal" has no place. Separate educational facilities are inherently unequal. Therefore, we hold that the plaintiffs and others similarly situated . . . are, by reason of the segregation complained of, deprived of the equal protection of the laws guaranteed by the Fourteenth Amendment. This disposition makes unnecessary any discussion whether such segregation also violates the Due Process Clause of the Fourteenth Amendment.[2]

There are in the Court's argument five points to be noticed: (1) the focus is solely upon education—it is 'in the field of public education' that 'the "separate but equal" doctrine has no place'; (2) it is taken as axiomatic, and there is no disputing it, that when a state undertakes a program of public education it must be available to all on equal terms; (What this means is the crucial point.) (3) segregation in education is constitutionally bad because it

---

[1] WECHSLER 43.   [2] 347 U.S. pp. 492–5.

'generates a feeling of inferiority'; (4) 'separate educational facilities are inherently unequal'; and (5) the issue is disposed of
entirely on equal protection grounds.

Considering the focus of the opinion, Professor Wechsler seems
entirely justified in his criticism of the Court's *per curiam* extension
of the ruling to other public facilities in later cases.[1] But I think
that one can explain this focus and that one may infer from the
Court's actions that *Plessy* v. *Ferguson*[2] is in effect overruled
'in form'.[3]

The effects of segregation on Negro children and, in particular,
whether segregation 'generates a feeling of inferiority' are topics
that have been widely discussed. The testimony of 'modern
authority' has been raked over the coals. Professor Black thinks
that this testimony did no more than to demonstrate what is
obvious to every sane man.[4] Professor Cahn believes that the
Court made no more than a passing reference, 'alluding to them
graciously as "modern authority".'[5] He thinks that the belief that
the Court's judgment was a result, either entirely or in major part,
of the opinions of the social scientists is both erroneous and
dangerous. Nor is Professor Wechsler without his doubts. 'Much
depended', he says, 'on the question that the witness had in mind,
which rarely was explicit.' And this is not all. '[I]f the harm that
segregation worked was relevant, what of the benefits that it
entailed: sense of security, the absence of hostility? Were they
irrelevant?'[6]

To me, what is least satisfying about the opinion in *Brown* is
the unclarity of the relationship between the Court's judgment that
segregated schools generate a feeling of inferiority and its judgment
that separate educational facilities are 'inherently unequal.' Is the
second meant to follow from the first? What then is the force of the
word 'inherently? Although I agree that segregation does stig-
matize Negroes with a badge of inferiority, and although I also
tend to accept the argument of some that as a matter of fact
'separate but equal' facilities are rarely equal, I find it hard,
together with Professor Wechsler, to think that the decision really
turned upon the facts.[7] But I would phrase this in a slightly

---

[1] WECHSLER 31.   [2] 163 U.S. 537 (1896).
[3] *Contrast*, HAND (cited above p. 222 n. 7), p. 54.
[4] Black, *The Lawfulness of the Segregation Decisions* 69 YALE L. J. 421 (1960).
[5] Cahn, *Jurisprudence* 30 N.Y.U.L. REV. 150, 160 (1955).
[6] WECHSLER 44–45.   [7] ibid. p. 45.

different way: I do not think that the decision turned *merely* upon the Court's understanding of the facts; the element of principle plays a crucial role in the Court's reasoning.

Throughout one's reading of the opinion one must keep in mind the legal position of segregated schools before the *Brown* decision, the import of the 'separate but equal' doctrine. Under the fourteenth amendment, the pre-*Brown* doctrine was that the *only* requirement regarding public schools was that Negroes and whites may be treated in a separate manner so long as the schools in any given state were equal in facilities, etc., in that state. In other words, with *no need of any touch of a justification* it was permissible for a state to single out a group of individuals and educate them separately from other groups so long as there was equality of facilities, etc., apparently on the theory that no showing of injury, necessary to successfully challenging legislation on equal protection grounds, could be made. It is this *at the very least* which is no longer the legal position after *Brown*.

As I see it, the decision in *Brown* turns upon two separate points. First, that segregation in public schools is invalid because it is in principle a denial of equality: such schools are 'inherently unequal'. Second, that it is constitutionally bad because it generates a feeling of inferiority in the minority group, i.e., the group not politically dominant.[1] The first point is directed toward the item mentioned above. It holds, no matter what the feelings are which are generated. Segregation, with or without equal facilities, taken by itself and without some justification for meting out a *different* treatment to equals under the law, is constitutionally bad. What is affirmed here is the prima facie *right* of Negroes to attend the same school as whites; a right which they can be prevented from exercising only if some adequate justification can be given for so preventing them. Clearly, their race alone, under the fourteenth amendment, is certainly not sufficient as an adequate justification.

On the first point, then, I do not see how the Court could have validated segregated public schools, even granting equal facilities. The major premise of the decision is that when a state undertakes a program of public education it must be made available to all on equal terms. This proposition is really the individualization, for this case, of a more general one about state programs: they all must be made available to all on equal terms. So, if a state undertakes a

[1] Professor Wechsler's gloss. See ibid. p. 45.

program of home nursing care to poor, disabled persons, it, too, must be available to all on equal terms. (This is to be distinguished from another 'more general' proposition that home nursing care must be made available to all irrespective of their economic status.) *Disparity of treatment* of equals must be justified by the discriminator if *it* is to be principled. Could the Court here have acknowledged such disparity of treatment—and enforced separation, even if 'separate but equal', is just that—granted that Negroes have a legitimate claim to equal treatment under the fourteenth amendment?

As I reconstruct this aspect of the Court's reasoning, the equal protection and due process clauses of the fourteenth amendment are intimately related—and are they so separate anyway? It is interesting to note that in *Bolling* v. *Sharpe*,[1] dealing with segregated schools in the District of Columbia, the Court arrived at the same result as *Brown* on fifth amendment due process grounds. Finally, in *Cooper* v. *Aaron* the Court makes its stand clear: 'the right of a student not to be segregated *on racial grounds* in schools so maintained is indeed so fundamental and pervasive that it is embraced in the concept of due process of law.'[2] In sum, principled decision requires sameness of treatment in public education—unless some justification can be offered for the different treatment, and distinction of race *alone* is not an acceptable ground for permitting separate school facilities. This is implicit in the Court's opinion in *Brown*, although that opinion leaves much to be desired.

The *onus probandi* of providing a justification for racially segregated public schools fell on the states that maintained such schools. There are, of course, justifications for racially segregated schools that could conceivably be offered. It could be argued that Negroes and whites differ significantly in native intellectual

---

[1] 347 U.S. 497 (1953). The permissibility of the separation of children by 'normal geographic school districting' is implied in the Court's order handed down when the segregation cases were assigned in 1953 for reargument, *Brown* v. *Board of Educ.* 345 U.S. 972, 973 (1953). Interestingly, this is not mentioned in the subsequent opinions. I am not certain as to how this really does affect those cases in which a *de facto* segregation (as distinct from an 'enforced separation') results.

[2] 358 U.S. 1, 19 (1958). (My italics.) See generally the hindsight opinion of Professor Pollak in which he refers to the 'comprehensive standards which the Fourteenth Amendment imposes on all state activity'. Pollak (cited above p. 227 n. 4) pp. 24–30.

Q

capacity, so that the purposes of education would be frustrated by integration. Such ploys ring a familiar bell, having been used by European countries to justify the domination of their colonies. But even if it were granted that this is true—which it is not—the measure of the sincerity of the discriminator would be whether he is prepared to maintain classes of Negroes and whites who possess a low level of intelligence. It is fairly evident that this ploy amounts to little more than dodging the issue. It could, again, be argued that although Negroes *do* have the right to attend integrated schools, because under the fourteenth amendment race is not an acceptable ground of distinction, the very attempt to integrate the schools is so fraught with danger to peace that Negroes ought to be prevented from exercising their right. But the weight of this argument would vary from community to community, and at best it only goes to the issue of how quickly integration ought to be instituted. I think that although the Court required (in the second *Brown* decision)[1] that it be done with all 'deliberate speed', the Court did, nevertheless, partially acknowledge some merit in this argument in recognizing that the variations in local conditions did affect the rate of integration. It is true that in *Cooper*, in its instructions to the district courts,[2] the Court excluded 'hostility to racial desegregation' as a relevant factor from a district court's consideration regarding the rate of desegregation. But this, I believe, wisely reflected the Court's realistic view that to recognize hostility to desegregation as a ground for delay could only result in a permanent deprivation of the right of Negro children in this context.

It is worth noting that the two examples given above as possible justifications for retaining segregated schools differ in a significant respect. The first makes reference to something within the sphere of education itself, while the second refers to some governmental objective outside of education as such. These represent two different forms of justification of exceptions to principle, but I shall not attempt to explore this any further here.

[1] 349 U.S. 294 (1955).
[2] '[A]District Court, after analysis of the relevant factors (which of course, excludes hostility to racial desegregation), might conclude that justification existed for not requiring the present nonsegregated admission of all qualified Negro children.' 358 U.S. at 7. It would naturally be self-defeating, in ordinary situations, to allow opposition to a principle to be a ground for making an exception to the principle.

This brings us to the second aspect of the *Brown* decision. Not only was the Court convinced as a matter of principle that Negroes have a prima facie right to sameness of treatment in public education, but the Court was also convinced that Negroes are positively harmed by such discrimination. This bodes ill for any conceivable justification for retaining enforced segregation. Obviously this fact weighed heavily in the minds of the members of the Court as they listened to and read the arguments put forth by counsel of states that practiced racial segregation. Even without it only the weightiest considerations could have overridden the right of Negroes to attend integrated schools; how much more so with it! Thus, even if one grants the benefits that Professor Wechsler alleges segregation might have entailed (sense of security and absence of hostility),[1] granting also the harms, the Court would have been hard put to see much merit in the purported justifications for segregation. Segregated schools are at best a mixed blessing to Negroes, and it is not clear that their virtues overbalance the vices to such an extent that, excluding other considerations, the right which Negroes have in principle ought to be denied them.[2]

Professor Wechsler suggests another approach to the issue of

---

[1] WECHSLER 45.

[2] I am not sure where this leaves the enforced separation of the sexes. Can some justification for it be found? An interesting area in which race and sex may be compared is that relating to juries. The Supreme Court has reversed the convictions of some Negroes when it was shown that the given state practiced a discriminatory racial policy in the selection of jurors. *Eubanks* v. *Louisiana*, 356 U.S. 584 (1958). In a recent case, *Hoyt* v. *Florida*, 368 U.S. 57 (1961), a woman who was convicted by an all-male jury of the baseball bat murder of her husband appealed on the ground that 'such jury was the product of a state jury statute which works an unconstitutional exclusion of women from jury service'. ibid. p. 58. Under that statute women are not required to serve on juries; they are permitted, however, to volunteer for service. But this was held not to be a purposeful or arbitrary discrimination. Writing for the Court, Mr. Justice Harlan said:

'Despite the enlightened emancipation of women from the restrictions and protections of bygone years, and their entry into many parts of community life formerly considered to be reserved to men, woman is still regarded as the center of home and family life. We cannot say that it is constitutionally impermissible for a State, acting in pursuit of the general welfare, to conclude that a woman should be relieved of the civic duty of jury service unless she herself determines that such service is consistent with her own special responsibilities.'

ibid. pp. 60–61. Perhaps this suggests the line of reasoning that would justify (for it clearly needs justification) the permissibility of the *enforced* separation of the sexes in schools.

segregation, and I shall conclude my remarks with a comment upon it.

For me [he says], assuming equal facilities, the question posed by state-enforced segregation is not one of discrimination at all. Its human and its constitutional dimensions lie entirely elsewhere, in the denial by the state of freedom to associate, a denial that impinges in the same way on any groups or races that may be involved. . . .

But if the freedom of association is denied by segregation, integration forces an association upon those for whom it is unpleasant or repugnant. Is this not the heart of the issue involved, a conflict in human claims of high dimension. . . . Given a situation where the state must practically choose between denying the association to those individuals who wish it or imposing it on those who would avoid it, is there a basis in neutral principles for holding that the Constitution demands that the claims for association should prevail? I should like to think there is, but I confess that I have not yet written the opinion. To write it is for me the challenge of the school-segregation cases.[1]

With all respect to Professor Wechsler, I do not see how one can say that the question 'is not one of discrimination *at all*'. Discrimination is certainly no less relevant than the freedom of association. Principled decision-making requires that the different treatment of equals be justified, and the *onus probandi* falls on the discriminator. As I see it, Professor Wechsler's question really comes down to this: is the 'evil' of the imposition of association on those who wish to avoid it sufficient to justify the different, and hence unequal, treatment of equals? Put this way, I suggest that a better constitutional case can be made for the negative answer. But in any event I should like to have more instruction on what kind of constitutionally protected right the freedom of association is. As far as I am aware it is no more than the right of individuals to combine for a common (legal) end,[2] which seems irrelevant to the question of segregated use of public facilities, assuming them to be equal. Moreover, how far can we extend the claim of those who wish to avoid an association that is unpleasant to them? Could this not lead to the invalidation of any form of compulsory education?

These remarks are the words of a friendly critic. I accept, in the only way I can understand it, Professor Wechsler's ideal of judicial decision-making. And it is important to recognize that it is an ideal that, as an ideal, is no less valid for its being so rarely realized in practice—if such be the case.

[1] WECHSLER 46–47. [2] See *NAACP* v. *Alabama*, 357 U.S. 449 (1958).

Legislative Intent

GERALD C. MacCALLUM, JR.[1]

INTRODUCTION

Appeals to legislative intent are a commonplace part of our judicial process. Nevertheless there are many unresolved disputes about the existence and discoverability of legislative intent. In 1930, Max Radin argued that the presence of genuine legislative intent in connection with a statute is at best a rare circumstance and that, in any event, the legislative intent could not be discovered from the records of the legislative proceedings.[2] This argument drew an immediate response from James Landis. Landis distinguished between two senses of 'intent'—'intent' as 'intended meaning' and 'intent' as 'purpose'. He maintained that legislative intent in the first sense (and apparently in the second also) is an ordinary although not invariable feature of legislative processes. Furthermore, he contended that this feature, when present, is clearly discoverable in the records of the legislative proceedings.[3]

The Radin–Landis dispute has had a curious history. Since 1930, treatises and articles on statutory interpretation have often

---

[1] Gerald C. MacCallum, Jr., A.B. 1950, M.A. 1954, Ph.D. 1961 U. Calif. Berkeley, is Associate Professor of Philosophy at the University of Wisconsin. The present essay appeared first in 75 YALE L. J. 754 (1966). Also of relevance by the author are: *Dworkin on Judicial Discretion* 60 J. PHILOSOPHY 638 (1963); *On Applying Rules* 32 THEORIA 196 (1966); *Negative and Positive Freedom* 76 PHILOSOPHICAL REV. 312 (1967). (Footnote by editor.)

[2] Radin, *Statutory Interpretation* 43 HARV. L. REV. 863 (1930). Radin also denied the relevance of appeals to legislative intent. This article, however, is only concerned with the prior questions of the existence and discoverability of legislative intent. For earlier criticisms of the notion of legislative intent, see SEDGWICK, THE INTERPRETATION AND CONSTRUCTION OF STATUTORY AND CONSTITUTIONAL LAW 327-8 (2d ed. 1874); Bruncken, *Interpretation of Written Law* 25 YALE L. J. 129 (1915); KOCOUREK, AN INTRODUCTION TO THE SCIENCE OF LAW 201 (1930).

[3] Landis, *A Note on 'Statutory Interpretation'*, 43 HARV. L. REV. 886 (1930).

mentioned the dispute and have sometimes taken sides. But commentators siding with Radin, although abandoning talk about legislative intent, proceed to talk freely about the 'legislative purposes', 'policies', and 'objectives' of statutes. Because it is not obvious that these expressions refer to anything different from legislative intent,[1] one would expect careful discussion of where the differences lie. In particular, one would expect to find a showing that arguments leading to the rejection of talk about legislative intent have no force against these new expressions. But no such showing is to be found in the leading discussions of the matter— including those by Willis,[2] Frankfurter,[3] Corry[4] and Radin himself.[5]

On the other hand, commentators siding with Landis have done so on the basis of inadequate arguments. For example, we find Radin falsely accused of assuming 'that the legislative intent is the sum of the total intents of the individual members of the legislature'.[6] This is accompanied by the mysterious assertion that the intention of the legislature is 'not a collection of subjective wishes, hopes and prejudices of individuals, but rather the objective footprints left on the trail of legislative enactment'.[7] Such a statement is mysterious because it appears to mistake what could at most be *evidence* of intent for intent itself. It is surely in need of further elucidation and support if it is to show Radin wrong.

Again, we find unsupported assumptions that statutes would be wholly meaningless in the absence of anything identifiable as legislative intent,[8] and that the meaning assigned to them 'must be one intended by the law-makers or the law-makers do not legislate'.[9] Such remarks raise interesting issues, but, as will be seen below, the arguments supporting them cannot stand.

---

[1] As Johnstone remarks, 'purpose' often seems simply another name for intent. Johnstone, *An Evaluation of the Rules of Statutory Interpretation* 3 KANS. L. REV. 1, 15 (1954). See also Bruncken (cited above p. 237 n. 2) p. 134.

[2] Willis, *Statute Interpretation in a Nutshell* 16 CAN. BAR. REV. 1 (1938).

[3] Frankfurter, *Some Reflections on the Reading of Statutes* 47 COLUM. L. REV. 527 (1947).

[4] Corry, *Administrative Law and the Interpretation of Statutes* 1 U. TORONTO L. J. 286 (1936). See also Corry, *The Use of Legislative History in the Interpretation of Statutes* 32 CAN. BAR. REV. 624 (1954).

[5] Radin, *A Short way With Statutes* 56 HARV. L. REV. 388 (1942).

[6] See 2 SUTHERLAND, STATUTES AND STATUTORY CONSTRUCTION 322 (3d ed. 1943). For what Radin actually says see Radin (cited above p. 237 n. 2) p. 870.

[7] ibid.   [8] cf. CRAWFORD, THE CONSTRUCTION OF STATUTES 255 (1940).

[9] ibid. p. 256.

These claims and counterclaims are fully representative of the curious career of the Radin–Landis dispute. Writers siding with Radin apparently find it impossible to reject every trace of what he rejected. Writers siding with Landis have done so on the basis of inadequate (although sometimes interesting) arguments. Clearly the issues raised by the dispute have not yet been satisfactorily resolved, and are still in need of careful discussion.

I

The most obvious difficulty with the notion of legislative intent concerns the relationship between the intent of a collegiate legislature and the intentions of the several legislators. Many difficulties would remain, however, if a legislature had only one authoritative member. We would profit, therefore, by asking what it could mean to speak of the legislative intent of a single legislator.

The fundamental question 'what was the legislator's intent' subsumes a number of more specific questions:

1. Was his intent to enact a statute—i.e., was the 'enacting' performance not, perchance, done accidentally, inadvertently or by mistake?
2. Was his intent to enact *this* statute—i.e., was this the *document* (the draft) he thought he was endorsing?
3. Was his intent to enact *this* statute—i.e., are the *words* in this document precisely those he supposed to be there when he enacted it as a statute?
4. Was his intent to enact *this* statute—i.e., do these words *mean* precisely what he supposed them to mean when he endorsed their use in the statute?
5. How did *he* intend these words to be understood?
6. What was his intent in enacting the statute—i.e., what did he intend the enactment of the statute to achieve?
7. What was his intent in enacting the statute—i.e., what did he intend the enactment of the statute to achieve *in terms of his own career*?[1]

Failure to distinguish between these more specific questions is

---

[1] Witherspoon, *Administrative Discretion to Determine Statutory Meaning: 'The Middle Road': I*, 40 TEXAS L. REV. 751, 796–800 (1962), distinguishes twenty-two 'forms or configurations of legislative purpose that may be discovered at work in any particular legislative process productive of a statute'. He does not attempt to order his list as I have, but I believe that it all lies somewhere within the range of my Nos. 3–6. Some of the entries are further specifications of what I have distinguished; but some of them also appear to conflate matters I wish to keep distinct; e.g., his Nos. 5–8 each could cover what I wish to distinguish above in (4) and (5).

responsible for much of the confusion in debates about the existence, discoverability and relevance of legislative intent. It is
therefore important to examine closely the relationships between
the more troublesome of these questions.

A. *The aims of the legislator:*
The distinction between

6. What did he intend enactment of the statute to achieve? and
7. What did he intend enactment to achieve in terms of his own
   career?

These questions distinguish between two kinds of reasons the
legislator may have for enacting a statute—reasons looking to the
effects of enactment upon the legal system, and reasons looking to
the effects of enactment on his own career.[1] This distinction is
crucial to any discussion of the relevance of legislative intent, since
judges and administrators are unlikely to regard as significant the
legislator's concern with his own career. The distinction is also
important when one is discussing the existence and discoverability
of legislative intent. To say there was no intent at all, for example, might mean that the enactment was motiveless, e.g., inadvertent
or accidental. On the other hand, it might mean that no intent of the
relevant sort was present, that the legislator had only his personal
career in mind when enacting the statute. Furthermore, depending
on the records available, one kind of intent might be discoverable
while the other is not. Thus the two must be kept distinct.

B. *Intent as intended meaning and intent as purpose:*
The distinction between

6. What did he intend the enactment of the statute to achieve? and
5. How did *he* intend these words to be understood?

Landis notes the way the distinction between intent as (intended)
meaning and intent as purpose becomes obscured when he says:

Purpose and meaning commonly react upon each other. Their exact

---

[1] cf. Radin (cited above p. 237 n. 2) p. 873. See de Sloovère, *Preliminary
Questions in Statutory Interpretation* 9 N.Y.U.L. REV. 407, 415 (1932), where his
remark about 'individual and combined motives' encourages, if it does not
actually constitute, a conflation of the questions.

differentiation would require an extended philosophical essay. . . . [T]he Distinction . . . is a nice one.[1]

Even though the distinction may be a 'nice one', no lengthy essay is needed to underscore the importance of distinguishing questions about the purposes of specific legislators from general questions about the meanings of statutory words. The major source of confusion has been the belief that we must always guide our understanding of statutory words by an understanding of legislative purposes, as though we could not understand the words without prior knowledge of the purposes.[2] This belief is most readily countered with the reminder that our primary source of 'evidence' of specific legislative purposes in connection with a statute generally lies in the words of the statute itself, and that these words could not provide such evidence if their meanings were not determined independently of consideration of the purposes in question.[3]

Confusion about the interplay between purpose and meaning has become so embedded in discussions of statutory interpretation that a more extended argument may be desirable. In particular, it may be helpful to show that the distinction between purpose and meaning exists even when the considerable concessions suggested by question (5) are made in the direction of establishing a connection between the purpose of a legislator and the meaning of what he says in a statute. Suppose we stipulate (i) that a legislator's words always mean precisely what he thinks they mean, and (ii) that the purposes in question concern the career of the statute rather then the career of the legislator. The first stipulation seems to go as far as possible in the direction of a tight connection between statutory meaning and the intentions or purposes of the legislator. The second stipulation restricts the purposes in question to those most generally thought to enter legitimately into issues of statutory interpretation. Even with these stipulations, however,

---

[1] See Note, *A Note on 'Statutory Interpretation'*, 43 HARV. L. REV. 886, 888 (1930).

[2] Cf. CRAWFORD (cited above p. 238 n. 8) pp. 255–6; Llewellyn, *Remarks on the Theory of Appellate Decision and the Rules or Canons About How Statutes are to be Construed* 3 VAND. L. REV. 395, 400 (1950); Witherspoon (cited above, p. 239 no. 1) p. 765.

[3] Cf. E. A. DREIDGER, THE COMPOSITION OF LEGISLATION 159 (1957). It is true that we sometimes allow our understanding of legislative purposes to shed light on puzzling passages in a statute. But we could not even attempt this if we did not believe we already understood most of the words in the statute.

one may show that persons normally need not be aware of legislative purposes in order to understand legislative words.

Although the problem is an 'interpreter's' problem, it will be helpful to consider the matter first from the point of view of the legislator, and on the simplifying assumption that he is the author of the statutes he enacts.[1] He is typically interested in enacting a piece of legislation because he wants to effect certain changes in society. The words he uses are the instruments by means of which he expects or hopes to effect these changes. What gives him this expectation or this hope is his belief that he can anticipate how others (e.g., judges and administrators) will understand these words. The words would be useless to him if he could not anticipate how they would be understood by these other persons. Insofar as this concern for how his words will be understood is a concern about the 'meaning' of his words, this 'meaning' must thus generally be determinable independently of consideration of his purposes; for, until he forms opinions about the 'meaning' of the words, he cannot consider whether they will serve his purpose.

The legislator can attempt to assure that his words will be correctly understood in various ways, e.g., by stipulation. But if he stipulates he must use other words about which he will have the same general concern. Ultimately, he must recognize that with the bulk of his words he cannot create but only can utilize the conventions in the light of which his words will be understood.[2] The

---

[1] Complications introduced by the presence of draftsmen who are not themselves legislators will be considered later in connection with the intentions of collegiate bodies such as modern legislatures.

[2] Of course, one convention of statutory interpretation might permit or require that one's understanding of statutory language be guided by consideration of the legislator's purpose. Cf., 2 SUTHERLAND (cited above p. 238 n. 6) p. 315. Such a convention would invite the legislator to attempt to lay down a trail of his 'purposes' for others to follow; hence the use, in jurisdictions where legislators believe that interpreters of statutes will seek and heed such 'evidence', of statutory preambles, carefully manufactured 'legislative histories', etc. The only feature of note about this convention is that it offers the legislator an opportunity to influence rather than merely to anticipate how his statutory words will be understood. In this respect, it is analogous to conventions for stipulation and for formal definition. Nevertheless, the 'trail' he is able to lay down, both within and outside of the statute, will be primarily if not exclusively a verbal one. As with stipulations, if the legislator believes he can influence the understanding of his statutory words, it is only because he has certain expectations about how certain other words will be understood. These expectations also must be formed independently of consideration of his purposes, because until he has the expectations he can have no notion of whether these other words will serve his purposes.

legislator will be interested primarily in the conventions of statutory interpretation—that is, in the current conventional approaches by judges, administrators, lawyers and citizens to the understanding of statutes. Although these conventions will not guarantee specific results, they are all that he has to work with.

Consider the matter now from the point of view of the interpreters of statutes. Maintaining a perspective favorable to the association of legislative purpose with statutory meaning, suppose that the interpreters declare themselves bound by what the legislator wanted at the time the statute was enacted. Suppose, in particular, that, rather than raising any questions about how the legislator *ought* to have expected his words to be understood, the interpreters assume that their only legitimate task is the discovery of the legislator's actual expectations.

Difficulties arise immediately. There may be a lack of fit between how the legislator expected the words of the statute to be understood, and what he hoped to achieve by means of the statute. That is, the statute itself, or some constituent parts of it, may have been poorly chosen instruments for the achievement of his goals— not in the sense that the words were not understood as he expected them to be, but rather in the sense that, even when the words *were* understood as he expected, behavior in accordance with this understanding did not produce the results he thought it would produce. There are, in short, at least *two* distinct ways in which things could go wrong from the legislator's point of view: (1) people might not understand the words of the statute in the way he thought they would, or (2) the behavior of people who understand the words as he thought they would and who act truly in accordance with this understanding, might not produce the results that the legislator anticipated. In the first case, the legislator would have made a mistake in predicting how his words would be understood; in the second case, he would have made a mistake in predicting what would happen if people behaved in certain ways.[1] The difference between the two kinds of mistakes is obscured for the

---

[1] The distinction between the two is clear enough even though there may be a large shadowy area between them where the legislator's expectations were not well formed, and where even he might not be able to say whether, on the one hand, his words had not been understood as he expected, or rather, on the other hand, that he had proposed in the statute an ineffective way of achieving what he wished to achieve. See HAGERSTROM, INQUIRIES INTO THE NATURE OF LAW AND MORALS 79–81 (Broad trans. 1953).

'interpreter', and his view of statutory interpretation is consequently muddied, if he supposes that an understanding of the legislator's 'purposes' is either a sufficient or normally necessary guide to how the legislator expected the words of the statute to be understood.

As the legislator may simply have misjudged the effectiveness of the statutory scheme in achieving the purported purpose, a resolve to interpret the words of the statute so that the statute *will be* an effective instrument for the achievement of the purpose would be simply a refusal to consider the possibility of this kind of legislative misjudgment. The importance of this observation lies in the fact that, where such legislative misjudgment has actually occurred, the method of interpretation under consideration may not produce an understanding of the words of the statute corresponding to that which the legislator expected—the very understanding that figured in his deliberate choice of those words. In the end, there may be nothing *wrong* with this; the legislator may be delighted with a method of interpretation which hides his own misjudgment. But are the interpreters really being faithful to the 'intentions' of the legislator when they interpret his words differently from what he had expected?[1] At the very least, this problem should be brought into the open and faced squarely—something that has not been done and is not likely to be done so long as intent as 'meaning' and intent as purpose are conflated.

One may wonder how intended legislative meaning could possibly be discovered *without* appeal to knowledge of legislative purpose. The answer is that discovery depends primarily upon our awareness of the linguistic conventions the legislator looked to in forming his expectations about how his words would be understood. Awareness of these conventions will provide us with good (although not infallible) grounds for believing we know what his expectations were. Moreover, there is no great problem in attaining this awareness. We know perfectly well how to tell whether a man speaks the same language as we do, and how to tell whether we can speak his language. Our capacity to do this provides us with a generally adequate basis for determining when the legislator and we are both familiar with the linguistic conventions in the light of which

[1] Hagerstrom apparently thinks that the whole 'intention' theory founders on just this issue. See HAGERSTROM (cited above p. 243 n. 1) pp. 99–101. And for people who come down on different sides of the question, see 2 AUSTIN, LECTURES ON JURISPRUDENCE 628–30 (5th ed. 1885); and Witherspoon (cited above p. 239 n. 1) pp. 831–2.

various understandings of his words will be formed, and for determining whether we can understand these conventions in the same ways. Further, if we are the specific audience to whom his remarks are directed, we are merely asking ourselves what our own linguistic conventions are, and how well he might have understood them. The fact that statutory language ordinarily serves us quite well in this respect indicates that we are able to use the same linguistic conventions as the legislator and to know that we are doing so.

In sum, for us as well as for the legislator, practical understanding of his language is ordinarily founded on a grasp of the linguistic conventions utilized, rather than a grasp of his specific purposes in enacting the statute. This explains both how his words can serve us as evidence of his purposes, and why there is ordinarily no need to search for his purposes in order to understand what he meant.

C. Can the legislator misunderstand his own words?

The distinction between

4. Do these words *mean* precisely what he supposed them to mean when he endorsed their use in the statute? and

5. How did *he* intend these words to be understood?

Question (4) pinpoints, as question (5) does not, the possibility that the *legislator* has misunderstood the words he used in a statutory document. Reading some discussions on statutory interpretation, one would think it impossible for a legislator to misunderstand what he has written or endorsed.[1] In these discussions, the entire burden of understanding or misunderstanding the statute seemingly is placed upon others—the judge, the lawyer, the citizen. The effective slogan of these discussions might well be that the words of the statute mean what their author–endorser (the legislator) intended them to mean. But, as we have seen, words in statutes are of use both to legislators and to others because they have acquired significance through the growth or stipulation of conventions regarding their use. Indeed, we could not recognize something *as* a word, rather than as merely a contour (or range of contours) of sounds or a certain form (or range of forms) of scribblings if we were not aware that sounds and scribblings with

[1] Cf. CRAWFORD (cited above p. 238 n. 8) p. 245; 2 SUTHERLAND (cited above p. 238 n. 6) pp. 315–16.

such contours and forms have a significance, function, or value resulting from the growth or stipulation of such conventions. *Our* belief that we can understand what a man says, and *his* belief that he will be understood, mutually depend upon the recognition, acceptance, and utilization of such conventions. Furthermore, as we have also noted, even when such conventions are stipulated by a speaker, the stipulations ultimately rely upon words whose meanings are not stipulated but are assumed to be already understood in the light of existing conventions. It follows that if a speaker is not understood as he expected to be, this may be because *he* misunderstood or because some member of his audience misunderstood linguistic conventions of which they should have been aware.

Of course, having recognized that a legislator might possibly misunderstand the conventions determining the commonly accepted significance of the words he uses, we might for some reason wish to give more importance to his (mistaken) beliefs about the significance of his words than to their actual significance —that is, we might feel bound more by what he *meant* to say than by what, on any ordinary view, he *did* say. We could remind ourselves of this with the slogan that the words in statutory documents mean what the legislators intended them to mean, and could regard as always authoritative, even when mistaken, the beliefs of legislators as to how their words would be understood, and, in particular, their beliefs as to the commonly accepted significance of their words.

The adoption of such a policy, however, would lead to practical and conceptual problems. The legislator's audience (judges, lawyers, administrators, citizens) would have to ignore what the legislator said (the commonly accepted significance of his words) and take upon itself the responsibility of seeking out what the legislator meant (what he expected them to understand). A serious attempt to fulfill this responsibility would, to say the least, require complex and tedious investigation.[1] Furthermore, if we insist that

---

[1] Judges and commentators, in protesting the seemingly overwhelming importance given to 'legislative intent' in statutory interpretation have sometimes been in part protecting against the placement of this responsibility on the interpreters of statutes. See, e.g., *Schwegmann Bros.* v. *Calvert Distillers Corp.* 341 U.S. 384, 395–6 (1951) (concurring opinion of Jackson, J.); *McBoyle* v. *United States* 283 U.S. 25, 27 (1931); Quarles, *Some Statutory Construction Problems and Approaches in Criminal Law* 3 VAND. L. REV. 531 (1950).

the audience is responsible for what the legislator meant rather than for what he said, we must concede that either (a) the statute consists of the string of words actually on the rolls, in which case that statute (i.e., that string of words) may not be binding, or (b) the statute is binding but may consist of a different string of words from that on the rolls.

Perhaps this analysis merely reveals that we are in a quandary when it comes to interpreting statutes. With statutes, some peculiar authority attaches to what the legislator *says* (for that is virtually all that most persons may have to go by), and some authority may attach also to what the legislator is *trying* to say (after all, under the separation-of-powers doctrine we have in some way obligated ourselves to submit to his wishes on certain matters).[1] But at least we need a formulation of the issues that allows us to see the quandary for what it is. Wholehearted acceptance of the slogan that statutory words mean what the legislator intended them to mean would make this insight impossible.

We have seen that appeals to the legislative intent of even a single legislator are attended by numerous difficulties and sources of confusion. But we have not yet approached the major problem about legislative intent. Judges and administrators appeal to the intent of entire *collegiate* legislatures. Many commentators believe that such appeals are futile—that it is senseless to speak of the intent of a collegiate legislature. Our examination of the intent of the single legislator is a prologue to this central controversy.

II

A. Introduction to the skeptical arguments

Does it make any sense at all to talk about the intentions of a collegiate legislature? Radin says:

A legislature certainly has no intention whatever in connection with words which some two or three men drafted, which a considerable number rejected, and in regard to which many of the approving majority might have had, and often demonstrably did have, different ideas and beliefs.[2]

---

[1] Crawford approaches the problem when he says 'And the meaning must be one intended by the law-makers or the law-makers do not legislate.' CRAWFORD (cited above p. 238 n. 8) p. 256. See also Frankfurter, *Forward to a Symposium on Statutory Construction* 3 VAND. L. REV. 365, 366 (1950); R. H. Jackson, *The Meaning of Statutes: What Congress Says or What the Court Says* 34 A.B.A.J. 535, 537–8 (1948). [2] Radin (cited above p. 237 n. 2) p. 870.

Stronger views have been taken. Kocourek's argument to the effect that such intentions 'never existed' is based upon an unsupported assertion that: 'Legislation is a group activity and it is impossible to conceive a group mind or cerebration.'[1] Willis says flatly and without argument: A composite body can hardly have a single intent.'[2] More recently D. J. Payne also appears to dismiss the possibility when he says: '[T]he legislature, being a composite body, cannot have a single state of mind and so cannot have a single intention.'[3]

Concerning at least the latter three views, there are two issues to be sorted out: (a) the extent to which they are based on the notion that two or more men cannot have the same intention, and (b) the extent to which they are based on the notion that a group of men is incapable of having an intention. Kocourek's remark appears to raise the second of these issues; Payne's, despite appearances, raises the first.

Although we shall deal with Payne's arguments more fully below, consider for a moment the supposition in (a). *Is* it possible for two or more men to 'have a single intention'? Anyone wishing to deny the possibility must tell us why we cannot truthfully say in the simple case of two men rolling a log toward the river bank with the purpose of floating it down the river that there is at least one intention both these men have—viz., to get the log to the river so that they can float it down the river. It would be unhelpful to reply that one man's intention cannot be identical with another man's because each is his own and not the other's. There is no reason to confine ourselves to counting intentions *only* in this way. Further, if we did so confine ourselves, the central claim that two men cannot have the same intention would turn out to be merely a disguised tautology.

B. *The deeper roots of skepticism*

The claim in (b) raises much more difficult issues. Should we

---

[1] KOCOUREK (cited above p. 237 n. 2) p. 201.

[2] Willis (cited above p. 238 n. 2) p. 3.

[3] Payne, *The Intention of the Legislature in the Interpretation of Statutes* 9 CURRENT LEGAL PROBLEMS 96, 97–8 (1956). I say 'appears to' because despite the above statement and several others equally strong, Payne also seems to endorse Gray's view that the intention of the legislature, far from being always nonexistent, is often perfectly obvious. ibid. 101–2. It also turns out, as we shall see below, that Payne's arguments don't support a conclusion as strong as that quoted in the text above.

agree that legislatures, being *groups* of men, cannot have intentions? One possible argument here might be: legislatures are not men; only men can have intentions; therefore, legislatures cannot have intentions.[1]

Kocourek makes a more specific claim that there are necessary conditions for having intentions—conditions absent in the case of legislatures. His candidates are mind and 'cerebration'.[2] But it is clear that the temptation to name these as necessary conditions lies only in thinking of them as preconditions for purposive behavior and for deliberation—two more immediate preconditions for having intentions. When one moves directly to a consideration of whether legislatures are capable of purposive behavior and deliberation, the reply that they are seems neither false nor (without further argument) only figurative. We do, after all, speak quite freely and precisely about legislatures deliberating, and this, aside from our talk about their debating, investigating, etc., implies a capacity for purposive behavior. Of course, if someone tried to elucidate such talk without any reference whatever to the deliberating, investigating, debating, etc. of officers, members, agents, or employees of the legislature, we might find this mysterious or unacceptable. But no one has proposed eliminating these references, and the point remains that we have clear notions of what it means to say that a *legislature* is doing these things and we know that legislatures sometimes do them. Thus, a protest that legislatures do not ever do them, or, perhaps, do not 'literally' do them, is not prima facie intelligible.

But the skeptic may argue that when he claims that a capacity to deliberate is a necessary condition for having intentions, he is not thinking of the deliberating in which legislatures are conventionally said to engage; rather, he is thinking of the deliberating

---

[1] But of course this argument will founder on the shoals of debate about whether things other than men, e.g., animals, have intentions.

Perhaps, however, the arguer means to say that talk about the intentions of legislatures involves a category mistake or a 'fallacy of composition'. Men have intentions, but legislatures are *associations* of men, etc. As it stands, the principle of the argument would have to be this: from the fact that X is a collection of Y's, it follows that predicates applicable to Y's (taken distributively) are *therefore* inapplicable to X. There are apparent counterexamples to the principle—e.g., Jones, the left tackle, is heavier this year than last; the team of which he is a member is also heavier this year than last. Responses to such counterexamples will hardly avoid raising the complex issues discussed below.

[2] See text accompanying note 1, p. 248 above.

R

engaged in by individual men. Though the former normally requires at least some cases of the latter, the two are not sufficiently alike for him.

The skeptic may feel that the notion of intention and the allied notions of deliberation, etc. are stretched 'too far' when applied to legislatures. Although no one can say precisely how far is 'too far', the line of reply to the skeptic is clear. Legislatures are not men, and if only men clearly have intentions, then one's arguments must cultivate analogies between legislatures and men—the point being to argue that legislatures are enough like men in important respects to be counted as having intentions. Such arguments cannot lead to a *discovery* that legislatures might, after all, have intentions. Rather, the arguments can at most persuade us that it would not, under certain circumstances, be unreasonable to attribute intentions to legislatures—because the expression 'intention of the legislature' could still have practicable and reasonable applications without moving from what many people now understand it to mean, and *also* without moving too far from what they understand such an expression as 'intention of Jones' to mean. This is a long road, requiring travel through considerable detail about legislative procedures and the practices of judges, administrators, etc. Furthermore, it is a road that does not lead to neat and decisive results. Perhaps, however, this road can be avoided, and the skeptics challenged in another manner.

C. The importance of legal and linguistic conventions

There have long been arguments about the extent to which any organization or association (e.g., a company, corporation, club, union, team, etc., as well as legislature) can, not being a man, nevertheless behave like or be treated as a man. The view that some can is buttressed by modern law, which treats certain types of organizations and associations in ways that could be variously described as (i) treating them *for certain purposes* as (or as though they were) men, and (ii) treating them *in certain respects* as (or as though they were) men. Furthermore, in everyday speech we sometimes speak of them in ways suggesting the appropriateness of such treatment, and suggesting furthermore the appropriateness of ascribing intentions to them—e.g., we speak of them as *competing* with each other, *attempting* this, *succeeding* in that. The prevailing tendency in most of these cases has been to accept the talk,[1] but, when pressed, to attempt to 'translate' it into talk about the intentions or behavior of various members, employees, officers, agents, or trustees of the organization or association in question. The claim is then common (at least in the Fiction, Bracket, and Purpose Theories of the nature of corporate personality)[2] that the 'translation' provides the truth behind claims about the organizations which, if taken literally, would simply be fictions.

The skeptic thinks that statements of the form—'The intention of the legislature is X'—are 'fictional' or at best 'figurative', and that they cannot be true if taken 'literally'. But he would be careless to assert this in the absence of any clear understanding of the 'literal' significance of the statements. Since these statements have been made for several centuries without special stipulation as to their meaning, what plausible account of their present 'literal' significance would show them to be fictional or figurative? The considerations involved can perhaps be made clearer by an examination of talk about the *activities* of legislatures. Why should we agree that claims such as—'the legislature enacted a sales tax bill in 1961' —must, when taken literally, be fictions or only 'figurative' even though there are perfectly well-established legal criteria for determining what can count as an act of the legislature? It is true that in order for a legislature to have acted, it is necessary that certain men have acted. But (i) it would be a mistake to say that the legislature's having acted was nothing more than these men having acted.[3] And (ii) there is nothing fictional about the legal

---

[1] The acceptance with respect to corporations has sometimes been justified by an appeal notably absent in discussions of legislative intent—viz., by arguing that the extent to which corporations may reasonably be treated in this way is simply a matter of public policy. Thus, for example, against the claim that corporations, *unlike* men, are solely creatures of law and hence incapable of illegal intent, one might argue that *as a matter of public policy* it would be better to treat corporation as *like* men in this respect; this would bring corporate assets and perhaps even corporate officers within easier reach of sanctions against behavior contrary to the public interest. In contrast to this approach, the dispute concerning legislative intent has almost universally been treated as though it were a factual and not a policy issue. The leading question has not been, 'what is to be gained by treating legislatures as capable of intent?' Rather it has been 'Are legislatures capable of intent?'

[2] Cf. PATON, A TEXTBOOK OF JURISPRUDENCE 365–76 (3d ed. Derham 1964).

[3] It would miss the role of rules in determining which of the activities of these men could count as activities of the legislature. See H. L. A. Hart's discussion of this point with respect to corporations in HART, DEFINITION AND THEORY IN JURISPRUDENCE 21–24 (1953).

significance of the criteria for determining whether the legislature acted.

In view of well-established legal criteria for telling when legislatures have acted, and in view of the obvious truth that these criteria are often satisfied, it seems futilely dogmatic to insist without special excuse that statements about legislatures having acted can never be *literally* true. Such statements may sometimes be false, but their *sense* when taken 'literally' is surely a matter of which conventions are well established in, or have been stipulated for, the relevant linguistic community. The question now is whether there are any such conventions with respect to legislative intentions, and if so, how well established are they?

It is important to be clear about what is being asked. We are not asking whether legislatures are conventionally supposed to have intentions; nor are we asking whether there is 'evidence' that is conventionally supposed to be good evidence of the presence of such intentions. Rather, we are asking whether there are any generally accepted conventions concerning *what it would be like for a legislature to have an intention*—i.e., concerning the conditions that actually would constitute a case of a legislature's having an intention.

The importance of keeping these questions distinct is shown by the recent, and otherwise highly rewarding, discussion of similar problems by Witherspoon.[1] Witherspoon seems to consider the matter of legislative purpose from a standpoint much like the above. But he does not focus the issue sharply enough; as a result he moves too far too fast. He points to the undeniable fact that courts, administrative agencies, legislators, scholars and practitioners talk in terms of legislative purpose; he concludes that, given such firmly established practices, there are such things as legislative purposes.[2] This is an error; one could, if allowed to select the appropriate linguistic communities, use the same kind of argument to prove the existence of Santa Claus, Zeus, and dragons. The fact that people talk about certain things as though they existed does not warrant the conclusion that these things exist. Nor does the fact that people conventionally appeal to certain kinds of data as good evidence for the existence of something, warrant the conclusion that these data are indeed good

---

[1] Witherspoon (cited above p. 239 n. 1) pp. 756–8, 790–1.
[2] ibid. pp. 789–91.

evidence for the existence of that thing. The crucial task is to discover generally accepted conventions concerning *what it would be like* for a legislature to have an intention or a purpose. Only then (barring objections of the types sketched in Section B above) can one go on in an intelligent way to discuss whether there ever are such things, and to discuss what should be accepted as good evidence of them.

What are the facts, then? It is obvious that there is considerable disagreement within the legal community as to whether legislatures ever have intentions. There is also disagreement as to what would be adequate evidence of the presence of such intentions. But is there any appreciable disagreement on *what it would be like* for a legislature to have an intention? The answer to this question appears initially to be 'no'. With the exception of Kocourek and Bruncken,[1] we have found no author reluctant to agree that a legislature should be admitted to have an intention *vis-à-vis* a statute if each and every member of the legislature had that intention.[2] Furthermore, we have found very few authors showing any unwillingness to accept an even weaker condition—namely, that a legislature should be acknowledged to have an intention *vis-à-vis* a statute in case each of the majority who voted for the statute had that intention.[3] Virtually all the persons who have discussed the issue of legislative intent seem to *assume* that the fulfillment of this last condition is sufficient to support claims about the intention of a legislature. No one, as far as we have been able to discover, thinks

[1] Bruncken's acceptance of the unanimity and majority models of legislative intent is clearly a concession he makes for the sake of further argument. See Bruncken (cited above p. 237 n. 2) p. 130.

[2] There may be difficulties with this if it is taken straightforwardly, but these difficulties have not troubled the skeptics. For example, a legislature can enact a bill into law; a legislator (that is, a member of a legislative assembly) cannot. He can only vote for the bill in the hope that it will be enacted into law. Thus, for example, a legislator can at most intend by his vote to help enact the legislation with a view to what it would, if enacted, achieve. The achievement of the latter is what the legislature might be said to intend; a contribution to the achievement of the latter might be what the legislator intends. In what follows, I shall suppose such shifts to be understood.

[3] Of course, Kocourek would be unwilling. Bruncken considers it a concession. Bruncken (cited above p. 237 n. 2) p. 130. Radin did not come down decisively either way. Radin (cited above p. 237 n. 2) p. 870. Corry shows a decided reluctance to accept it. Corry, *The Use of Legislative History in the Interpretation of Statutes* 32 CAN. BAR. REV. 624, 625–6 (1954). However, he did not show this reluctance earlier. Corry, *Administrative Law and the Interpretation of Statutes* I U. TORONTO L. J. 286, 290 (1936).

it necessary even to *argue* the point. All the hullabaloo has been about whether that many legislators ever do share any significant intentions *vis-à-vis* a statute, and whether, if they do, we can ever know of it.

This apparent agreement should be approached cautiously. Perhaps it is only a product of the confidence of many skeptics that they need not go so far as to question it because they can show that the majority of legislators never share intentions. It is therefore desirable initially to see whether such confidence is misplaced, or whether it is indeed unnecessary to investigate the (provisional?) agreement. We shall consider this by way of a detailed examination of the arguments used by Payne to support his skeptical position. His arguments are not only the most substantial yet to be offered on the subject, but they also share crucial claims with the bulk of commentators, both pro and con, on this problem. One caveat: Payne thinks of legislative intent more or less in terms of our question (5)—i.e., in terms of how the legislature intended the (general) words of a statute to be understood. Perhaps he would extend the argument to include other items on our list, but this is uncertain.

D. *The futility of the common skeptical arguments*

Payne accepts without question the common view that the intentions of a legislature relative to a statute must be identified with the intentions of those legislators who voted for the bill, and further that the intentions of the legislature are the intentions those legislators share. But he claims that the legislature cannot have a single state of mind.

Context does much to fix the extension of a general word, but even the fullest consideration of context generally leaves an uncertain fringe of meaning, and it is this uncertain fringe of meaning which gives rise to so many problems of statutory interpretation. For example, is linoleum "furniture"? . . . It is impossible to decide such questions by reference to the intention of the legislature since the mental images of the various members of the legislature who vote for a bill containing such a general word will exhibit the same imprecision and lack of agreement as found in the common usage of the word. This would be true even if every member of the legislature voting for the bill reflected at length on the extension of the particular general word, *for reflection would not necessarily entail agreement.*[1]

[1] Payne (cited above p. 248 n. 3) p. 98 (my italics).

What Payne says here seems quite sensible, but the italicized portion shows his error. He has tried to move from saying that reflection does not entail agreement to saying that, even with reflection, agreement is impossible. This move is illegitimate, and consequently he has not shown that there *cannot* be a single state of mind (agreement).

Notice next that his claim about the unlikelihood or impossibility of a single state of mind is indeterminate. This is revealed by his concentration in the above passage upon borderline or 'fringe areas' of the extensions of general words. The question which should be asked about his claim is—a single state of mind pertaining to what? The whole extension of the word? Or only some part of that extension? It is surely not necessary for persons to agree in *all* cases in order for them to agree in *some* cases. What Payne has done here (and does elsewhere in his essay)[1] is to claim that there cannot *ever* be agreement, although he demonstrates only that there cannot *always* be agreement. But surely, if agreement among the legislators is a prerequisite of legislative intent, a person who wishes to claim that there is legislative intent in this or that specific case is not bound to claim that there is always intent in every case. It is true that some persons may have committed themselves to the view that there is *always* intent of the sort Payne is discussing;[2] his argument might shake them. But he is very far from having shown that there cannot sometimes be such intent, or even that there cannot often be such intent.

Consider next his supposition, shared without argument by Radin, Jones, de Sloovère, and perhaps Landis, that in order for several legislators to have the same intention relative to the understanding of a general work in a statute, it is necessary for them to have had the same 'mental images', at least relative to the instant case.[3] Payne argues:

[1] ibid. pp. 101–2.
[2] Perhaps such a view is implied by Crawford and Llewellyn. See note 2, p. 241 above.
[3] See Radin (cited above p. 237 n. 2) pp. 869–70. Landis is chary of this kind of talk, but his discussion of 'determinates' implies a similar view. Landis, *A Note on "Statutory Interpretation"* 43 HARV. L. REV. 886, 889 (1930). For other examples of the view in question, see Jones, *Statutory Doubts and Legislative Intention* 40 COLUM. L. REV. 957, 967 (1940); and de Sloovère, *Extrinsic Aids in the Interpretation of Statutes* 88 U. PA. L. REV. 527, 533–8 (1940). Perhaps Frankfurter would also be sympathetic to this view; see Frankfurter (cited above p. 282 n. 2).

How can it be said that [the legislator] has any intention in respect of a particular covered by the general word which did not occur to his mind. . . ? [I]t would, I suggest, be a strange use of language to say that the user of such a general word "intends" it to apply to a particular that never occurred to his mind.[1]

Payne has only the vestige of a good point here. The behavior of a man who took Payne seriously could be extraordinary. Suppose that, needing a large number of ashtrays for an impending meeting in a building unfamiliar to me, I ask my assistant to scout around and bring back all the ashtrays he can find in the building. He comes back empty-handed, saying the following: 'I found a good many ashtrays, but naturally wanted to bring back only those you intended me to bring back. So, as I picked up each one, I asked myself—did he intend me to bring this ashtray back? Upon doing this, I realized in each case that it would certainly be a strange use of language to say that you "intended" me to bring back that ashtray, as it was virtually certain that the thought of that ashtray had never occurred to you—after all, you had never even been in this building before. In the end, therefore, I found it most sensible to return without any.'

Clearly, such behavior would be idiotic. But it is also true that my assistant could have erred at the opposite extreme. Suppose he had ripped built-in ashtrays off the walls of the building, snatched ashtrays from persons using them and removed a hundred thousand ashtrays from a storage room. In each of these situations I might protest that I had not intended him to do that, and that he should have known better than to think I did. The ground for the latter claim, however, would not be that he should have realized that the thought of those particular ashtrays had never occurred to me; after all, he was already virtually certain of this. Rather, the ground would be that, given the circumstances, he should have understood that I did not need a hundred thousand ashtrays and that my interest in having ashtrays was not so pressing as to require

---

[1] Payne (cited above p. 248 n. 3) p. 101. But he also says later (p. 105):

'A statute is a formal document intended to warrant the conduct of judges and officials, and if any intention can fairly be ascribed to the legislature, it is that the statute should be applied to situations not present to the mind of its members.'

The whole challenge lies, if one is to make sense of Payne's arguments, in understanding how the claims in these two sets of remarks are related to each other; but he does not enlighten us here. Perhaps he is moving toward the agency theory discussed below.

him to rip them off walls, etc. It is true that I might say that the thought never occurred to me that there were any built-in ashtrays in the building; or, the thought never occurred to me that he would snatch ashtrays out of people's hands. Thus, I might react against the claim that I had intended x by making statements roughly in the form: 'The thought of such a thing as x never occurred to me.' But the point of this remark is not merely that the thought of such a thing as x had not occurred to me; there is also a clear suggestion that *if* such a thought had occurred to me I would have *excepted* such things as x.[1] Without this further suggestion, my remark would surely seem pointless.

The mere fact that the thought of such a thing as x hadn't occurred to me does not imply anything about what I did or did not intend. It follows that in our ashtray case the thought of this or that kind of ashtray, or the thought of getting ashtrays in this or that kind of circumstance, need not have occurred to me in order for me to have intended that my assistant get such ashtrays or get ashtrays under such circumstances. Payne, Radin and others who have discussed legislative intent in terms of 'mental images', 'mental pictures', and 'the contents of the mind of the legislator' have been fundamentally wrong in certain important respects. If, as the above discussion shows, a legislator voting for a bill need not actually have thought of each and every particular that he can reasonably be said to have intended the words of the bill to cover, nor thought of each and every *type* of particular, then the mere fact that two legislators have not thought of the same particulars or of particulars of the same types in connection with some general word in a bill shows neither that they disagreed nor that they agreed in their intention to have those particulars or particulars of those types covered by the bill. Of course, what a legislator did

---

[1] Note also that the key phrase is not that which Payne's remarks suggest: for, 'such a thing as X' refers to a *type* of particular rather than to a particular. (Furthermore, some of the types referred to were types of circumstances rather than types of ashtrays.)

Radin, and by implication Landis, may have had this in mind when discussing the 'determinate' as the issue in litigation. They may, that is, have been referring to issue-types. More likely, they may have been counting issues in such a way that one and the same issue could appear in many cases. But if they were doing either, then Radin's talk about 'mental images' and 'pictures' becomes inappropriate, as Payne rightly recognizes and argues. See Payne (cited above p. 238 n. 3) p. 99; see also Radin (cited above p. 237 n. 2) p. 869; Landis (cited above p. 237 n. 3) p. 887.

think of does make a difference. But what he did not think of does not make a difference *unless* he would have excepted it had he thought of it.

But how are we to *know* whether he would have excepted it? Supposing that we cannot interview him (or that, if we did, he and we might find it difficult to distinguish between his intention *then* and his decision *now*), would not we always be uncertain? Hagerstrom, in the course of arguing against certain appeals to the intention of the legislator, thinks so.[1] In an interesting discussion of the 'unprovided-for case', he concludes that in reality the decisive factor is only the degree to which the *interpreter's feelings of value* are shocked. If, for example, my assistant, while out gathering ashtrays for me, were to be shocked by the idea of snatching ashtrays from people currently using them, he will impute to me an intention not to have him do that, even though I had made no mention of such a case but had merely said 'bring back all the ashtrays you can find'.

But such results are not inevitable. My assistant may react differently. He may be a very crude fellow, or one who places a much greater importance on having ashtrays for the meeting than I do. In either case, *he* might not be disturbed at all by the thought of snatching ashtrays from people; but, knowing me, he might think: 'That silly old fool *would* be shocked by this, so I'd better not do it.' We can also imagine the reverse—that is, a case where the assistant *is* shocked, but, realizing that I would not be, steels himself to the task.

Imputed intentions may require a fair degree of intimacy with the person whose intentions are being considered. Even then, there may be circumstances in which the imputations would be highly uncertain. These two considerations are important— especially in dealing with the intentions of legislators *vis-à-vis* circumstances that, so far as we can tell, they did not contemplate or foresee. The interpreter of a statute may be remote in time, place, social stratum or background from many or all of the legislators who had a hand in enacting the statute. There may only be a small range of cases in which he can reasonably impute to them approval or disapproval of various outcomes. But there will

---

[1] HAGERSTROM (cited above p. 243 n. 1) pp. 82–83. For other discussions of this point see HART & SACKS, THE LEGAL PROCESS 97–98 (Tent. ed. 1958); and Witherspoon (cited above p. 239 n. 1) pp. 776–82.

surely be such a range, provided that the interpreter is not completely ignorant of the beliefs and attitudes of these men. The
frequency with which such imputations may be made depends
upon the cases that arise; there may be many or few cases within
the range of reasonable imputation.[1]

What, however, of cases where the uncontemplated and unfore-
seen things, circumstances, or types thereof are such that the
legislator would not unhesitatingly have designated them by the
general words he used? To return to the ashtrays example, suppose
that when I asked my assistant to bring back all the ashtrays he
could find, it never occurred to me that he might run across some
items that were for me not clearly ashtrays, but were enough like
ashtrays to have made me hesitate over them.[2] If he ran across
such items, neither he nor I might be clear about whether I had
intended him to bring them back. Insofar as I was not certain
whether they *were* ashtrays, I could not be certain that I had
intended him to bring them back; insofar as I was not certain they
were not ashtrays, I could not be certain that I had not intended him
to bring them back. Thus, the question of whether I would have
excepted them if I had thought of them may have no decisive
answer.

A common move at this point is to claim that I had no intentions
whatever in connection with such cases.[3] This is misleading. The
occurrence of such a case may be an occasion for abandoning
reliance upon what was intended; but the abandonment should
not be justified by denying that one had any intentions at all in
connection with the case; it should be justified simply by pointing
out that the applicability of one's intentions to the instant case is
not clear, and that appeal to intentions therefore does not afford
guidance in the case. The undecidability is not due to limitations

[1] Perhaps it is worth pointing out that the imputation spoken of here is not
what Cohen calls 'legisputation'. Cohen, *Judicial 'Legisputation' and Dimensions
of Legislative Meaning* 36 IND. L. J. 414, 418 (1961). While it agrees with 'legisputation' in referring to probable legislative meaning, it concerns meaning at the
time of enactment and not what the legislature would have thought if it had 'the
awareness of the problems that hindsight now permits'. See also, Bruncken
(cited above p. 237 n. 2) p. 135; Curtis, *A Better Theory of Legal Interpretations*
3 VAND. L. REV. 407, 412 (1950).
[2] As almost everyone recognizes, this is the type of circumstance faced by the
Court in *McBoyle v. United States*, 283 U.S. 25 (1930).
[3] Cf. Gray's oft-quoted remark in THE NATURE AND SOURCES OF LAW 173 (2d
ed. 1921).

on our tools of investigation (e.g., that we do not have total recall); rather it is due both to the fact that there are limitations on the preciseness of the intentions a person can have, and to the fact that new experience can challenge the rationale of old classifications. But it is misleading in such circumstances to claim that we had no intentions whatsoever. This claim suggests something quite false—that there is no connection between the circumstances and our intentions—whereas, the whole problem lies in the fact that there is a connection but one which is not clear enough to afford us guidance when we appeal to the intentions.

It is now timely to reconsider the crucial assumption on which all the arguments and counterarguments were based—the agreement that an intention *vis-à-vis* a bill shared by all the legislators in the majority voting for the bill would count as an intention of the legislature. As previously noted, one might argue that this agreement has only been provisional. One might claim that Radin, Payne and other skeptics stop here only because they believe they can, even on this assumption, show the impossibility of such a thing as an intention of a legislature.[1] But the examination of Payne's arguments shows the skeptical arguments to be insufficient. Thus, we are forced to confront the agreement in question, and consider its status. Is it only provisional? *Would* most or all of the skeptics retreat to some position behind it? What would this position be?

E. The path of further argument

The skeptic might argue that the widespread agreement about the conditions under which a legislature can have an intention was *unreasonable*. His grounds could be any or all of the following:

1. That not even the majority condition is taken seriously by a significant section of the legal community (viz., judges and administrators)—that even though legislative intent is possible and its occurrence not in every respect infrequent, conventional appeals to it are clearly fictional in the sense of being based upon wholly inadequate evidence of its presence.
2. That no other models of legislative intent could find serious support in legislative, judicial and administrative practices.
3. That all models in the end make the obviously unsound move of treating legislatures as human beings.

[1] The clearest case of this attitude is in Bruncken (cited above p. 237 n. 2) p. 130.

4. That, in view of the difficulty of using any of the models proffered to arrive at plausible accounts of what 'legislative intent' could mean, there are no policy considerations sufficient to support continued use of the expression.

The first argument should be approached cautiously. Commentators using it generally exhibit a fatal tendency to assume that the majority condition discussed above is not merely a sufficient but also a necessary condition for legislative intent. They have failed to recognize that acceptance of weaker and perhaps even quite different conditions might be reasonable, and that, therefore, the common run of claims about legislative intent may not be so strikingly irresponsible or 'fictional' after all.

But this defense merely calls in the second argument: *are* there any other such conditions? This is a difficult question. Support for the 'literal truth' of claims that legislatures have *acted* comes from the citation of explicit legal rules (for example, constitutional ones) setting out the circumstances under which the behavior of legislators will count as an act by a legislature. It is true that even the rules for determining when a legislature has acted (such as rules determining the circumstances under which an 'enacting' vote can be taken on a bill, the ways of casting and tallying votes, the proportion of affirmative votes needed for enactment) are sometimes difficult to interpret and apply; but legislators clearly go to great lengths to establish explicitly and precisely the conditions under which the legislature will be regarded as having enacted a statute. They have not, however, given any such formal and extended consideration to the conditions under which the legislature will be regarded as having an intention, except perhaps the intention to enact the statute itself and to use the words appearing in the statute. The acceptance by the legislators of a majority of affirmative votes as constituting (under certain conditions) the enactment of a statute, sheds no light whatever on what they would accept as constituting a legislative intent outside of an intent to enact the statute itself. There is no evidence, indeed, that any legislature has, for its own use, attempted to establish *formal* criteria for the determination of legislative intent *vis-à-vis* statutes other than the use of statements of intent somewhere within the statutes themselves.[1]

[1] This is not surprising. One can imagine that authoritative expressions about legislative intent outside the individual statutes would fare no better before

Although legislatures have not provided criteria for the determination of legislative intent, there are relevant judicial and
administrative practices. Not only do judges and administrators
regularly refer to 'the intentions of the legislature', but, in various
jurisdictions at various times, more or less regular use is made of
'presumptions' as to the intentions of the legislature—e.g., that
there is no intent to interfere with the common law unless explicitly stated. Use is also made of appeals to records of legislative
proceedings as 'evidence' of the intentions of the legislature.

The third argument was that all models of legislative intent will
in the end make the unsound move of treating legislatures as human
beings. As shown earlier, the roots of this argument are very deep.
We shall not pursue the matter further, except to suggest below
some relevant analogies and disanalogies to legal treatments of
persons and to suggest in closing some possible variations in our
attitudes toward the issue.

The fourth argument was that, in view of the difficulties in
arriving at plausible accounts of what 'legislative intent' could
amount to on any of the models put forward, there are no policy
considerations sufficient to support continued use of the expression.
Although considerations bearing on this argument will also be
mentioned briefly at various stages of the discussion below, it will
be raised again directly only at the end of the paper.

F. Models of legislative intent

The following discussion of models of legislative intent attempts to
discover what support each can muster against the above arguments.

1. *The majority model.* Consider initially the following straightforward argument for the sufficiency of the majority model of
legislative intent. On the supposition that judges and administrators believe themselves to have a legitimate interest in the
intentions of the legislature, if there were any such intentions, they
might argue as follows:

'The idea of a legislature intending x without *any* of its members,
officers or agents intending x would hardly give us even a beginning
for an acceptable account of the intentions of the legislature. But, if
at least some member(s), officer(s) or agent(s) of the legislature
must intend x, then which and how many? Given that our interest

---

judges, administrators and the public than statutory preambles. They too
would require 'interpretation' if we were to take them seriously.

is in the intentions of the legislature concerning a statute enacted by it, we may start by considering the conditions under which the statement "The legislature enacted the statute" is true. What, in short, counts as a legislature's enacting a statute?

'The important thing is to see what, in accordance with constitutional and legislative rules, results in and amounts to the enactment of a statute. Ordinarily this has to do with majorities of affirmative votes by the legislators, taken and tallied under specified conditions.[1] But, if such a coincidence in behavior (voting affirmatively) by a majority of the legislators is sufficient for and equivalent to saying that the *legislature* has acted (i.e., has enacted a piece of legislation), then a coincidence in the intentions of those very same legislators *vis-à-vis* the bill and their affirmative votes for it should be sufficient in determining what the *legislature* intended (if anything) by the act or relative to the act.

'The main principle behind our argument is as follows: When there is a group, organization or association recognized by a legal system as a unit for the assignment of rights, powers, duties, etc. (e.g., the *legislature* has the legal capacity to legislate, and the legislators do not, either separately or collectively, *except* when acting in such a way that they constitute a legislature), certain activities on the part of officers, agents or employees of the organization will in certain circumstances be recognized at law as resulting in and amounting to acts of the organization. In such cases, it is reasonable to identify as the intention of the organization in so acting at least whatever intentions are shared by those of its officers, agents, etc., who have discretionary powers in determining or contributing to the determination of what the group does. This is a conventional approach to the intentions of corporations.[2] It should apply to legislatures as well.'

From the viewpoint of judges and administrators, this hypothesized argument might seem reasonable. But do the actual practices of these officials support the majority model argued for? Anyone taking a close look at current judicial and administrative practices must conclude that these practices have only the slightest

[1] Excluding executive endorsement or acquiescence (the expression 'intention of the legislature' does not require us to consider them), and leaving open whether we would allow something to count as a statute if it were not subsequently enrolled or promulgated. Accounting for bicameral legislatures would, of course, complicate but not vitiate the argument.

[2] See GRAY (cited above p. 259 n. 3) p. 55.

relationship to that model. While judges and administrators obviously utilize evidence of the intentions of various individual legislators, they make no serious attempts to discover the actual intentions of the voting majorities; further, our records of legislative proceedings are still not sufficient to support such an enterprise. There are presumptions galore about what, in the light of our records, the legislators must have been aware of and agreed with, but the realities of legislative processes are such that few of these presumptions are thought to be reliable *enough*.

This may persuade some commentators that courts and administrators generally have not been genuinely interested in the intentions of legislatures. But the behavior of judges and administrators *vis-à-vis* legislative intent would clearly be capricious and irresponsible only if they believed that the majority model set out necessary as well as sufficient conditions for the existence of legislative intent. There is no reason to suppose the judges and administrators believe this, nor did 'their' argument above suppose it. Thus there is no good reason to believe that their behavior is either capricious or irresponsible until it is seen to be so in the light of a model plausibly supposed to be their model of the *minimal* conditions for the existence of legislative intent.

Of course, it may not be necessary to move immediately to searching for such a weaker model. Instead we may attempt to uphold the majority model, but restrict the scope of its legitimate application. The conventional move by commentators is to reject appeals to legislative intentions in favor of appeals to legislative purposes.[1] For these commentators, appeals to the former are appeals to the aims of the *details* of statutes, whereas appeals to the latter are appeals to the much more highly generalized purposes behind the statutes, taken as wholes.[2]

---

[1] This is characteristic of the writers cited above pp. 238 n. 2–5.

[2] See, e.g., Corry, *Administrative Law and the Interpretation of Statutes* 1 U. TORONTO L. J. 286, 290–2 (1936):
'Even the majority who vote for complex legislation do not have any common intention *as to its detailed provisions*. Though the intention of the legislature is a fiction, the purpose or object of the legislation is very real. *No enactment is ever passed for the sake of its details; it is passed in an attempt to realize a social purpose.* It is what is variously called the aim and object of the enactment, the spirit of the legislation, the mischief and the remedy.' (My italics.)
It is not always clear when a commentator is in fact making this move. Talk about the (general) purposes of the statute sometimes seems to refer to what the statute was designed to achieve and sometimes to the purposes interpreters can

The motive behind such a move is obvious. It is an attempt to show that judicial and administrative practices do support the majority model of legislative intent if the applicability of the model is restricted to the more highly general intentions of the legislators.[1] The argument is that, in view of modern legislative processes, coincident purposes among the legislators regarding the highly general aims of a statute are more likely than coincident purposes regarding the specific aims of portions of the statute. Thus, special investigations of each legislator in the majority relative to such more 'general' purposes are not needed.[2]

Is it a valid presumption that consensus among the legislators on various purposes of a statute is more likely in proportion to the generality of the purposes? A distinction must be drawn between a purpose that a legislator actually has, and a purpose that he is aware of as one he is supposed to have or is presumed to have. For, as one considers purposes of greater and greater generality, it becomes more and more likely—not so much that the legislators share those purposes—but rather that they are aware of them as purposes that others have, or as purposes that they themselves are presumed to have. One of Witherspoon's examples of such a general 'purpose' is:

To have the statutory formula so administered as to avoid specific procedural or substantive evils collateral to the main purposes of the statute: e.g., undue federal intrusion into matters normally committed to resolution by state authority.[3]

It is easy to imagine a legislator knowing that he is supposed or presumed to have this purpose or that others have it, but it is also

[1] Witherspoon in fact extends this generality to consideration, not merely of specific aims *vis-à-vis* a particular statute, but also to whole programs of statute-making, and even to the aims of the legislative process itself, as seen in the light of the traditional functions of legislatures. See Witherspoon (cited above p. 239 n. 1) pp. 758, 795–805, 831–2.

[2] Another argument sometimes made in support of the restriction is that highly general aims are more important to the legislators themselves than specific aims. Cf. Witherspoon (cited above p. 239 n. 1) pp. 790, 812, 827. See also HART & SACKS (cited above p. 258 n. 1) p. 1285, where the authors say that 'the probative force of materials from the internal legislative history of a statute varies in proportion to the *generality* of its bearing upon the purpose of the statute or provision in question'. (Emphasis added.) They are here seemingly appealing to both of the above considerations.

[3] Witherspoon (cited above p. 239 n. 1) pp. 799–800.

find for the statute. See Radin (cited above p. 238 n. 5) pp. 422–3, 406, 408, 411, 419.

S

easy to imagine him not having it—even though he votes for the legislation in question. Some commentators, realizing that more legislators are likely to be *aware* of such purposes than are aware of the specific purposes of the details of the legislation in question, have either (i) too facilely assumed that being aware of the purpose is equivalent to having it, or (ii) too facilely assumed that silence in the face of knowledge that one may possibly be presumed to share a certain purpose is a good sign that one actually does share the purpose. In fact, there seems little reason to believe that the generality of the purpose alone much increases the confidence with which we can say that the voting majority has it.

It is not much easier to learn about the general purposes of legislators than to learn about the specific intentions of legislators. Thus, even if we look only at general purposes, current judicial and administrative practices are insufficient to support the majority model. We must search for another model of legislative intent which comports more closely with judicial and administrative behavior.

2. *The agency model.* It is possible that judges and administrators use an agency model of legislative intent. This model recognizes that legislatures delegate certain responsibilities (such as filling in the statutory details) to various persons (legislative draftsmen, committee chairmen, judges, administrators), and that this may justify appealing to the intentions of these persons as the intentions of the legislature regarding the aims of statutes or the details thereof.

Few commentators have explicitly appealed to the agency model, but several have touched on it. Driedger appears to identify the intention of the legislature with the intentions of the draftsmen. The competent draftsman

has in his mind a complete legislative scheme and he attempts to give expression to that scheme in a logical and orderly manner; every provision in the statute must fit into that scheme, and the scheme is as complete as he can conceive it.

It is this legislative scheme that should be regarded as the purpose, object, intent, spirit, of the Act.[1]

The following remark by Judge Learned Hand suggests identifying the intentions of the legislature with the intentions of legislative committees. He says:

[1] DREIDGER (cited above p. 241 n. 3) p. 161. See also Bruncken (cited above p. 237 n. 2) p. 130.

[Courts] recognize that while members deliberately express their personal position upon the general purposes of the legislation, as to the details of its articulation they accept the work of the committees; so much they delegate because legislation could not go on in any other way.[1]

A remark by de Sloovère, taken in isolation, suggests turning in quite a different direction—viz., to the interpreter, or at least to a class of interpreters. He says:

The only legislative intention, whenever the statute is not plain and explicit, is to authorize the courts to attribute a meaning to a statute within the limitations prescribed by the text and by the context. . . . In other words, a single meaning which the text will reasonably bear must, if genuine, be considered not as the conclusion which the legislature would have arrived at, *but one which the legislature by the text has authorized the courts to find.*[2]

These remarks suggest that the legislature delegates certain responsibilities to other persons in connection with statutes, and in doing so, the legislature exhibits its intention to rely on the judgment and discretion of these persons concerning how to achieve what the legislature wants the statute to achieve. Consequently, the judgment of these persons, having been authorized by the legislature, may stand for the judgment of the legislature. These persons now have somewhat, if not actually, the status of agents of the legislature.[3] Thus, our discovery of what these persons intended in attempting to carry out the assignment of the legislature (e.g., to draft a bill that would, in their judgment, achieve what the legislature wanted to achieve; to interpret the language of the bill so as, in their judgment, to achieve what the legislature wanted to achieve)

[1] *SEC* v. *Collier*, 76 F.2d 939, 941 (2d Cir. 1935). At least one commentator agrees that Judge Hand's statement here implies agency. See Johnstone (cited above p. 238 n. 1) p. 14.

[2] de Sloovère, *Preliminary Questions in Statutory Interpretation* 9 N.Y.U.L.Q. REV. 407, 415 (1932). (Emphasis added). See also Curtis (cited above p. 259 n. 1) p. 425; and, in comment on Curtis' view, Clark, *Special Problems in Drafting and Interpreting Procedural Codes and Rules* 3 VAND. L. REV. 493, 494–5, 503, 506 (1950). But de Sloovère clearly disclaims that the result of such authorization accords with any supposed legislative intention.

[3] 'An agent. . . is one who acts as a conduit pipe through which legal relations flow from his principal to another. Agency is created by a juristic act by which one person (the principal) gives to another (the agent) the power to do something for *and in the name of* the principal so as to bind the latter directly.' PATON (cited above p. 251 n. 2) p. 285. (My italics.)

is a discovery of intentions that the legislature stood behind, wished us to attend to, wished us to regard as authoritative as their own—indeed, wished us to regard *as* their own. These intentions may therefore be taken as, and in fact are, the intentions of the legislature.

The agency model *would* render rational the present 'investigations' of judges and administrators into legislative intent, and it would do this without reliance on so many presumptions about the significance of the silence of individual legislators. Investigations of the intentions of 'agents' would be sufficient to establish (because they would be equivalent to) the intentions of the legislature. However, the agency model is extremely perilous. It not only requires us to consider whether any of its variations are persuasively similar to typical agency situations, but it confronts us with difficult problems concerning agency itself and in particular concerning the reasonableness of identifying the will of the agent with the will of his principal. Consider the following:

(a) If the legislature is to be thought of as the principal, we presumably would need to know how to identify the actions and intentions of this principal. But, what model of the *latter* are we to use? We would need to feel at home with some *other* model of legislative intention and purpose before we could get on with establishing the plausibility of this new model. Presumably, this earlier model would be the majority model. But the adequacy of this model has not yet been decisively established.

(b) Even within the traditions of agency the proposal that the actions and judgment of an agent be taken for the actions and judgment of his principal is open to charges of fictionalizing every bit as severe as the initial charges concerning the intentions of legislatures (and by way of them, concerning the nature of corporate personalities).[1] For example, as with the initial controversy, there would be difficulties about whether analogies sufficiently strong to support a claim of identity could be found between the relationship of a principal to his own acts and his relationship to the acts of his agent.[2] Also there will be a worry similar to our earlier worry about the *explicitness* of the legal rules supporting the claims made—that is, a worry about the character

---

[1] Cf. HOLMES, COLLECTED LEGAL PAPERS 49 (1952).
[2] Ibid. pp. 52–53, where he is patently exploring precisely this.

of the 'juristic act' by which a person designates someone as his agent, and about the degree of explicitness needed in such a 'bestowal' of power.[1]

(c) Finally, and closely connected with this last point, each variation of the agency-model—delegation to committee, to courts, etc.—would have to be examined separately in order to discover the justifiability of saying that such a specific 'bestowal' of power had actually been made by the legislature.

The strongest case for the bestowal of such power could surely be made in the case of legislative reliance upon draftsmen and committee chairmen. In view of the realities of legislative proceedings, it is certainly plausible to say that legislatures go very far in relying on the judgment and discretion of such persons.[2] When it comes to the interpreters of statutes such as judges and administrators, the claim that legislatures have bestowed such power seems highly dubious. Hagerstrom, for example, gives such a claim short shrift. He says:

> Such a general authorization cannot usually be shown to exist. It is a mere fiction motivated by desire to defend the will-theory, and it may be compared with similarly motivated fictions concerning customary law as the general will.[3]

It should be noted, too, that Hagerstrom is here talking about a well-hedged and limited authorization.

One might counter, however, by claiming that the authorization need not be explicit. In the law of agency, after all, the authorization is not always explicit either—as in instances of so-called 'agency of necessity'.[4] It would surely be a matter of 'necessity' that the best judgment of judges and administrators be relied upon by legislatures. But this argument appears to go too far. We would not want in any wholesale way to hold legislatures responsible for what judges and administrators make out of statutes.

So much, then, for various models of legislative intent and for

---

[1] Cf. PATON (cited above p. 251 n. 2) p. 287.

[2] Cf. Witherspoon, *Administrative Discretion to Determine Statutory Meaning: 'The Low Road'* 38 TEXAS L. REV. 392, 430 (1959). It should be noted, however, that the work of draftsmen and committee chairmen has no legal effect until endorsed by the legislature. This is a striking *dis*analogy with the customary situation in agency.

[3] HAGERSTROM (cited above p. 243 n. 1) p. 93.

[4] See PATON (cited above p. 251 n. 2) p. 287.

the justifiability of *de novo* introduction of the use of such models. We have seen that one strongly justified model of such intentions (the majority model) finds little serious support in current judicial and administrative investigations of the intentions of legislatures. We have also seen that the model fitting these investigations best (the agency model) is also the most difficult to justify. But, while the arguments on behalf of either model cannot be decisive, neither are they negligible. In the end our use of either or both of the models may depend simply upon how many ragged edges we are willing to tolerate in the conceptual framework we use to approach legal problems; or, alternatively, our use may depend, as will be suggested below, on how far we are willing to go in developing our legal institutions in such a way as to eliminate these ragged edges.

G. *The significance of model-entrenchment*

Our exploration of the justifiability of talk about legislative intentions cannot stop here. The 'realism' of such talk must be examined not only from the standpoint of the reasonableness of *introducing* such talk in light of our present institutions and practices; it must also be examined from the standpoint of how the reasonableness of such talk is supported by the fact that it is already a well-established part of the legal environment. That is, one should consider whether the established use of *references* to legislative intent does not itself produce conditions under which the references become more reasonable as the practice of making them becomes entrenched.

Quite apart from any consideration of whether starting the practice was a good idea in the first place, once it *has* been started it provides part of the institutional background against which legislators recognize themselves to be acting when proposing, investigating, discussing, and voting for bills. For example, all legislators now understand that views of the intentions of the legislature may well be formed in the light of certain standard presumptions (e.g., that there is no intent to interfere with the common law unless explicitly stated) and 'investigations' (e.g., of debates and committee reports on the bill). If the legislators have a capacity to contribute to the materials and to rebut the presumptions they know will be used by judges and administrators as indicia of the intentions of the legislature, their behavior will influence what the intentions of the legislature can reasonably be said to be.

At present, judicial and administrative uses of materials and presumptions are not always clear or predictable enough to provide a guide for the legislators. But one *can* describe circumstances in which the picture would be much clearer. Courts and administrators could establish much greater regularity in their use of preparatory materials and of 'presumptions' concerning legislative intent—a regularity sufficient to enable trained persons to predict with reasonable accuracy what the outcomes of these uses would be in specific cases.[1] Furthermore, legislatures could control the issuing of preparatory materials with a view to their use in just such ways by judges and administrators. In such circumstances, judicial and administrative investigations of the 'intentions of the legislature' would surely look more realistic and reasonable than they do today. Even today, however, circumstances provide *some* reason, although perhaps not *enough* reason, to say that realistic references to legislative intent can be made. Even now these references are made in an institutional environment which to some extent sustains their reasonableness.[2]

CONCLUSIONS

We have proposed several models of legislative intent and have examined (1) whether judges and administrators actually could

---

[1] Cf. Horack, *Cooperative Action for Improved Statutory Interpretation* 3 VAND. L. REV. 382, 387 (1950); Mayo, *The Interpretation of Statutes* 29 AUSTL. L. J. 204 (1955); Jackson (cited above p. 247 n. 1) pp. 537–8. And, for an extreme view, see Silving, *A Plea for a Law of Interpretation* 98 U. PA. L. REV. 499, 512 (1950).

[2] Notice in particular how present practices strengthen the temptation of all participants to treat legislatures as persons. When attempting to discover the intentions of a person *vis-à-vis* an action of his, we would think it helpful to be privy to his deliberations (if any) on whether to engage in that action. On analogy, when attempting to discover the intentions of a legislature *vis-à-vis* a statute, we obviously think it helpful to be privy to *its* deliberations on whether to enact the statute. Clearly, insofar as judges and administrators appeal to proceedings on the floor of the house, they are appealing to the deliberations of the legislature (as well as to the deliberations of the legislators). This is just what one would do, if he could, when attempting to learn more about the intentions of any creature. Furthermore, insofar as the investigator thinks that being privy to such deliberations would be helpful, it is not because he supposes that the picture gained will be clear, unequivocal and decisive. Deliberations of individuals on important acts may well be rehearsals of pros and cons quite as indefinite in character as the proceedings of many legislative deliberations.

be regarded as taking any of them seriously, and (2) whether they would be justified in taking any of them seriously. As predicted, the results of this examination are not conclusive. No one model of legislative intent is either so strongly or so weakly supported as to make its use either unproblematic or absurd. This is not surprising, given that the controversy about the intentions of legislatures has gone on for so long. But it is an important result to reach and to substantiate. We too often continue to demand clear-cut and decisive answers in the face of facts that simply will not support such answers, thus perpetuating controversy (because there always *is* something to be said for the other side) and rendering ourselves ineffective in dealing with the matters at hand. Our detailed discussion of the controversy over the existence and discoverability of legislative intent enables us to understand, for example, the inappropriateness of treating it only as a straightforward controversy over facts. Instead of continuing to ask only— *Are* legislatures capable of intent?—we should also shift to such questions as the following:

(a) Are there any policy considerations sufficient to justify continuance of references to legislative intent in view of the difficulties exposed? What, after all, *hangs* on whether the references are continued? This is essentially an inquiry into the *relevance* of appeals to legislative intent—an inquiry that has not been embarked upon here. But it is an inquiry given a new twist by what we have shown. The question is no longer simply: (i) Supposing that there is a legislative intent, what hangs on appealing to it? It is rather: (ii) Does enough hang on such appeals to make their continuance worth while even in the face of the difficulties exposed?

But, we may also ask: (b) Is it worth our while in terms of the ideological and practical importance of such appeals, to seek institutional changes strengthening the analogies between these appeals and appeals to intentions elsewhere in law and in life generally (this being the same for us as increasing the rationality of the appeals)? It is important to notice that the difficulties exposed above are not unavoidable facts of life; legislatures and the institutional environments in which they operate are, in a sense, our creatures and can be altered. Depending upon the model of legislative intent one has in mind (and I should emphasize that only the most obvious ones have been examined here), one may seek to bring the appeals closer to the conditions under which we attribute intentions to corporations, to principals via the intentions of their agents, or, above all, to individual men. The institutional changes accomplishing this could amount to such diverse measures as the fixing of formal limits on what may count as good evidence of legislative intent on the one hand, and alterations in the operating procedures of legislatures on the other.

The Obligation to Obey the Law

RICHARD A. WASSERSTROM[1]

I

The question of what is the nature and extent of one's obligation to obey the law is one of those relatively rare philosophic questions which can never produce doubts about the importance of theory for practice. To ask under what circumstances, if any, one is justified in disobeying the law, is to direct attention to problems which all would acknowledge to be substantial. Concrete, truly problematic situations are as old as civil society.

The general question was posed—though surely not for the first time—well over two thousand years ago in Athens when Crito revealed to Socrates that Socrates' escape from prison could be easily and successfully accomplished. The issue was made a compelling one—though once again surely not for the first time— by Crito's insistence that escape was not only possible but also *desirable*, and that disobedience to law was in *this* case at least, surely justified. And the problem received at the hand of Socrates —here perhaps for the first time—a sustained theoretical analysis and resolution.

Just as the question of what is the nature and extent of one's obligation to obey the law demanded attention then—as it has throughout man's life in the body politic—it is no less with us today in equally vexing and perplexing forms. Freedom rides and

[1] Richard A. Wasserstrom, B.A. 1957 Amherst College, M.A. 1958, Ph.D. 1960 U. of Michigan, LL.B. 1960 Stanford Law School, is Professor of Philosophy and Law, U.C.L.A. School of Law and Department of Philosophy. The essay reprinted here is from 10 U.C.L.A. L. REV. 780 (1963). In addition, Mr. Wasserstrom has written: *Strict Liability in the Criminal Law* 12 STAN. L. REV. 731 (1960); THE JUDICIAL DECISION: TOWARD A THEORY OF LEGAL JUSTIFICATION (1961); *Rights, Human Rights, and Racial Discrimination* 61 J. PHILOSOPHY 628 (1964); *H. L. A. Hart and the Doctrines of Mens Rea and Criminal Responsibility* 35 U. CHI. L. REV. 92 (1967). (Footnote by editor.)

sit-ins have raised the question of whether the immorality of segregation may justify disobeying the law. The all too awesome horrors of a nuclear war have seemed to some to require responsive action, including, if need be, deliberate but peaceful trespasses upon government-owned atomic testing grounds. And the rightness of disobedience to law in the face of court-ordered school integration has been insisted upon by the citizens of several states and acted upon by the governor of at least one.[1]

The problem is one of present concern and the questions it necessarily raises are real. But even if the exigencies of contemporary life were not such as to make this topic a compelling one, it is one which would still be peculiarly ripe for critical inquiry. In part this is so because despite their significance many of the central issues have been relatively neglected by legal or political philosophers and critics. Many of the important questions which bear upon the nature and extent of one's obligation to obey the law have been dealt with summarily and uncritically; distinguishable issues have been indiscriminately blurred and debatable conclusions gratuitously assumed.

More important is the fact that historically the topic has generally been examined from only one very special aspect of the problem. Those philosophers who have seriously considered questions relating to one's obligation to obey the law have considered them only in the context of revolution. They have identified the conditions under which one would, if ever, be justified in disobeying the law with the conditions under which revolution would, if ever, be justified; and they have, perhaps not surprisingly, tended thereby to conclude that one would be justified in disobeying the law if, and only if, revolution itself would in that case be justified.[2]

To view the problem in a setting of obedience or revolution is surely to misconstrue it. It is to neglect, among other things, something that is obviously true—that most people who disobey the law are not revolutionaries and that most acts of disobedience of the law are not acts of revolution. Many who disobey the law are,

---

[1] This is to say nothing of the stronger claim, involved in many of the war crimes prosecutions, that one does have a duty to disobey the law and, therefore, that one can be properly punished for having obeyed the law.

[2] See, e.g., AUSTIN, THE PROVINCE OF JURISPRUDENCE DETERMINED 53–55 (1954); HUME, A TREATISE OF HUMAN NATURE, bk. III, §§ 9, 10; LOCKE, THE SECOND TREATISE OF GOVERNMENT, chs. 18, 19.

of course, ordinary criminals: burglars, kidnappers, embezzlers, and the like. But even of those who disobey the law under a claim of justification, most are neither advocates nor practitioners of revolution.[1]

If the traditional, philosophical treatment of this subject is unduly simplistic and restrictive, contemporary legal thought is seldom more instructive. It is distressing, for one thing, that those whose daily intellectual concern is the legal system have said so little on this subject. And it is disturbing that many of those who have said anything at all appear so readily to embrace the view that justified disobedience of the law is a rare, if not impossible, occurrence. What is so disturbing is not the fact that this view is held—although I think it a mistaken one—but rather that such a conclusion is so summarily reached or assumed.[2]

I must make it clear at the outset that it is not my purpose to devote the remainder of this article to a documentation of the claims just made concerning either historical or contemporary thought. I do not wish to demonstrate that people in fact do believe what they appear to believe about the possibility of justified

---

[1] A subject which has surely not received the philosophical attention it deserves is that of the nature of revolution. What, for instance, are the characteristics of a revolution? Must the procedures by which laws are made or the criteria of validity be altered? Or is it sufficient that the people who occupy certain crucial offices be removed in a manner inconsistent with existing rules? Must force or resistance accompany whatever changes or alterations are made? Whatever the answers may be to questions such as these, it is, I think, plain that particular laws may be disobeyed under a claim of justification without any of these features being present. One can *argue* that for one reason or another, any act of disobedience must necessarily lead to revolution or the overthrow of the government. But then this is an argument which must be demonstrated.

[2] Professor Henry Hart, for example, in his extremely stimulating analysis of the aims of the criminal law, seems to hold such a view. Professor Hart believes that the criminal law ought only be concerned with that conduct which is morally blameworthy. From this he infers that no real problem can ever be presented by laws which make knowledge of the illegality of an action one of the elements of the offense. And this is so because the 'knowing or reckless disregard of legal obligation affords an independent basis of blameworthiness *justifying the actor's condemnation as a criminal*, even when his conduct was not intrinsically antisocial'. Hart, *The Aims of the Criminal Law* 23 LAW & CONTEMP. PROB. 401, 418 (1958). (My italics.) Some such view can also be plausibly attributed to, among others, Professor Lon Fuller, see text at section II, and Professor Herbert Wechsler, see text at section IV. Of course, all of these scholars, or any other person holding such a view, might well insist that the position is tenable only if an important qualification is made; namely, that the legal system in question be that of an essentially democratic society. For a discussion of this more restricted claim, see text at section IV.

disobedience to law. Nor do I wish to show why it is that people have come to believe what they appear to believe. Rather, in very general terms I am concerned here with *arguments*—with those arguments which have been or which might be given in support of the claim that because one does have an obligation to obey the law, one ought not ever disobey the law.

To describe the focus of the article in this manner is, however, to leave several crucial matters highly ambiguous. And thus, before the arguments can be considered properly, the following matters must be clarified.

A. There are several different views which could be held concerning the nature of the stringency of one's obligation to obey the law. One such view, and the one which I shall be most concerned to show to be false, can be characterized as holding that one has an *absolute* obligation to obey the law. I take this to mean that a person is never justified in disobeying the law; to know that a proposed action is illegal is to know all one needs to know in order to conclude that the action ought not to be done;[1] to cite the illegality of an action is to give a sufficient reason for not having done it. A view such as this is far from uncommon. President Kennedy expressed the thoughts of many quite reflective people when he said:

. . . [O]ur nation is founded on the principle that observance of the law is the eternal safeguard of liberty and defiance of the law is the surest road to tyranny.

The law which we obey includes the final rulings of the courts as well as the enactments of our legislative bodies. Even among law-abiding men few laws are universally loved.

But they are universally respected and not resisted.

Americans are free, in short, to disagree with the law, but not to disobey it. For in a government of laws and not of men, no man, however prominent or powerful, and no mob, however unruly or boisterous, is entitled to defy a court of law.

If this country should ever reach the point where any man or group of men, by force or threat of force, could long deny the commands of our court and our Constitution, then no law would stand free from

---

[1] Because I am concerned with the question of whether one is ever *morally justified* in acting illegally, I purposely make the actor's knowledge of the illegality of the action part of the description of the act. I am not concerned with the question of whether ignorance of the illegality of the action ought to excuse one from moral blame.

doubt, no judge would be sure of his writ and no citizen would be safe from his neighbors.[1]

A more moderate or weaker view would be that which holds that, while one does have an obligation to obey the law, the obligation is a prima facie rather than absolute one. If one knows that a proposed course of conduct is illegal then one has a good—but not necessarily a sufficient—reason for refraining from engaging in that course of conduct. Under this view, a person may be justified in disobeying the law, but an act which is in disobedience of the law does have to be justified, whereas an act in obedience of the law does not have to be justified.

It is important to observe that there is an ambiguity in this notion of a prima facie obligation. For the claim that one has a prima facie obligation to obey the law can come to one of two different things. On the one hand, the claim can be this: the fact that an action is an act of disobedience is something which always does count against the performance of the action. If one has a prima facie obligation to obey the law, one always has that obligation—although, of course, it may be overridden by other obligations in any particular case. Thus the fact that an action is illegal is a relevant consideration in every case and it is a consideration which must be outweighed by other considerations before the performance of an illegal action can be justified.

On the other hand, the claim can be weaker still. The assertion of a prima facie obligation to obey the law can be nothing more than the claim that as a matter of fact it is *generally* right or obligatory to obey the law. As a rule the fact that an action is illegal is a relevant circumstance. But in any particular case, after deliberation, it might very well turn out that the illegality of the action was not truly relevant. For in any particular case the circumstances might be such that there simply was nothing in the fact of illegality which required overriding—e.g., there were no bad consequences at all which would flow from disobeying the law in this case.

The distinction can be made more vivid in the following fashion. One person, *A*, might hold the view that any action in disobedience of the law is intrinsically bad. Some other person, *B*,

---

[1] N.Y. TIMES, Oct. 1, 1962, p. 22, col. 6. The same qualification must be made here as was made above in note 2, p. 276. President Kennedy may well have meant his remarks to be applicable only to the legal system which is a part of the set of political institutions of the United States.

might hold the view that no action is intrinsically bad unless it has the property, P, and that not all actions in disobedience of the law have that property. Now for A, the fact of disobedience is *always* a relevant consideration,[1] for B, the fact of disobedience may always be initially relevant because of the existence of some well-established hypothesis which asserts that the occurrence of any action of disobedience is correlated highly with the occurrence of P. But if in any particular case disobedience does not turn out to have the property, P, then, upon reflection, it can be concluded by B that the fact that disobedience is involved is not a reason which weighs against the performance of the act in question. To understand B's position it is necessary to distinguish the relevance of *considering* the fact of disobedience from the relevance of the fact of disobedience. The former must always be relevant, the latter is not.

Thus there are at least three different positions which might be taken concerning the character of the obligation to obey the law or the rightness of disobedience to the law. They are: (1) One has an absolute obligation to obey the law; disobedience is never justified. (2) One has an obligation to obey the law but this obligation can be overridden by conflicting obligations; disobedience can be justified, but only by the presence of outweighing circumstances. (3) One does not have a special obligation to obey the law, but it is in fact usually obligatory, on other grounds, to do so; disobedience to law often does turn out to be unjustified.

B. It must also be made clear that when I talk about the obligation to obey the law or the possibility of actions which are both illegal and justified, I am concerned solely with *moral obligations* and *morally justified* actions. I shall be concerned solely with arguments which seek to demonstrate that there is some sort of a connection between the legality or illegality of an action and its morality or immorality. Concentration on this general topic necessarily renders a number of interesting problems irrelevant. Thus, I am not at all concerned with the question of why, in fact, so many people do obey the law. Nor, concomitantly, am I concerned with the non-moral reasons which might and do justify obedience to law—of these, the most pertinent is the fact that highly unpleasant consequences of one form or another are typically inflicted upon those

---

[1] To repeat, though, it surely is not necessarily conclusive, or sufficient, since an action in obedience to the law may under some other description be worse, or less justifiable, than disobedience.

who disobey the law. Finally there are many actions which are immoral irrespective of whether they also happen to be illegal. And I am not, except in one very special sense, concerned with this fact either. I am not concerned with the fact that the immorality of the action itself may be a sufficient reason for condemning it regardless of its possible illegality.

C. My last preliminary clarification relates to the fact that there is a variety of kinds of legal rules or laws and that there is a variety of ways in which actions can be related to these rules. This is an important point because many moral philosophers, in particular, have tended to assimilate all legal rules to the model of a typical law or legal order which is enforced through the direct threat of the infliction by the government of severe sanctions, and have thereby tended to assume that all laws and all legal obligations can be broken or disobeyed only in the manner in which penal laws can be broken or disobeyed. That this assimilation is a mistake can be demonstrated quite readily. There are many laws that, unlike the typical penal law, do not require or prohibit the performance of any acts at all. They cannot, therefore, be disobeyed. There are laws, for example, that make testamentary dispositions of property ineffective, unenforceable, or invalid, if the written instrument was not witnessed by the requisite number of disinterested witnesses. Yet a law of this kind obviously does not impose an obligation upon anyone to make a will. Nor, more significantly, could a person who executed a will without the requisite number of witnesses be said to have disobeyed the law. Such a person has simply failed to execute a valid will.[1]

[1] See HART, THE CONCEPT OF LAW 27–48 (1961), particularly for the clearest and fullest extant philosophical analysis of the important distinguishing characteristics of different kinds of legal rules.

In this connection a stronger point than the one made above can be made. It is that there are many laws which, if they can be disobeyed at all, cannot be disobeyed in the way in which the typical criminal law can be disobeyed. For there are many laws that either impose or permit one to impose upon oneself any number of different legal obligations. And with many of these legal obligations, regardless of how created, it seems correct to say that one can breach or fail to perform them without thereby acting illegally or in disobedience of the law. One's obligation to obey the law may not, therefore, be coextensive with one's legal obligations. In the typical case of a breach of contract, for example, the failure to perform one's contractual obligations is clearly a breach of a legal obligation. Yet one can breach a contract and, hence, a legal obligation without necessarily acting illegally. This last assertion is open to question. And arguments for its correctness would not here be germane. It is sufficient to recognize only that failing to honor or perform some types of legal obligations may be a

The foregoing observations are relevant largely because it is important to realize that to talk about disobeying the law or about one's obligation to obey the law is usually to refer to a rather special kind of activity, namely, that which is exemplified by, among other things, actions in violation or disobedience of a penal law. It is this special type of activity which alone is the concern of this article.

II

One kind of argument in support of the proposition that one cannot be justified in disobeying the law is that which asserts the existence of some sort of *logical* or conceptual relationship between disobeying the law and acting immorally.[1] If the notion of illegality entails that of immorality then one is never justified in acting illegally just because part of the meaning of *illegal* is *immoral*; just because describing an action as illegal is—among other things—to describe it as unjustified.[2]

A claim such as this is extremely difficult to evaluate. For one has great difficulty in knowing what is to count as truly relevant—let

[1] It is worth emphasizing that I am not at all interested in the claim—which in many ways is an odd one to belabor—that there is a logical relationship between disobeying the law and acting illegally. See, e.g., Carnes, *Why Should I Obey the Law* 71 ETHICS 14 (1960).

[2] Professor Fuller may hold to some version of this view in his article, *Positivism and Fidelity to Law—A Reply to Professor Hart* 71 HARV. L. REV. 630, 656 (1958), where, after characterizing the position of legal positivism as one which says that 'On the one hand, we have an amoral datum called law, which has the peculiar quality of creating a moral duty to obey it. On the other hand, we have a moral duty to do what we think is right and decent.' Professor Fuller goes on to criticize this bifurcation of law and morality on the grounds that ' "The dilemma" it states has the verbal formulation of a problem, but the problem it states makes no sense. It is like saying I have to choose between giving food to a starving man and being mimsey with the borogroves. I do not think it unfair to the positivistic philosophy to say that it never gives any coherent meaning to the moral obligation of fidelity to law.'

Others who at least suggest adherence to such a position are: BAIER, THE MORAL POINT OF VIEW 134 (1958); NOWELL-SMITH, ETHICS 236–7 (1959); and WELDON, THE VOCABULARY OF POLITICS 57, 62, 66–67 (1953). And there are surely passages in Hobbes that could also be read in this way. See, e.g., HOBBES, LEVIATHAN, chs. XIII, XVIII. The claim that *illegal* entails *immoral* is closely related to, but surely distinguishable from, the position that Professor Fuller, among many others, may also hold, namely, that there are certain minimum 'moral' requirements that must be met before any rule can be a law.

quite different kind of activity from violating or disobeying a law or order which is backed up, in some very direct fashion, by a governmentally threatened severe sanction.

T

alone decisive—evidence of its correctness. There is, nevertheless, a supporting argument of sorts which can be made. It might go something like this:

It is a fact which is surely worth noticing that people generally justify action that *seems to be* illegal by claiming that the action *is not really* illegal. Typically an actor who is accused of having done something illegal will not defend himself by pointing out that, while illegal, his conduct was nevertheless morally justified. Instead, he will endeavor to show in one way or another that it is really inaccurate to call his conduct illegal at all. Now it looks as though this phenomenon can be readily accounted for. People try to resist the accusation of illegality, it might be argued, for the simple reason that they wish to avoid being punished. But what is interesting and persuasive is the fact that people try just as hard to evade a charge of illegality even in those situations where the threat of punishment is simply not an important or even relevant consideration.

The cases of the recent sit-ins or freedom rides are apt. To be sure, the claim was that the preservation of segregated lunch-counters, waiting rooms, and the like was morally indefensible. But an important justification for the rightness of the actions employed in integrating these facilities in the fashion selected rested upon the insistence that the perpetuation- of segregation in these circumstances was itself illegal. One primary claim for the rightness of freedom rides was that these were not instances of disobeying the law. They were instead attempts to invoke judicial and executive protection of legal, indeed constitutional, rights. While there were some, no doubt, who might have insisted upon the rightness of sit-ins even if they were clearly illegal, most people were confident of the blamelessness of the participants just because it was plain that their actions were not, in the last analysis, illegal. Were it evident that sit-ins were truly illegal many might hold a different view about the rightness of sitting-in as a means to bring about integrated facilities.

Language commonly invoked in the course of disputes between nations furnishes another equally graphic illustration of the same point. In the continuing controversy over the status of Berlin, for instance, both the United States and Russia have relied upon claims of legality and have been sensitive to charges of illegality, to an appreciably greater extent than one would otherwise have supposed. And much the same can be said of the more recent dispute between India and China. Now if nations which have little to fear in the way of the imposition of sanctions for acting illegally are nevertheless extraordinarily sensitive to charges of illegal conduct, this also may be taken as evidence of the fact that *illegality* implies *immorality*.

Wholly apt, too, was the controversy over the Eichmann trial. To some, the fact that the seizure and trial of Eichmann by Israel was illegal was sufficient to cast grave doubts upon the justifiability of the proceedings. To others, the charge of illegality made it necessary to demonstrate that nothing really illegal had occurred. What is significant about all this is the fact that all of the disputants implicitly acknowledged that illegality was something which did have to be worried about.

Such in brief is the argument which might be advanced and the 'evidence' which might be adduced to support it. I think that such an argument is not persuasive, and I can best show this to be so in the following fashion.

Consider the case of a law that makes it a felony to perform an abortion upon a woman unless the abortion is necessary to preserve *her* life. Suppose a teenager, the daughter of a local minister, has been raped on her way home from school by an escapee from a state institution for mental defectives. Suppose further that the girl has become pregnant and has been brought to a reputable doctor who is asked to perform an abortion. And suppose, finally, that the doctor concludes after examining the girl that her life will not be endangered by giving birth to the child.[1] An abortion under these circumstances is, it seems fair to say, illegal.[2] Yet, we would surely find both intelligible and appealing the doctor's claim that he was nonetheless justified in disobeying the law by performing an abortion on the girl. I at least can see nothing logically odd or inconsistent about recognizing both that there is a law prohibiting this conduct and that further questions concerning the rightness of obedience would be relevant and, perhaps, decisive. Thus I can see nothing logically odd about describing this as a case in which the

[1] These facts are taken from Packer & Gampell, *Therapeutic Abortion: A Problem in Law and Medicine* 11 STAN. L. REV. 417 (1959), where they are introduced in a different context.

[2] Such would seem to be the case in California, for example, where CAL. PEN. CODE § 274 makes the performance of an abortion a felony unless the abortion is necessary to preserve the life of the pregnant woman.

performance of the abortion could be both illegal and morally justified.[1]

There is, no doubt, a heroic defense which can be made to the above. It would consist of the insistence that the activity just described simply cannot be both illegal and justified. Two alternatives are possible. First, one might argue that the commission of the abortion would indeed have been justified if it were not proscribed by the law. But since it is so prohibited, the abortion is wrong. Now if this is a point about the appropriateness of kinds of reasons, I can only note that referring the action to a valid law does not seem to preclude asking meaningful questions about the obligatoriness of the action. If this is a point about language or concepts it does seem to be perfectly intelligible to say that the conduct is both illegal and morally justified. And if this is, instead, an *argument* for the immorality of ever disobeying a valid law, then it surely requires appreciable substantiation and not mere assertion.

Second, one might take a different line and agree that other questions can be asked about the conduct, but that is because the commission of the abortion under these circumstances simply cannot be illegal. The difficulty here, however, is that it is hard to understand what is now meant by *illegal*. Of course, I am not claiming that in the case as I have described it, it is clear that the performance of the abortion must be illegal. It might not be. But it might be. Were we to satisfy all the usual tests that we do invoke when we determine that a given course of conduct is illegal, and were someone still to maintain that because the performance of the abortion is here morally justified it cannot be illegal, then the burden is on the proponent of this view to make clear how we are to decide when conduct is illegal. And it would further be incumbent upon him to demonstrate what seems to be highly dubious, namely, that greater clarity and insight could somehow be attained through a radical change in our present terminology. It appears to

---

[1] I am supposing, of course, that one would regard the performance of the abortion—in the absence of the relevant penal law—as clearly morally justified. If one disagrees with this assessment of the morality of the case, then some other example ought to be substituted. One likely candidate, drawn from our own history, is that of the inherent rightness in refusing to return an escaped Negro slave to his 'owner'. If one believes that refusing to do so would be clearly justifiable, then consider whether the existence of the fugitive slave laws necessarily rendered a continued refusal unjustified.

be a virtually conclusive refutation to observe that there has never been a legal system whose criteria of validity—no matter how sophisticated, how rational and how well defined—themselves guaranteed that morally justified action would never be illegal.

Thus an argument as strong as any of the above must fail. There is, of course, a weaker version which may be more appealing. If it is true that there is something disturbing about justifying actions that are conceded to be illegal, then one way to account for this is to insist that there is a logical connection between the concepts involved, but it is something less than the kind of implication already discussed. Perhaps it is correct that *illegal* does not entail *immoral*; *illegal* might nevertheless entail *prima facie immoral*. The evidence adduced tends to show that among one's moral obligations is the prima facie duty to obey the law.[1]

Once again, it is somewhat difficult to know precisely what to make of such a claim. It is hard to see how one would decide what was to count as evidence or whether the evidence was persuasive. At a minimum, it is not difficult to imagine several equally plausible alternative explanations of the disturbing character of accusations of illegal activity. In addition, to know only that one has a prima facie duty to obey the law is not to know a great deal. In particular, one does not know how or when that obligation can be overridden. And, of course, even if it is correct that acting illegally logically implies acting prima facie immorally, this in no way shows that people may not often be morally justified in acting illegally. At most, it demands that they have some good reason for acting illegally; at best, it requires what has already been hypothesized, namely, that the action in question, while illegal, be morally justified.

Thus, it is clear that if the case against ever acting illegally is to be made out, conceptual analysis alone cannot do it. Indeed, arguments of quite another sort must be forthcoming. And it is to these that I now turn.

III

One such argument, and the most common argument advanced, goes something like this: The reason why one ought never to

---

[1] Sir W. David Ross, for example, suggests that the obligation to obey the law is a prima facie obligation which is a compound of three more simple prima facie duties. ROSS, THE RIGHT AND THE GOOD 27–28 (1930).

disobey the law is simply that the consequences would be disastrous if everybody disobeyed the law. The reason why disobedience is never right becomes apparent once we ask the question 'But what if everyone did that?'

Consider again the case of the doctor who has to decide whether he is performing an illegal abortion. If he only has a prima facie duty to obey the law it looks as though he might justifiably decide that in this case his prima facie obligation is overridden by more stringent obligations. Or, if he is simply a utilitarian, it appears that he might rightly conclude that the consequences of disobeying the abortion law would be on the whole and in the long run less deleterious than those of obeying. But this is simply a mistake. The doctor would inevitably be neglecting the most crucial factor of all, namely, that in performing the abortion he was disobeying the law. And imagine what would happen if everyone went around disobeying the law. The alternatives are obeying the law and general disobedience. The choice is between any social order and chaos. As President Kennedy correctly observed, if any law is disobeyed, then no law can be free from doubt, no citizen safe from his neighbor.

Such an argument, while perhaps overdrawn, is by no means uncommon.[1] Yet, as it stands, it is an essentially confused one. Its respective claims, if they are to be fairly evaluated, must be delineated with some care.

At a minimum, the foregoing attack upon the possibility of justified disobedience might be either one or both of two radically different kinds of objection. The first, which relates to the consequences of an act of disobedience, is essentially a *causal* argument. The second questions the *principle* that any proponent of justified disobedience invokes. As to the causal argument, it is always relevant to point out that any act of disobedience may have certain consequences simply because it is an act of disobedience. Once the occurrence of the act is known, for example, expenditure

---

[1] Socrates, for instance, supposes that were he to escape he might properly be asked: 'What are you about? Are you going by an act of yours to overturn us—the laws and the whole state, as far as in you lies? Do you imagine that a state can subsist and not be overthrown, in which the decisions of law have no power, but are set aside and overthrown by individuals?' PLATO, CRITO. Analogous arguments can be found in, for example: AUSTIN, THE PROVINCE OF JURISPRUDENCE DETERMINED 52–53 (1954); HOBBES, LEVIATHAN, ch. XV; HUME, A TREATISE OF HUMAN NATURE, bk. III, pt. II, 3, 6, 8, 9; TOULMIN, AN EXAMINATION OF THE PLACE OF REASON IN ETHICS 151 (1950).

of the state's resources may become necessary. The time and energy of the police will probably be turned to the task of discovering who it was who did the illegal act and of gathering evidence relevant to the offense. And other resources might be expended in the prosecution and adjudication of the case against the perpetrator of the illegal act. Illustrations of this sort could be multiplied, no doubt, but I do not think either that considerations of this sort are very persuasive or that they have been uppermost in the minds of those who make the argument now under examination. Indeed, if the argument is a causal one at all, it consists largely of the claim that any act of disobedience will itself cause, to some degree or other, general disobedience of all laws; it will cause or help to cause the overthrow or dissolution of the state. And while it is possible to assert that any act of disobedience will tend to further social disintegration or revolution, it is much more difficult to see why this must be so.

The most plausible argument would locate this causal efficacy in the kind of example set by any act of disobedience. But how plausible is this argument? It is undeniable, of course, that the kind of example that will be set is surely a relevant factor. Yet, there is nothing that precludes any proponent of justified disobedience from taking this into account. If, for example, others will somehow infer from the doctor's disobedience of the abortion law that they are justified in disobeying *any* law under *any* circumstances, then the doctor ought to consider this fact. This is a consequence—albeit a lamentable one—of his act of disobedience. Similarly, if others will extract the proper criterion from the act of disobedience, but will be apt to misapply it in practice, then this too ought to give the doctors pause. It, too, is a consequence of acting.[1] But if the argument is that disobedience would be wrong even if no bad example were set and no other deleterious consequences likely, then the argument must be directed against the principle the doctor appeals to in disobeying the law, and not against the consequences of his disobedience at all.

As to the attack upon a principle of justified disobedience, as a principle, the response 'But what if everyone disobeyed the law?' does appear to be a good way to point up both the inherent inconsistency of almost any principle of justified disobedience and the

[1] For a very special and related version of this argument, see section V below (p. 302).

manifest undesirability of adopting such a principle. Even if one need not worry about what others will be led to do by one's disobedience, there is surely something amiss if one cannot consistently defend his right to do what one is claiming he is right in doing.

In large measure, such an objection is unreal. The appeal to 'But what if everyone did that?' loses much, if not all, of its persuasiveness once we become clearer about what precisely the 'did that' refers to. If the question 'But what if everyone did that?' is simply another way of asking 'But what if everybody disobeyed the law?' or 'But what if people generally disobeyed the laws?' then the question is surely quasi-rhetorical. To urge general or indiscriminate disobedience to laws is to invoke a principle that, if coherent, is manifestly indefensible. It is equally plain, however, that with few exceptions such a principle has never been seriously espoused. Anyone who claims that there are actions that are both illegal and justified surely need not be thereby asserting that it is right generally to disobey all laws or even any particular law. It is surely not inconsistent to assert both that indiscriminate disobedience is indefensible and that discriminate disobedience is morally right and proper conduct. Nor, analogously, is it at all evident that a person who claims to be justified in performing an illegal action is thereby committed to or giving endorsement to the principle that the entire legal system ought to be overthrown or renounced. At a minimum, therefore, the appeal to 'But what if everyone did that?' cannot by itself support the claim that one has an absolute obligation to obey the law—that disobeying the law can never be truly justified.

There is, however, a distinguishable but related claim which merits very careful attention—if for no other reason than the fact that it is so widely invoked today by moral philosophers. The claim is simply this: While it may very well be true that there are situations in which a person will be justified in disobeying the law, it is surely not true that disobedience can ever be justified solely on the grounds that the consequences of disobeying the particular law were in that case on the whole less deleterious than those of obedience.[1]

---

[1] This is a particular illustration of the more general claim that for one reason or another utilitarianism cannot be a defensible or intelligible moral theory when construed as permitting one's moral obligation to do any particular action

This claim is particularly relevant at this juncture because one of the arguments most often given to substantiate it consists of the purported demonstration of the fact that any principle which contained a proviso permitting a general appeal to consequences must itself be incoherent. One of the most complete statements of the argument is found in Marcus Singer's provocative book, *Generalization in Ethics*:

> Suppose, . . . that I am contemplating evading the payment of income taxes. I might reason that I need the money more than the government does, that the amount I have to pay is so small in comparison with the total amount to be collected that the government will never miss it. Now I surely know perfectly well that if I evade the payment of taxes this will not cause others to do so as well. For one thing, I am certainly not so foolish as to publicize my action. But even if I were, and the fact became known, this would still not cause others to do the same, unless it also became known that I was being allowed to get away with it. In the latter case the practice might tend to become widespread, but this would be a consequence, not of my action, but of the failure of the government to take action against me. Thus there is no question of my act being wrong because it would set a bad example. It would set no such example, and to suppose that it must, because it would be wrong, is simply a confusion. . . . Given all this, then if the reasons mentioned would justify me in evading the payment of taxes, they would justify everyone whatsoever in doing the same thing. For everyone can argue in the same way— everyone can argue that if he breaks the law this will not cause others to do the same. The supposition that this is a justification, therefore, leads to a contradiction.

I conclude from this that, just as the reply "Not everyone will do it" is irrelevant to the generalization argument, so is the fact that one knows or believes that not everyone will do the same; and that, in particular, the characteristic of knowing or believing that one's act will remain exceptional cannot be used to define a class of exceptions to the rule. One's knowledge or belief that not everyone will act in the same way in similar

---

to be overridden by a direct appeal to the consequences of performing that particular action. For recent statements of the claim see, e.g., NOWELL-SMITH (cited above p. 281 n. 2) RAWLS, *Two Concepts of Rules* 64 PHILOSOPHICAL REV. 3 (1955), in OLAFSON, SOCIETY, LAW, AND MORALITY 420 (1961); SINGER, GENERALIZATION IN ETHICS 61–138, 178–216 (1961); TOULMIN (cited above p. 286 n. 1) pp. 144–65; Harrison, *Utilitarianism, Universalisation, and Our Duty To Be Just* 53 ARISTOTELIAN SOC'Y PROCEEDINGS 105 (1952–53).

For some criticisms of this restriction on utilitarianism see, e.g., WASSERSTROM, THE JUDICIAL DECISION 118–37 (1961). But see Hart, *Book Review*, 14 STAN. L. REV. 919, 924–6 (1962).

circumstances cannot therefore be regarded as part of the circumstances of one's action. One's belief that not everyone will do the same does not make one's circumstances relevantly different from the circumstances of others, or relevantly different from those in which the act is wrong. Indeed, on the supposition that it does, one's circumstances could never be specified, for the specification would involve an infinite regress.[1]

Singer's argument is open to at least two different interpretations. One quite weak interpretation is this: A person cannot be morally justified in acting as he does unless he is prepared to acknowledge that everyone else in the identical circumstances would also be right in acting the same way. If the person insists that he is justified in performing a certain action because the consequences of acting in that way are more desirable than those of acting in any alternative fashion, then he must be prepared to acknowledge that anyone else would also be justified in doing that action whenever the consequences of doing that action were more desirable than those of acting in any alternative fashion. To take Singer's own example: A person, A, could not be morally justified in evading the payment of his taxes on the grounds that the consequences of nonpayment were *in his case* more beneficial, all things considered, than those of payment, unless A were prepared to acknowledge that any other person, X, would also be justified in evading his, i.e., X's taxes, if it is the case that the consequences of X's nonpayment would in X's case be more beneficial, all things considered, than those of payment. If this is Singer's point, it is, for reasons already elaborated, unobjectionable.[2]

But Singer seems to want to make a stronger point as well. He seems to believe that even a willingness to generalize in this fashion could not justify acting in this way. In part his argument appears to be that this somehow will permit everyone to justify nonpayment of taxes; and in part his argument appears to be that there is a logical absurdity involved in attempting to make the

---

[1] SINGER (cited above p. 288 n. 1) pp. 149–50.

[2] Neither Singer nor I have adequately refuted the confirmed ethical egoist who insists that he is prepared to generalize but only in the sense that X's nonpayment is justified if, and only if, the consequences of X's nonpayment would in X's case be more beneficial *to A* than those of payment. This is a problem which surely requires more careful attention than it typically receives. It will not do simply to insist that the egoist does not understand ordinary moral discourse. Instead, what must be demonstrated are the respects in which the egoist's position is an inherently unjust one. But to make this showing is beyond the scope of this article.

likelihood of other people's behavior part of the specification of the relevant consequences of a particular act. Both of these points are wrong. To begin with, on a common sense level it is surely true that the effect which one's action will have on other people's behavior is a relevant consideration. For as was pointed out earlier, if *A* determines that other people will be, or may be, led to evade *their* taxes even when the consequences of nonpayment will in their cases be less beneficial than those of payment, then this is a consequence of *A*'s action which he must take into account and attempt to balance against the benefits which would accrue to society from his nonpayment. Conversely, if for one reason or another *A* can determine that his act of nonpayment will not have this consequence, this, too, must be relevant. In this sense, at least, other people's prospective behavior is a relevant consideration.

More importantly, perhaps, it is surely a mistake—although a very prevalent one in recent moral philosophy—to suppose that permitting a general appeal to consequences would enable everyone to argue convincingly that he is justified in evading his taxes. Even if I adopt the principle that everyone is justified in evading his taxes whenever the consequences of evasion are on the whole less deleterious than those of payment, this in no way entails that I or anyone else will always, or ever, be justified in evading my taxes. It surely need not turn out to be the case—even if no one else will evade his taxes—that the consequences will on the whole be beneficial if I succeed in evading mine. It might surely be the case that I will spend the money saved improvidently or foolishly; it might very well be true that the government will make much better use of the money. Indeed, the crucial condition which must not be ignored and which Singer does ignore is the condition which stipulates that the avoidance of one's taxes in fact be optimific, that is, more desirable than any other course of conduct.

The general point is simply that it is an empirical question—at least in theory—what the consequences of any action will be. And it would surely be a mistake for me or anyone else to suppose that that action whose consequences are most pleasing to me—in either the short or long run—will in fact be identical with that action whose consequences are on the whole most beneficial to society. Where the demands of self-interest are strong, as in the case of the performance of an unpleasant task like paying taxes, there are particular reasons for being skeptical of one's conclusion that the consequences of nonpayment would in one's own case truly be beneficial. But once again there is no reason why there might not be cases in which evasion of taxes would be truly justified, nor is there any reason why someone could not consistently and defensibly endorse nonpayment whenever these circumstances were in fact present.

There is one final point which Singer's discussion suggests and which does appear to create something of a puzzle. Suppose that I believe that I am justified in deliberately trespassing on an atomic test site, and thereby disobeying the law, because I conclude that this is the best way to call attention to the possible consequences of continued atmospheric testing or nuclear war. I conclude that the consequences of trespassing will on the whole be more beneficial than any alternative action I can take. But suppose I also concede— what very well may be the case—that if everyone were to trespass, even for this same reason and in the same way, the consequences would be extremely deleterious. Does it follow that there is something logically incoherent about my principle of action? It looks as though there is, for it appears that I am here denying others the right to do precisely what I claim I am right in doing. I seem to be claiming, in effect, that it is right for me to trespass on government property in order to protest atomic testing only if it is the case that others, even under identical circumstances, will not trespass. Thus, it might be argued, I appear to be unwilling or unable to generalize my principle of conduct.

This argument is unsound, for there is a perfectly good sense in which I am acting on a principle which is coherent and which is open to anyone to adopt. It is simply the principle that one is justified in trespassing on government property whenever—among other things—it happens to be the case that one can say accurately that others will not in fact act on that same principle. Whether anyone else will at any given time act on any particular principle is an empirical question. It is, to repeat what has already been said, one of the possible circumstances which can be part of the description of a class of situations. There is, in short, nothing logically self-contradictory or absurd about making the likelihood of even identical action one of the relevant justifying considerations. And there is, therefore, no reason why the justifiability of any particular act of disobedience cannot depend, among other things, upon the probable conduct of others.

IV

It would not be at all surprising if at this stage one were to feel considerable dissatisfaction with the entire cast of the discussion so far. In particular, one might well believe that the proverbial dead horse has received still another flaying for the simple reason that no one has ever seriously argued that people are never justified in disobeying the law. One might insist, for instance, that neither Socrates nor President Kennedy were talking about all law in all legal systems everywhere. And one might urge, instead, that their claims concerning the unjustifiability of any act of disobedience rest covertly, if not overtly, on the assumption that the disobedience in question was to take place in a society in which the lawmaking procedures and other political institutions were those which are characteristic of an essentially democratic, or free, society. This is, of course, an important and plausible restriction upon the original claim, and the arguments which might support it must now be considered.

While there are several things about a liberal, democratic or free society which might be thought to preclude the possibility of justified disobedience, it is evident that the presence of all the important constitutive institutions *cannot* guarantee that unjust or immoral laws will not be enacted. For the strictest adherence to principles of representative government, majority rule, frequent and open elections and, indeed, the realization of all of the other characteristics of such a society, in no way can insure that laws of manifest immorality will not be passed and enforced. And if even the ideal democratic society might enact unjust laws, no existing society can plausibly claim as much. Thus, if the case against the possibility of justified disobedience is to depend upon the democratic nature of the society in question, the case cannot rest simply on the claim that the only actions which will be made illegal are those which are already immoral.

What then are the arguments which might plausibly be advanced? One very common argument goes like this: It is, of course, true that even democratically selected and democratically constituted legislatures can and do make mistakes. Nevertheless, a person is never justified in disobeying the law as long as there exist alternative, 'peaceful' procedures by which to bring about the amendment or repeal of undesirable or oppressive laws. The genuine possibility that rational persuasion and argument can bring a majority to favor any one of a variety of competing views, both requires that disapproval always be permitted and forbids that disobedience ever be allowed. This is so for several reasons.

First, it is clearly unfair and obviously inequitable to accept the results of any social decision-procedure only in those cases in which the decision reached was one of which one approves, and to refuse to accept those decisions which are not personally satisfying. If there is one thing which participation, and especially voluntary participation, in a decision-procedure entails, it is that all of the participants must abide by the decision regardless of what it happens to be. If the decision-procedure is that of majority rule, then this means that any person must abide by those decisions in which he was in a minority just as much as it means that he can insist that members of the minority abide when he is a member of the majority.

As familiar as the argument is, its plausibility is far from assured. On one reading, at least, it appears to be one version of the universalization argument. As such, it goes like this. Imagine any person, A, who has voted with the majority to pass a law making a particular kind of conduct illegal. A surely would not and could not acknowledge the right of any person voting with the minority justifiably to disobey that law. But, if A will not and cannot recognize a right of justified disobedience here, then A certainly cannot consistently or fairly claim any right of justified disobedience on his part in those cases in which he, A, happened to end up being in a minority. Thus, justified disobedience can never be defensible.

This argument is fallacious. For a person who would insist that justified disobedience was possible even after majoritarian decision-making could very plausibly and consistently acknowledge the right of any person to disobey the law under appropriate circum- stances regardless of how that person had voted on any particular law. Consider, once again, the case already put of the doctor and the pregnant girl. The doctor can surely be consistent in claiming both that circumstances make the performance of the illegal abortion justified and that any comparable action would also be right irrespective of how the actor, or the doctor, or anyone else, happened to have voted on the abortion law, or any other law. The point is simply that there is no reason why any person cannot consistently: (1) hold the view that majority decision-making is the best of all forms of decision-making; (2) participate voluntarily in the decision-making process; and (3) believe that it is right for *anyone* to disobey majority decisions whenever the relevant moral circumstances obtain, e.g., whenever the consequence of obedience to that law at that time would on the whole be more deleterious than those of obedience.

But this may be deemed too facile an answer; it also may be thought to miss the point. For it might be argued that there is a serious logical inconsistency of a different sort which must arise whenever a voluntary participant in a social decision-procedure claims that not all the decisions reached in accordance with that procedure need be obeyed. Take the case of majority rule. It is inconsistent for anyone voluntarily to participate in the decision-process and yet at the same time to reserve the right to refuse to abide by the decision reached in any particular case. The problem is not an inability to universalize a principle of action. The problem is rather that of making any sense at all out of the notion of having a majority decide anything—of having a procedure by which to make group decisions. The problem is, in addition, that of making any sense at all out of the fact of voluntary participation in the decision-procedure—in knowing what this participation can come to if it does not mean that every participant is bound by all of the decisions which are reached. What can their participation mean if it is not an implicit promise to abide by all decisions reached? And even if the point is not a logical one, it is surely a practical one. What good could there possibly be to a scheme, an institutional means for making social decisions, which did not bind even the participants to anything?

The answer to this argument—or set of arguments—is wholly analogous to that which has been given earlier. But because of the importance and prevalence of the argument some repetition is in order.

One can simply assert that the notion of any social decision-making procedure is intelligible only if it entails that all participants always abide by all of the decisions which are made, no matter what those decisions are. Concomitantly, one can simply insist that any voluntary participant in the decision-process must be consenting or promising to abide by all decisions which are reached. But one cannot give as a plausible reason for this assertion the fact that the notion of group decision-making becomes incoherent if anything less in the way of adherence is required of all participants. And one cannot cite as a plausible reason for this assertion the fact that the notion of voluntary participation loses all meaning if anything less than a promise of absolute obedience is inferred.

It is true that the notion of a group decision-making procedure would be a meaningless notion if there were no respects in which a group decision was in any way binding upon each of the participants. Decisions which in no way bind anyone to do anything are simply not decisions. And it is also true that voluntary participation is an idle, if not a vicious, act if it does not commit each participant to something. If any voluntary participant properly can wholly ignore the decisions which are reached, then something is surely amiss.

But to say all this is not to say very much. Group decision-making can have a point just because it does preclude any participant from taking some actions which in the absence of the decision, he might have been justified in performing. And voluntary participation can still constitute a promise of sorts that one will not perform actions which, in the absence of voluntary participation, might have been justifiable. If the fact of participation in a set of liberal political institutions does constitute a promise of sorts, it can surely be a promise that the participant will not disobey a law just because obedience would be inconvenient or deleterious to him. And if this is the scope of the promise, then the fact of voluntary participation does make a difference. For in the absence of the participation in the decision to make this conduct illegal, inconvenience to the actor might well have been a good reason for acting in a certain way. Thus, participation can create new obligations to behave in certain ways without constituting a promise not to disobey the law under any circumstances. And if this is the case, adherence to a principle of justified disobedience is not inconsistent with voluntary participation in the decision-making process.

Indeed, a strong point can be made. The notion of making laws through voluntary participation in democratic institutions is not even inconsistent with the insistence that disobedience is justified whenever the consequences of disobedience are on the whole more beneficial than those of obedience. This is so because a promise can be a meaningful promise even if an appeal to the consequences of performing the promise can count as a sufficient reason for not performing the promise.[1] And if this is the case for promises

[1] The point here is analogous to that made in the discussion of Singer's argument. Moral philosophers have often argued that one cannot appeal simply to the consequences of performing or not performing a particular promise as a reason for not performing that promise. And the reason why this is so is that the notion of having promised to do something would be unintelligible if the promisor could always, when the time came for performance, be excused if it were the case that the consequences of nonperformance were more beneficial than those of performance. This would make promising unintelligible, so the argument goes, because promising entails or means obligating oneself to do something. But if the appeal to consequences is what is to be determinative of one's obligations, then the promise becomes a wholly superfluous, meaningless act. Rawls, for instance, puts the point this way: 'Various defenses for not keeping one's promise are allowed, but among them there isn't the one that, on general utilitarian grounds, the promisor (truly) thought his action best on the whole, even though there may be the defense that the consequences of keeping one's promise would have been *extremely* severe. While there are too many complexities here to consider all the necessary details, one can see that the general defense isn't allowed if one asks the following question: what would one say of someone who, when asked why he broke his promise, replied simply that breaking it was best on the whole? Assuming that his reply is sincere, and that his belief was reasonable (i.e., one need not consider the possibility that he was mistaken), I think that one would question whether or not he knows what it means to say "I promise" (in the appropriate circumstances). It would be said of someone who used this excuse without further explanation that he didn't understand what defenses the practice, which defines a promise, allows to him. If a child were to use this excuse one would correct him; for it is part of the way one is taught the concept of a promise to be corrected if one uses this excuse. The point of having the practice would be lost if the practice did allow this excuse.' Rawls (cited above p. 288 n. 1) p. 17, in OLAFSON (cited above p. 288 n. 1) pp. 429–30.

Now I am not concerned to dispute Rawls' remark if taken as descriptive of our institution of promising. For what I am here concerned with is the claim, implicit throughout, that promising would be a meaningless or pointless activity if the excuse were permitted. I should say though that the passage quoted from Rawls is not, I think, central to his main argument. I think I can show this to be a mistake through the following two examples.

(1) *A* has promised *B* that he will mow *B*'s lawn for *B* on Sunday. On Sunday, *A* is feeling lazy and so he refuses to mow the lawn.

(2) *A* is sitting home on Sunday, feeling lazy, when *B* calls him up and asks him to come over and mow *B*'s lawn. *A* refuses to mow the lawn.

Ceteris paribus, it would be the case that *A* is wrong in refusing to mow *B*'s lawn in example (1) but not blamable for refusing to mow *B*'s lawn in example (2). Why is this so? Because *A*'s promise to mow *B*'s lawn creates an obligation which in the absence of such a promise is nonexistent. If this is so, then permitting the general utilitarian defense does not make a promise a meaningless gesture. This is so because there are many situations in which, in the absence of having promised to do so, we are not, for example, obligated to inconvenience ourselves simply for another's convenience. Personal inconvenience then might be one excuse which must be inconsistent with the practice of promising, even if the general appeal to consequences is not. Thus, promising would and could have a real point even if the general appeal to consequences were a good defense.

U

generally, it can be no less the case for the supposed promise to obey the law.

Finally, even if it were correct that voluntary participation implied a promise to obey, and even if it were the case that the promise must be a promise not to disobey on consequential grounds, all of this would still not justify the conclusion that one ought never to disobey the law. It would, instead, only demonstrate that disobeying the law must be prima facie wrong, that everyone has a prima facie obligation to obey the law. This is so just because it is sometimes right even to break one's own promises. And if this, too, is a characteristic of promises generally, it is, again, no less a characteristic of the promise to obey the law.

The notions of promise, consent, or voluntary participation do not, however, exhaust the possible sources of the obligation to obey the laws of a democracy. In particular, there is another set of arguments which remains to be considered. It is that which locates the rightness of obedience in the way in which any act of disobedience improperly distributes certain burdens and benefits among the citizenry. Professor Wechsler, for example, sees any act of disobedience to the laws of the United States as 'the ultimate negation of all neutral principles, to take the benefits accorded by the constitutional system, including the national market and common defense, while denying it allegiance when a special burden is imposed. That certainly is the antithesis of law'.[1]

On the surface, at least, Professor Wechsler's claim seems overly simple; it appears to be the blanket assertion that the receipt by any citizen, through continued, voluntary presence of benefits of this character necessarily implies that no act of disobedience could be justified. To disobey any law after having voluntarily received these benefits would be, he seems to suggest, so unjust that there could never be overriding considerations. This surely is both to claim too much for the benefits of personal and commercial security and to say too little for the character of all types of disobedience. For even if the receipt of benefits such as these did simply impose an obligation to obey the law, it is implausible to suppose that the obligation thereby imposed would be one that stringent.

But there is a more involved aspect of Professor Wechsler's thesis—particularly in his insistence that disobedience of the law,

---

[1] Wechsler, *Toward Neutral Principles of Constitutional Law* 73 HARV. L. REV. 1, 35 (1959).

where benefits of this kind have been received, is the negation of all neutral principles. I am not at all certain that I understand precisely what this means, but there are at least two possible interpretations: (1) Unless everyone always obeyed the law no one would receive these obviously valuable benefits. (2) Since the benefits one receives depend upon the prevalence of conditions of uniform obedience, it follows that no one who willingly receives these benefits can justly claim them without himself obeying. The first has already been sufficiently considered.[1] The second, while not unfamiliar, merits some further attention.

In somewhat expanded form, the argument is simply this. What makes it possible for any particular person to receive and enjoy the benefits of general, personal and economic security is the fact that everyone else obeys the law. Now, if injustice is to be avoided, it is surely the case that any other person is equally entitled to these same benefits. But he will have this security only if everyone else obeys the law. Hence the receipt of benefits at others' expense requires repayment in kind. And this means universal obedience to the law.[2]

---

[1] See section III above (p. 285).

[2] For a somewhat related characterization of the source of the obligation to obey the law, see Hart, *Are There Any Natural Rights?* 64 PHILOSOPHICAL REV. 175, 185 (1955), in OLAFSON, SOCIETY, LAW, AND MORALITY 173, 180–1 (1961): 'A third very important source of special rights and obligations which we recognize in many spheres of life is what may be termed mutuality of restrictions. . . . In its bare schematic outline it is this: when a number of persons conduct any joint enterprise according to rules and thus restrict their liberty, those who have submitted to these restrictions when required have a right to a similar submission from those who have benefited by their submission. The rules may provide that officials should have authority to enforce obedience and make further rules, and this will create a structure of legal rights and duties, but the moral obligation to obey the rules in such circumstances is *due to* the co-operating members of the society, and they have the correlative moral right to obedience. In social situations of this sort (of which political society is the most complex example) the obligation to obey the rules is something distinct from whatever other moral obligations there may be for obedience in terms of good consequences (e.g., the prevention of suffering); the obligation is due to the co-operating members of the society as such and not because they are human beings on whom it would be wrong to inflict suffering.'

I would point out only two things. First, as Professor Hart himself asserts—in a passage not quoted—the existence of this right in no way implies that one is never justified in disobeying the law. The right which any participating member has in others' obedience can justifiably be infringed in appropriate circumstances. Second, and here perhaps Professor Hart disagrees for reasons already elaborated, there is no reason that I can see why an appeal to the consequences of disobeying a particular law cannot be a sufficient justification for infringing upon that

There are two features of this argument which are puzzling. First, it is far from clear that the benefits of security received by anyone necessarily depend upon absolute obedience on the part of everyone else. It just might be the case that an even greater quantum of security would have accrued from something less than total obedience. But even if I am wrong here, there is a more important point at issue. For reasons already discussed, it is undeniable that even in a democracy a price would be paid for universal obedience—the price that might have to be paid, for instance, were the doctor to refuse to perform the abortion because it was illegal. If this is so, then the fact that a person received benefits from everyone else's obedience does not necessarily entail that it is unjust for him to fail to reciprocate in kind. The benefit of general security might not have been worth the cost. A greater degree of flexibility on the part of others, a general course of obedience except where disobedience was justified, might have yielded a greater benefit. People may, in short, have done more or less than they should have. And if they did, the fact that anyone or everyone benefited to some degree in no way requires that injustice can only be avoided through like and reciprocal conduct. If it is better, in at least some circumstances, to disobey a law than to obey it, there is surely nothing unjust about increasing the beneficial consequences to all through acts of *discriminate* disobedience.

If the argument based upon the effect of receipt of certain benefits is therefore not very persuasive, neither in most cases is the argument which is derived from the way in which any act of disobedience is thought to distribute burdens unfairly among the citizenry. The argument can be put very briefly: If there is one thing which any act of disobedience inevitably does, it is to increase the burdens which fall on all the law-abiding citizens. If someone disobeys the law even for what seems to be the best of reasons, he inevitably makes it harder—in some quite concrete sense—on everyone else. Hence, at a minimum this is a good reason not to disobey the law, and perhaps a sufficient reason as well.

This argument is appealing because there is at least one kind of case it fits very well. It is the case of taxation. For suppose the following, only somewhat unreal, conditions: that the government

---

right. It is surely conceivable, at least, that this is all the submission to rules which anyone ought to have given, and hence all the submission which anyone is entitled to expect from others.

is determined to raise a specified sum of money through taxation, and that, in the long, if not the short, run it will do so by adjusting the tax rate to whatever percentage is necessary to produce the desired governmental income. Under such circumstances it could plausibly be argued that one of the truly inevitable results of a successfully executed decision to evade the payment of one's taxes—a decision made, moreover, on ostensibly justifiable grounds—is that every other member of society will thereby be required to pay a greater tax than would otherwise have been the case. Thus in some reasonably direct and obvious fashion any act of disobedience—particularly if undetected—does add to the burdens of everyone else. And surely this is to make out at least a strong case of prima facie injustice.

Now, for reasons already elaborated, it would be improper to conclude that evasion of one's taxes could never be justified. But the argument is persuasive in its insistence that it does provide a very good reason why evasion always must be justified and why it will seldom be justifiable. But even this feature of disobedience is not present in many cases. Tax evasion, as opposed to other kinds of potentially justified disobedience, is a special, far from typical case. And what is peculiar to it is precisely the fact that any act of disobedience to the tax laws arguably shifts or increases the burden upon others. Such is simply not true of most types of acts of disobedience because most laws do not prohibit or require actions which affect the distribution of resources in any very direct fashion.

Thus, if we take once again the case of the doctor who has decided that he is justified in performing an illegal abortion on the pregnant girl, it is extremely difficult, if not impossible, to locate the analogue of the shifting of burdens involved in tax evasion. How does the performance of the abortion thereby increase the 'costs' to anyone else? The only suggestion which seems at all plausible is that which was noted earlier in a somewhat different context. Someone might argue that it is the occurrence of illegal actions which increase the cost of maintaining a police force, a judiciary and suitable correctional institutions. This cost is a burden which is borne by the citizenry as a whole. And hence, the doctor's illegal acts increase their burdens—albeit very slightly. The difficulty here is threefold. First, if the doctor's act is performed in secret and if it remains undetected, then it is hard to see how there is any shift of economic burden at all. Second, given the fact that police forces, courts and prisons will always be necessary as long as unjustified acts of disobedience are a feature of social existence, it is by no means apparent that the additional cost is anything but truly de minimis.[1] And third, the added costs, if any, are in the doctor's case assumed by the doctor *qua* member of the citizenry. He is not avoiding a burden; at most he adds something to everyone's—including his own—existing financial obligations. Thus, in cases such as these, it is not at all evident that disobedience need even be prima facie unjust and hence unjustified.

V

There is one final argument which requires brief elucidation and analysis. It is in certain respects a peculiarly instructive one both in its own right and in respect to the thesis of this article.

It may be true that on some particular occasions the consequences of disobeying a law will in fact be less deleterious on the whole than those of obeying it—even in a democracy. It may even be true that on some particular occasions disobeying a law will be just whereas obeying it would be unjust. Nevertheless, the reason why a person is never justified in disobeying a law—in a democracy —is simply this: The chances are so slight that he will disobey only those laws in only those cases in which he is in fact justified in doing so, that the consequences will on the whole be less deleterious if he never disobeys any law. Furthermore, since anyone must concede the right to everyone to disobey the law when the circumstances so demand it, the situation is made still worse. For once we entrust this right to everyone we can be sure that many laws will be disobeyed in a multitude of cases in which there was no real justification for disobedience. Thus, given what we know of the possibilities of human error and the actualities of human frailty, and given the tendency of democratic societies to make illegal only those actions which would, even in the absence of a law, be unjustified, we can confidently conclude that the consequences will on the whole and in the long run be best if no one ever takes

[1] Curiously, perhaps, given a legal system in which laws are in general good and hence in which the possibility of justified disobedience is rare, the special or added cost of an occasional act of justified disobedience is diminished still further.

it upon himself to 'second-guess' the laws and to conclude that in his case his disobedience is justified.[1]

The argument is, in part, not very different from those previously considered. And thus, what is to be said about it is not very different either. Nonetheless, upon pain of being overly repetitive, I would insist that there is a weak sense in which the argument is quite persuasive and a strong sense in which it is not. For the argument makes, on one reading, too strong an empirical claim—the claim that the consequences will in the long run always in fact be better if no one in a democracy ever tries to decide when he is justified in disobeying the law. As it stands, there is no reason to believe that the claim is or must be true, that the consequences will always be better. Indeed, it is very hard to see why, despite the hypothesis, someone might still not be justified in some particular case in disobeying a law. Yet, viewed as a weaker claim, as a summary rule, it does embody a good deal that is worth remembering. It can, on this level, be understood to be a persuasive reminder of much that is relevant to disobedience: that in a democracy the chances of having to live under bad laws are reduced; that in a democracy there are typically less costly means available by which to bring about changes in the law; that in a democracy—as in life in general—a justified action may always be both inaptly and ineptly emulated; and that in a democracy—as in life in general— people often do make mistakes as to which of their own actions are truly justified. These are some of the lessons of human experience which are easy to forget and painful to relearn.

But there are other lessons, and they are worth remembering too. What is especially troubling about the claim that disobedience of the law is never justified, what is even disturbing about the claim that disobedience of the law is never justified in a democratic or liberal society, is the facility with which its acceptance can lead to the neglect of important moral issues. If no one is justified in disobeying the Supreme Court's decision in *Brown* v. *Board of Educ.*[2] this is so because, among other things, there is much that is wrong with segregation. If there was much that was peculiarly wrong in Mississippi, this was due to the fact, among other facts,

---

[1] For fuller analyses and assessments of this argument in different contexts see, e.g., Rawls (cited above p. 288 n. 1); WASSERSTROM (cited above p. 288 n. 1) pp. 118–71.

[2] 347 U.S. 483 (1954).

that a mob howled and a governor raged when a court held that a person whose skin was black could go to a white university. Disobeying the law is often—even usually—wrong; but this is so largely because the illegal is usually restricted to the immoral and because morally right conduct is still less often illegal. But we must always be sensitive to the fact that this has not always been the case, is not now always the case and need not always be the case in the future. And undue concentration upon what is wrong with disobeying the law rather than upon the wrong which the law seeks to prevent can seriously weaken and misdirect that awareness.

Bibliographical Notes

ANALYTIC PHILOSOPHY

Several of the most influential thinkers were Bertrand Russell (1872–), G. E. Moore (1873–1959), Ludwig Wittgenstein (1889–1951), John Wisdom (1904–). J. L. Austin (1911-60), and Gilbert Ryle (1900–). Russell, Moore, Wittgenstein and Wisdom taught at Cambridge; Austin and Ryle at Oxford. In the 1930s, the Cam began to flow into the Isis, and the center of analytic philosophy moved from Cambridge to Oxford. Today there are signs of back flow.

For introductory treatments of modern analytic philosophy, and for extensive bibliographies, see URMSON, PHILOSOPHICAL ANALYSIS: ITS DEVELOPMENT BETWEEN THE TWO WORLD WARS (1956); G. J. WARNOCK, ENGLISH PHILOSOPHY SINCE 1900 (1958); M. WARNOCK, ETHICS SINCE 1900 (1960); Quinton, *Contemporary British Philosophy*, in A CRITICAL HISTORY OF WESTERN PHILOSOPHY 530 (O'Connor ed. 1964).

LEGAL PHILOSOPHY

Throughout this book, there are many references to writings of contemporary legal philosophers, and in the opening footnote to each of the essays included here, other relevant writings of the author have been listed. For further references, see Summers, *The New Analytical Jurists* 41 N.Y.U.L. REV. 861, 863–5 (1966).

While modern analytic philosophy has provided much stimulus and example, the legal philosophy represented here is not without other antecedents. In particular, relevant writings of Jeremy Bentham (1748–1832) should be mentioned: THE COMMENT ON THE COMMENTARIES (Everett ed. 1928); A FRAGMENT ON GOVERNMENT (Montague ed. 1891); AN INTRODUCTION TO THE PRINCIPLES OF MORALS AND LEGISLATION (Hafner Library ed. 1948); (the two preceding works, edited by Wilfred Harrison, are published in one volume by Basil Blackwell (1948)); and THE LIMITS OF

JURISPRUDENCE DEFINED (Everett ed. 1945). There is also much of interest scattered through the Bowring edition of BENTHAM'S WORKS (1841). And there is further unpublished work to be incorporated in the new edition of Bentham's writings now under way. See generally, Hart, *Bentham: Lecture on a Master Mind* 48 PROCEEDINGS OF THE BRITISH ACADEMY 297 (1962).

GENERAL SOURCES

Philosophy Journals

Much work of relevance appears not in books but in philosophy journals. The principal ones are: ANALYSIS, AUSTRALIAN JOURNAL OF PHIL., ETHICS, INQUIRY, J. OF PHIL., MIND, MONIST, PHILOSOPHY, PHIL. and PHEN. RESEARCH, PHIL. QUARTERLY, PHIL. REVIEW, REVIEW OF METAPHYSICS, and THEORIA. There is no comprehensive index to all these journals.

Legal Periodicals

Legal periodicals in which relevant writing may appear number more than one hundred. Fortunately, there is a comprehensive index to all these periodicals called, simply: INDEX TO LEGAL PERIODICALS. Work of interest may be indexed both under the general topic *jurisprudence* and under some more specific topic, e.g., *punishment, natural law*. The INDEX is available in almost all law libraries.

Political Science Journals

Sometimes relevant articles in 'political theory' appear in these journals. Among the principal ones are: AMERICAN POLITICAL SCIENCE REVIEW, AUSTRALASIAN JOURNAL OF POLITICS AND HISTORY, JOURNAL OF POLITICS, POLITICAL QUARTERLY, POLITICAL SCIENCE QUARTERLY, POLITICAL STUDIES, and PUBLIC LAW. Several of these journals are indexed in INDEX TO LEGAL PERIODICALS.

Other

Each year, the New York University School of Law publishes its ANNUAL SURVEY OF AMERICAN LAW. The essay on jurisprudence which appears there is usually written by Mr. Graham Hughes and includes both analytical commentary and bibliographical material. Similarly, Mr. J. Roland Pennock edits the annual 'Nomos' volume of the American Society of Political and Legal Philosophy which each year includes essays by different authors on a single theme. See also, the three collections each entitled PHILOSOPHY, POLITICS AND SOCIETY edited by Messrs. Laslett and Runciman, and the various entries under *Law, Philosophy of*, in THE ENCYCLOPEDIA OF PHILOSOPHY (Edwards ed. 1967).

There is no English language periodical devoted exclusively to legal philosophy. But ARCHIV FÜR RECHTS-UND SOZIALPHILOSOPHIE frequently includes contributions by American and British authors.